Nietzsche
and
Paradox

Nietzsche
and
Paradox

Rogério Miranda de Almeida

Translated by
Mark S. Roberts

State University of New York Press

Published by
State University of New York Press, Albany

© 2006 State University of New York

For information, address State University of New York Press,
194 Washington Avenue, Suite 305, Albany, NY 12210-2384

Production by Michael Haggett
Marketing by Susan M. Petrie

Library of Congress Cataloging-in-Publication Data

Almeida, Rogério Miranda de.
    [Nietzshe et le paradoxe. English]
    Nietzsche and paradox / Rogerio Miranda de Almeida ; translated by
Mark S. Roberts.
        p. cm.
    Includes bibliographical references and index.
    ISBN-13: 978-0-7914-6889-0 (hardcover : alk. paper)
    ISBN-10: 0-7914-6889-5 (hardcover : alk. paper)
    1. Nietzsche, Friedrich Wilhelm, 1844–1900. I. Title.

B3317.A42613 2006
193—dc22
                                                                        2005037170

10 9 8 7 6 5 4 3 2 1

To Mazrcelo Fabri,
Moacir Bandin
and Germano Rigacci, Jr.

Contents

Preface

These reflections are not intended to present an explication, still less a synthesis of Nietzsche's philosophy. Given the extremely fragmentary and diffuse character of his thought, such an undertaking would be doomed to fail from the very outset. Our proposal here is, rather, to focus on paradox, or the paradoxes that Nietzsche expresses through his writing, and thus through the great diversity of perspectives and rereadings operative in the domains of art, science, religion, morality, philosophy, and culture in general.

If one conceives, as we do, the Nietzschean text as divergent and as what resists or escapes the order of discourse as such, it would be a mistake to seek a ground or a model that guarantees and explicates the plurality of meanings that engender the unfolding of his writing. In other words, Nietzschean thought discloses itself only to the extent that, paradoxically, it is masked, reread, *reiterated*, and stripped of all constraint, all mastery and interpretation.

To be sure, the traditional commentators on Nietzsche are unanimous in admitting that his oeuvre contains "contradictions" and ambiguities. But these contradictions invoke, as often as not, "apparent contradictions" in the sense that they would be—unknown to Nietzsche himself—a logical thread carrying these texts to a coherent and continuous whole. Among these authors are Karl Jaspers, Martin Heidgegger, Walter Kaufmann, Jean Wahl, and, more recently, Wolfgang Müller-Lauter. In his book, *Nietzsche: His Philosophy of Contradictions and Contradictions of His Philosophy* (first German edition, 1971), Müller-Lauter sees in the Will to Power the concept by which all Nietzsche's contradictions would be explained. Yet our purpose is not, at least not primarily, to establish a confrontation between Nietzsche's writings and his commentators.

As a matter of fact, the principal themes of the Nietzschean oeuvre that we develop—that is, the will to power, the relation of forces, nihilism, and the eternal return—are extremely problematic and subject to diverse interpretations. And this is the case because Nietzsche himself continually reiterates, rereads, and creates new perspectives on the art of poetry, fiction, invention, interpretation, and construction. But the art of construction presupposes the force of destruction and imposes a new meaning. This is why a thought that moves in and from one relation of forces, and that is itself force, can only be expressed through the writing of paradox, that is, through the constant play of inclusions, exclusions, ruptures, renewals, and reevaluations. It is true that Nietzsche's first insights progress explicitly from the very beginning of his work, but they remain nevertheless problematic and ambiguous; for it is precisely in the development and movement of his writing that other evaluations, other tables of values and other visions are set in motion. Consequently, to evaluate for him is to appropriate a meaning, to impart a new interpretation, to create a world of values, that, in turn, is constantly re-created, reinvented, and repeated, in difference.

If there is a problem occupying the center of the Nietzschean question, it is the problem of the relation of forces and what is derived from them: the creation-destruction of interpretations. Thus, one can understand why the question of morality extends throughout all his works, since what is at play in the different domains of art, religion, science, philosophy, and culture is the universe of forces from and by which judgments and values are constantly established, transformed, and superseded. In this perspective, the Nietzschean text remains open and receptive to a plurality of readings, for insofar as the means behind the different forces are expressed, the text is at the same time writing, reading, enchaining, and a constant movement of success and failure.

Thus, our own text would perhaps have been on the verge of filling a gap, but one's pleasure is all the more extreme when there is a multiplicity of meanings and interpretations to overcome. It follows, then, that we cannot and will not *conclude*. In fact, the last chapter points, following Nietzsche, toward other directions, aspiring to go beyond all limits, all resistance, and all opposition.

Acknowledgments

The author writes in the original that he has followed the French translation of the Colli-Montinari edition of Nietzsche's complete works (Édi-
tions Gallimard), and that he has taken the liberty to modify certain passages. English speakers, however, do not have the advantage of a complete
translation of the Colli-Montinari edition (though one is underway at
Stanford University Press). I have thus substituted, wherever possible,
Walter Kaufmann's English translations of Nietzsche's works, which are
generally considered standard. In cases where no Kaufmann translation
exists, I have tried to substitute the clearest and most readable translation
possible. Where there is no English translation at all (e.g., some of the various posthumous fragments), I have translated the material myself.

I would like to thank Lysane Fauvel for checking the English translations of the untranslated passages from Nietzsche's *Nachlass*. I would also
like to extend my gratitude to David B. Allison for his many valuable suggestions regarding the form and content of Nietzsche's work, and his help
in tracking down some of the references in the *KSA*. Saint Vincent College (Latrobe, Pennsylvania) and the Archabbey connected to the college
have been extremely generous in supporting my work. George Leiner,
chair of the Philosophy Department at Saint Vincent, has also been helpful in the completion of the translation. And, last, but certainly not least,
I would like to acknowledge the book's author, Rogério Miranda de
Almeida, for his many helpful suggestions, corrections, and comments.

List of Abbreviations

BT	*The Birth of Tragedy* (1872)
UO	*Unmodern Observations* (1873–1876)
HAH	*Human, All Too Human* (1878)
AOM	*Assorted Opinions and Maxims* (1879 in HAH II, 1886)
WS	*The Wanderer and His Shadow* (1880 in HAH II, 1886)
D	*Daybreak* (1881)
GS	*The Gay Science* (1882)
Z	*Thus Spoke Zarathustra* (1883–1885)
BGE	*Beyond Good and Evil* (1886)
GM	*On the Geneology of Morals* (1887)
CW	*The Case of Wagner* (1888)
TI	*Twilight of the Idols* (1888—This is the last book published by Nietzsche himself. The official date of publication was 1889).
AC	*The Antichrist* (1895)
EH	*Ecce Homo* (1908)
NW	*Nietzsche contra Wagner* (1895)
WP	*The Will to Power* (1901)
WLN	*Writings from the Late Notebooks* (Various dates)
KSA	*Kritische Studienausgabe*—German edition of Nietzsche's complete works (1988)
PTAG	*Philosophy in the Tragic Age of the Greeks* (Posthumous writing of 1872)
TGS	*The Greek State* (1872)

1

The Birth of Tragedy

> Whoever does not merely comprehend the Dionysian but comprehends him-
> self in the word "Dionysian" needs no refutation of Plato or Christianity or
> Schopenauer—he *smells the decay.*
>
> —*EH-BT*, 2

Nietzsche published *The Birth of Tragedy* in January 1872. The book
belongs with *Unmodern Observations* (1873–1876) and the contempora-
neous posthumous writings and fragments in what is now usually considered Nietzsche's early period. In fact, one already finds in these writings the important insights that will be revealed in the progressive
development of his work. To be sure, these early writings do not have the
critical inspiration of *Human, All Too Human* (1878–1880), a work situated at the very axis of this development. Nor do they have the breath, the
violence or tension of the later texts, those of 1888, where polemics and
aggressivety reach a paroxysm and a style unequaled in beauty. These early
themes, however, are no less fundamental to Nietzschean thought because
they are already expressed, either explicitly or implicitly, in *The Birth of
Tragedy*. This is precisely why, in the first chapter, we will center our questions on this work, without overlooking the other writings of the same
period or other later periods that relate, directly or indirectly, to these
important themes.

    In this difficult to understand work—despite the clarity of its com-
position—Nietzsche not only brings another perspective to the origin of

tragedy, but he also asserts, with remarkably original insights, the relations between art and science, Greek civilization and the modern era, and tragic wisdom and theoretical knowledge. Indeed, the question of tragic wisdom insofar as it is an affirmation of life, the *Yes*, is even of greater importance to Nietzsche than the origin of tragedy and the opposition between Apollo and Dionysus. "What is essential to that theory—asserts Nietzsche sixteen years later—is the conception of art in its relation to life. One sees there, as much psychologically as physiologically, the great *stimulant*, what *drives* one eternally to life, to eternal life . . ."[1]

Formally, *The Birth of Tragedy* consists of twenty-five chapters or sections. The first six sections are introductory and not of particular interest stylistically. The heart of the work can be found in sections 7 through 15. They treat the birth and the death of tragedy. With Socrates as the principal adversary, these sections focus on the relations between art and science, understood as dialectic, as logic and theory.[2] As Nietzsche himself even acknowledges:

> The critique of Socrates constitutes the central part of the book. Socrates, the adversary of tragedy who destroys the demonic instincts— art's preventive. Socratism, the great misunderstanding of the life of art, representing morality, dialectics, the frugality of the theoretician, a form of lassitude: the famous Greek serenity is only a *twilight* . . .[3]

The nine following sections, with the exception of 24, appear quite meager in comparison with Nietzsche's philosophical genius. They obviously run counter to the new problematic that he will eventually introduce. Following a posthumous fragment, it seems that Nietzsche intended to finish the first work at section 14: "'Socrates, practice music?,' as the final chapter."[4] And, in fact, he regrets this most bitterly in an *Attempt at a Self-Criticism*, written sixteen years later:

> But there is something far more worse in this book, something I now regret more than that I obscured and spoiled Dionysian premonitions with Schopenhauerian formulations: namely, that I *spoiled* the grandiose *Greek problem*, as it had risen before my eyes, by introducing the most modern of problems! That I appended hopes where there was no ground for hope, where everything pointed all too plainly to an end! That on the basis of the latest German music I began to rave about "the German spirit" as if that were in the process even then of discovering and finding itself again.[5]

Nietzsche was thus counting on the renewal of tragic wisdom, on the rebirth of Dionysian music through German music, "in its vast solar orbit from Bach to Beethoven, from Beethoven to Wagner."[6] These latter considerations were too *modern*. They too readily accepted the imminent revival of Hellenic antiquity. They contributed to Wagnermania. They fueled and fomented as if they were a phenomenon of *ascendant* life and not a symptom of *decadence*. Nietzsche would say of the book in general:

> To say it once more: today I find it an impossible book: I consider it badly written, ponderous, embarrassing, image-mad and image-confused, sentimental, and in places saccharine to the point of effeminacy, uneven in tempo, without the will to logical cleanliness, very convinced and therefore disdainful of proof, suspicious even of the *propriety* of proof, a book for initiates . . .[7]

What, then, are the challenges, what are the questions underlying the "metaphysics of the artist" and of that work that sets it forth through an aesthetic problematic? What reasons lead us to maintain, at this point, that it is a question of a relation of forces, of multiple forces that are made patently visible with the later, skillfully polemical writings? We now anticipate immediately that the aesthetic, cultural, metaphysical, and religious problems concealed by morality, express themselves only through a relation of forces and can only be thought through a thought that is itself *paradoxical*. This is what we will now try to elucidate.

APOLLO AND DIONYSUS

Nietzsche opens the first chapter of *The Birth of Tragedy* with a statement that appears in some ways to be the primary intuition guiding the reader through his reflections on the origin and the death of tragic art: "We have gained much for the science of aesthetics, once we perceive not merely by logical inference, but with the immediate certainty of vision, that the continuous development of art is bound up with the *Apollonian* and *Dionysian* duality—just as procreation depends on the duality of the sexes, involving perpetual strife with only periodically intervening reconciliations."[8] It is in fact these two deities that tie together the two worlds of Greek art: the Apollonian plastic art, and the Dionysian nonplastic art. Apollo is the god of beautiful illusion, of measured restraint, the sculptor god, the "glorious divine image of the *principium individuationis*, through whose gestures and eyes all the joy and wisdom of 'illusion,' together with its beauty, speak to us."[9] To render these two impulses more accessible, Nietzsche represents them as two distinct aesthetic worlds: Apollo, that of the dream and Dionysus, that of intoxication and ecstacy which, through its own artistic power, breaks the bonds of the *principium individuationis* and makes manifest the most intimate ground of man, things, nature, and the primordially One.

A number of Nietzsche interpreters see in the opposition between Apollo and Dionysus a kind of dialectical progression in the course of which Dionysus takes on the bearing, assumes the attributes of Apollo, is set in opposition to Socrates so as to lead to a later and more fundamental opposition: "*Dionysus verses the Crucified*," a passage that closes *Ecce Homo.* Among these interpreters we find Gilles Deleuze and Walter Kaufmann. Deleuze sees in Nietzsche's work an anti-Hegelian project, while Kaufmann tries to turn Nietzsche into a "monistic dialectician." In a certain way, it is Nietzsche himself who favors these interpretations, for he admits in reference to *The Birth of Tragedy*: "it (this work) smells offensively Hegelian, and the cadaverous perfume of Schopenhauer sticks only to a few."[10]

In reality, *The Birth of Tragedy* does not present a uniform, regular, and continuous progression of these two opposed gods converging in a synthesis of Dionysus.[11] In fact, despite the terms and ideas of "duality" and "opposition" used in the text, a closer reading of *The Birth of Tragedy* would, rather, reveal a certain hesitation or refusal on Nietzsche's part to characterize either one of these two drives in an exclusive way, or to oppose them too simply. Thus, Dionysus "In his existence as a dismembered god, . . . possesses the dual nature of a cruel, barbarized demon and a mild, gentle ruler."[12] But this does not apply only to Dionysus; Apollo, too, connected to the spell of the beautiful illusion, is clothed in fearful and appalling attributes.[13] Now separate, now together, here in open struggle, there reconciled, these two gods nevertheless bear common traits of one through the other, of one in the other. Although the Dionysian appears in the Greek Apollonian as "titanic" and "barbaric," he is incapable of dissimulating the affinity that is attached to that very ground he rejects: "And behold: Apollo could not live without Dionysus! The 'titanic' and 'barbaric' were in the last analysis as necessary as the Apollonian!"[14] Apollo, of course, appears as the principle of individuation, by which he carries out the ends of the primordially One and achieves, through the illusion he creates in tragedy, the victory over the Dionysian, that is, over the primordial element in music. Yet it is of no small importance that this illusion is broken and annihilated; it is as if the destruction of the visible was the very condition necessary to open access to the heart of true being: "And thus the Apollonian illusion reveals itself as what it really is—the veiling during the performance of the tragedy of the real Dionysian effect; but the latter is so powerful that it ends by forcing the Apollonian drama itself into a sphere where it begins to speak with Dionysian wisdom and even denies itself and its Apollonian visibility."[15] And yet, the accord by which tragedy is achieved could never be known without the interaction of these two realms of art: that of Apollo and that of Dionysus.

Schopenhauer's influence and that of Kant—by way of his influence on Schopenhauer—run throughout *The Birth of Tragedy*. Through Apollonian illusion and Dionysian music, tragic wisdom reveals the most intimate ground of things, nature, the willed one, and the primordially One. Moreover, Dionysian music appears to us as the mirror of the universal will, for the eternal truth that springs from the will itself is reflected and reproduced in it. But in chapter 5, Nietzsche already distances himself from Schopenhauer, and in chapter 7, his own position is even more clearly articulated. Here he proposes that the metaphysical comfort embodied in tragedy and which is incarnated in the satyric chorus is pure pleasure—pleasure in its indestructible power that, despite the changing character of phenomena, affirms life. To be sure, the profound Hellene who the chorus comforts and who looks boldly into the terrible destructive forces of history and nature, courts the danger "of longing for a *Buddhistic negation* of the will."[16] But art comes to his rescue, it saves him: "Art saves him, and through art—life."[17] For Nietzsche, then, art admits of the universal suffering, accepts and assumes it, but transfigures it in the affirmation, in the *Yes* to life. This is why fifteen years later he would say: "Tragic art, rich in these two experiences, is defined as the reconciliation of Apollo and Dionysus. Dionysus imparts the most profound meaning to appearance, and that appearance can nevertheless be denied with *sensual pleasure*. This is directed, like the tragic vision of the world, against the Schopenhauerean doctrine of *resignation*."[18]

In the later chapters, Nietzsche will no longer be content to question the relations between the Apollonian and Dionysian, nor will he settle on merely establishing that tragedy reproduces the universal will, where the artist and Dionysian spectator look boldly into the primordially One and transfigure suffering through art. It would be a further step for him to try to grasp that original phenomenon that is Dionysian art and to understand what constitutes the pleasure we experience through this type of art.

Indeed, in the musical tragedy, where Apollonian art is perfected by justifying the world of individuation, the spectator contemplates the world transfigured on the stage, and yet he denies it: "He sees the tragic hero before him in epic clearness and beauty, and nevertheless rejoices in his annihilation. . . . He sees more extensively and profoundly than ever, and yet wishes he were blind."[19] But the tragic artist also creates the figures that his Dionysian drive devours, so as to foreshadow, behind the annihilation of the phenomenal world, "the highest artistic primal joy, in the bosom of the primordially One."[20]

But Nietzsche wants to avoid any moral account regarding the pleasure one feels before the world of the stage, even given the fact that for most, as in the case of aesthetics, it is often under the effect of moral delight, of a catharsis or a consolation that the tragic myth appears. For him, tragedy is not a "pathological discharge," but, rather, a form of superior art. And it is only in the sphere of aesthetics itself that he can find an explanation of the pleasure peculiar to tragedy. "How can the ugly and the disharmonic, the content of the tragic myth, stimulate aesthetic pleasure?"[21]

To resolve this difficult problem, Nietzsche resorts to musical dissonance, since music is the language most apt to reproduce the universal will, to manifest the ground of things and to confirm that *the world and existence can only be justified as aesthetic phenomena*. With this as support, Nietzsche will go on to state that the pleasure aroused by the tragic myth and that provoked by dissonance have a common origin (*Heimat*), that is, the Dionysian. This knowledge, combined with the primordial delight (*Urlust*) experienced in suffering, gives rise to music and tragic myth. An experience comparable to what occurs in the use of musical dissonance also appears in tragedy. There, we wish to see all while desiring to get beyond the visible, and in music one experiences the desire to hear and at the same time go beyond the audible. This experience of the destruction of visibility and audibility as a condition of and passageway to primordial delight (*Urlust*), or more precisely, that destruction being itself a pleasure, is reaffirmed in a posthumous fragment of 1888, which reads: "In the same way, pleasure is given far more primitively than pain. Pain, in such a case, is only contingent, an after-affect of pleasure (of the will to become, to grow, to shape, that is, to *create*. But this act of creation also includes destruction.)."[22]

This is why, in *The Birth of Tragedy*, Nietzsche links the Dionysian state with that "striving for the infinite," that "wing beat of longing" that accompanies the highest state of pleasure. It is Dionysus who, through the play of the construction and destruction of the phenomenal world, opens a passageway to primordial delight. But this construction-destruction is itself delight, for, like in Heraclitus, the world-building force can be compared to a playing child who places stones here and there, and builds sand hills only to overturn them again.[23] Thus, for Dionysus, the world is a huge backgammon game, the kingdom of a child, who overturns and builds and overturns anew. This is the incessant desire to become, to create and to destroy in voluptuous delight. "In the same way, pleasure is given far more primitively than pain. Pain, in such a case, is only contingent, an after-affect of the will to pleasure (of the will to become, to grow, to shape, that is, to *create*). But this act of creation also includes destruction."[24] In this sense appearance becomes a provisional solution, grasping each moment, denied each moment, sought after when it is denied, in affirmation and will. This is a succession of visions and transfigurations that are promulgated eternally and can never be overcome.

This conception of art as play, introduced by Nietzsche in *The Birth of Tragedy*, will be unique to him and developed up to the point of his later writings: art as the play of deception, as illusion, fiction and lie; art as the great stimulant of life, as the great *Yes* to life. In fact, the will to appearance is, for Nietzsche, more profound, more originary, and more primitive than the will to be: "and being itself is only a form of the will to illusion."[25] Apollo and Dionysus are thus presented in the *Birth of Tragedy* in opposition and reconciled, one assuming the traits of the other, taking part in the attributes of the other, in an exchange that is continuously regenerated, continuously renewed. This is why Aeschylus's Prometheus wears both the mask of Apollo and Dionysus: the titanic effort to carry humanity higher and higher, farther and farther constitutes, for Nietzsche, the common trait between the Promethian and the Dionysian, whereas in his profound demand for justice, Aeschylus also reveals Prometheus's paternal descent from Apollo, the god of just limits and established measures. This Promethian nature is the bearer of both Dionysian and Apollonian attributes, expressed by Nietzsche in the conception: "All that exists is just and unjust and equally justified in both."[26]

Even if the name Apollo is blurred as the early work progresses, and fades away much to Dionysus's profit, this does not imply absolutely a determination on Nietzsche's part to show the shift of these two forces as a movement toward Absolute Knowing—a movement where Dionysus would represent the synthesis that would redeem Apollo as the *one* of these moments. Even so, there are a number of interpreters who try to affix a design to these two drives that sustains a certain reading of Hegel. It is as if Nietzsche's work could only be understood as a reaction in favor of or against Hegel, for or against the dialectic.

Thus, for Gilles Deleuze, the antithesis Dionysus-Apollo will be replaced by the complementary Dionysus-Ariadne, and the opposition Dionysus-Socrates will be substituted for a more fundamental one, that which closes *Ecce Homo*: "Dionysus versus the Crucified. . . ."[27] At another level of interpretation, but fully utilizing Hegelian concepts that contrast largely with the aims, method and development central to Nietzsche, Bernard Pautrat asserts: "The more one moves away from the strict problematic of *The Birth*—and of its ontological 'ground'—the greater the stress on the one of the couple's terms, to the point of the *complete effacement* of the other. In the later texts, where the idea of the Dionysus-philosopher is developed, the name of Apollo is virtually absent, simply because it has become useless."[28] Thus: "There is no Apollo-philosopher to the extent there is never something else, where Platonism has not ceased to be the way of thinking. Now, what allows us to say that Platonism has always been the Apollonianism of thought, is that 'philosophical Dionysianism' which constitutes the Dionysian or tragic text, which recognizes in itself the power and the law of difference-in-itself, and thus welcomes Apollo as the name of one of these moments."[29]

Even more remarkably, however, in later text (Spring 1888), which forms part of a series of reflections on *The Birth of Tragedy*, Nietzsche continues to examine the ambiguous character of these two forces:

> This antinomic character of the Dionysian and Apollonian in the interior of the Greek soul is one of the great enigmas—in view of Greek genius—to which Nietzsche is drawn. At bottom, Nietzsche has tried to divine precisely why the Greek Apollonian became necessarily born out of a Dionysian subsoil; why the Greek Dionysian had to become Apollonian, that is, to destroy its will to monstrosity, multiplicity, chance and to turn against a will to measure, simplicity, harmonious integration in a rule and a conception. The unmeasurable, the savage, the Asiatic is the ground of his character: the courage of the Greek lies in his struggle against what he has of the Asiatic: beauty has not been given to him, no more than logic, or the natural evidence of morality—beauty has been conquered, willed, taken by force; it is his victory . . .[30]

This text demonstrates how Nietzsche himself refused to privilege one of these two forces to the exclusion of the other, or to purely and simply oppose them, though they more often express themselves in opposition or in open struggle. But the hostility is a way in which one recognizes oneself in difference. Here again Nietzsche accentuates their ambiguous character, as well as the flux and reflux that they maintain by relation to one another, the one unable to overcome the other, to live, to conceive without the other. This is why the Apollonian can only be born of Dionysian basis, a savage ground, the will to multiplicity, to chance, to disrupting, and to the unmeasured. The Dionysus-philosopher of the later texts—where Apollo appears to Pautrat as one of the moments overcome in the progress of the Spirit, and Dionysus as the Concept realized—is the Dionysus who guards over the ambiguous traits, both those of Apollo and Dionysus. Thus, one will find in *Twilight of the Idols*, also written in 1888, a portrait of Goethe painted in a wide variety of colors, which recalls the mixture and shimmering of colors constantly at play between these two drives. This portrait, which is cast in a rhetorical effusion rarely seen in the later works, ends in Nietzsche designating Goethe as a "spirit who has become free" and "stands amid the cosmos with a joyous and trusting fatalism. . . ." And he concludes: "Such a faith, however, is the highest of all possible faiths: I have baptized it with the name of *Dionysus*."[31]

This elaboration of the Dionysian phenomenon, as it appears in the later writings, rejoins, through changes and developments at work in Nietzschean thought, what was already expressed, either implicitly or explicitly, in *The Birth of Tragedy* and other related texts: an affirmative life force, Dionysus presented as the god of the overabundance of forces, through whom the good Hellene will be assured—thanks to the mysteries of sexuality—the eternal return of life, the triumphant *Yes* to life, and eternal life itself.

If there is a problem that haunted Nietzsche, it is that of the relation of forces and that of creation and destruction. But one cannot conceive creation and destruction in the Nietzschean oeuvre apart from this relation of forces. Nonetheless, how could a force or forces be able to assert themselves in difference while at the same time affirm that difference, or, in the case of nihilism, turn around against themselves?

As his prophet Zarathustra, the later Dionysus effectively possesses this power to embrace all spaces, to stride, swiftly, across all expanses, to descend to the lowest depths and ascend to the greatest heights, with playfulness and mischievousness, with grace and seriousness, the soul overflowing, open to willing-life and willing to become.

But that is the concept of Dionysus himself—. Another consideration leads to the very same result. The psychological problem in the type that is Zarathustra is how he that says No and *does* No to an unheard-of degree, to everything to which one has so far said Yes, can nevertheless be the opposite of a No-saying spirit; how the spirit who bears the heaviest fate, a fatality of a task, can nevertheless be the lightest and most transcendent—Zarathustra is a dancer—how he that has the hardest, most terrible insight into reality, that has thought the "most abysmal idea," nevertheless does not consider it an objection to existence, not even to its eternal recurrence—but rather one reason more for being himself the eternal Yes to all things, "the tremendous, unbounded saying Yes and Amen."—"Into the abysses I still carry the blessings of my saying Yes."—*But this is the concept of Dionysus once again.*[32]

JUSTIFICATION BY AESTHETICS AND THE QUESTION OF NATURE

Why did Nietzsche begin his philosophical work with an aesthetic problematic? Why does *The Birth of Tragedy* stress the fact that life, transfigured and affirmed by art, is the only satisfactory theodicy?

In fact, Nietzsche was often associated in his early period with the German Romantics. This was because the problematic of art was of primary importance in all his initial writings. But a sharper look turned toward the eighteenth century, and toward the influence of the Enlightenment on the nineteenth century, will help us to better understand why Nietzsche gave primacy to aesthetic values, without being part of the line of romantic philosophers beginning with Schelling. This question leads us to examine the conception of finality and, particularly, the way finality in nature was construed by the representatives of the *Aufklärung.* A text that reveals this spirit was published by Kant in the *Berlinische Monatsschrift* (1784) under the title: *Idea for a Universal History with a Cosmopolitan Intent.* In this text, composed of nine theses, one finds a theory of "purpose in nature," one that Nietzsche does not in any way sanction. In the first thesis Kant already speaks of "a leading thread of reason," an idea that will be restated and developed six years later in paragraph 83 of *The Critique of Judgment.* In the Fourth Thesis, the philospher asserts: "*The means which nature employs to accomplish the development of all faculties is the antagonism of men in society, since this antagonism becomes, in the end, the cause of a lawful order of society.*" Further on in the same thesis, we read:

In this way, the first true steps from barbarism to culture, in which the unique social worth of man consists, now occur, all man's talents are gradually developed, his taste is cultured, and through progressive enlightenment he begins to establish a way of thinking that in time can transform the crude natural capacity for moral discrimination into definite practical principles and thus transform a pathologically enforced agreement into a society, and, finally, into a moral whole.[33]

At the end of the Seventh Thesis, Kant maintains: "All good that is not grafted onto a morally-good character is nothing but illusion and glistering misery." And he ends the text, in the Ninth Thesis, by explicitly naming *providence*:

> Such a *justification* of nature—or better, of *providence*—is no unimportant motive for adopting a particular perspective in observing the world. For what use is it to laud and recommend observing the majesty and wisdom of creation in the non rational realm of nature, if that part of the great theatre of supreme wisdom that contains the purpose of all the rest—the history of the human race—should remain an endless reproach to it . . .[34]

We are well aware of the influence exercised by Shaftsebury's philosophy on the eighteenth century, not only in England but also in France, Germany, and particularly on Leibniz and the so-called precritical period of Kant. Kant's conception of beauty, even though it has undergone certain transformations and has been distanced from the model of the Cambridge philosophers, nevertheless sustains a perspective of immanence and finality that Shaftsebury himself maintained in his philosophy of nature. In this regard, Shaftsebury's *Hymn to Nature* played a considerable role in Herder's philosophy of nature and in that of the young Goethe.[35]

Now, nothing is more foreign to the basic method and thought of Nietzsche than to assign an ordered finality to nature, to endow it with some providence or a pedagogical and rational *telos*. These conceptions, which he attributes, either explicitly or implicitly, to the forces of morality, are revealed progressively as symptoms of decadence, as an expression of the negative forces of life that are disguised as noble, sublime, and "divine" appearances.

In *The Birth of Tragedy*, Nietzsche deliberately uses the terminology developed by Christian morality up to his time. In doing so, he acccentuates the change of values he introduced in such a terminology, even though the revaluation of all values is only clearly manifested in the later writings. Thus, already in chapter 3 of *The Birth of Tragedy*, he refers to art as what the Greeks, exceptionally gifted at suffering, have used to create the Olympian world as a mirror in which life appears transfigured in the joy, the incitement to survive, the affirmation and justification of life: "the only satisfactory theodicy." He stresses several times that the world and existence can only be justified insofar as they are treated as aesthetic phenomena.[36]

That same terminology and evaluation will be reiterated, sixteen years later, in a series of reflections on *The Birth of Tragedy*:

> *Art as the redemption of the man of knowledge*—of those who see the terrifying and questionable character of existence, who want to see it, the men of tragic knowedge.
> *Art as the redemption of the man of action*—of those who see the terrifying and questionable character of existence but live it, want to live it, the tragic-warlike man, the hero.
> *Art as the redemption of the sufferer*—as the way to states in which suffering is willed, transfigured, deified, where suffering is form of great delight.[37]

But does nature have any ends? Yes, but these ends remain hidden. In referring to the "naive" in art, Nietzsche explains it as the capacity of Apollonian culture to overcome the terrifying aspects of existence and the susceptibility to suffering by recourse to the most forceful and pleasurable illusions. But it is only rarely that the naive is attained—that one takes total possession of the transfiguration and beauty of mere appearance. "The Homeric 'naïveté' can be understood only as the complete victory of Apollonian illusion: this is one of those illusions which nature so frequently employs to achieve her own ends. The true goal is veiled by a phantasm: and while we stretch out our hands for the latter, nature attains the former by means of an illusion."[38]

For Nietzsche, Homer is the "naive" artist par excellence. He knows how to combat, through the mirroring play of beauty, the artistically correlative attitude for suffering and for the wisdom of suffering, in affirmation.

Curiously, in the same chapter and context in which he treats "naive" art in Apollonian civilization and the ends of nature, Nietzsche stresses, directly following the above quote, that "in order to glorify themselves, these creatures had to feel themselves worthy of glory; they had to behold themselves again in a higher sphere, without this perfect world of contemplation acting as a command or a reproach."[39] Notice the word "command" is not used here by chance.

In a writing of December 1872, that treats the origin of the ancient Greek state, Nietzsche refers unequivocally to the ends of nature, placing an accent on force, violence and the cruelty that form the basis of this origin: "Here again we see with what pitiless inflexibility Nature, in order to arrive at Society, forges for herself the cruel tool of the State—namely, that *conqueror* with the iron hand, which is nothing else than the objectification of the instinct indicated."[40] Here again one does not feel the presence of an ordered finality of nature that employs the antagonism and discord among men to lead them, through an "enlightened progression," to a moral whole or to a legal order of society. In fact, the idea of progress, of a legal order, and a "leading thread of reason," are totally excluded from Nietzsche's basic intent. This will appear even more evident in *Unmodern Observations*, where he is critical of the supposed superiority of modern civilization: "I do not necessarily mean religious dogmas only, but such claptrap notions as "progress," "general education," "nationalism," "modern state," "struggle of church and state (*Kulturkampf*)."[41]

It is clear that Nietzsche views nature as the setting for the State, but as a means of reaching its liberation in the world of art. Thus, for him, the suffering, which is already proper to human existence, must be increased to allow a small number of Olympians to bring forth art: ". . . then out of all that speaks the enormous necessity of the State, without which Nature might not succeed in coming, through Society, to her deliverance in semblance, in the mirror of genius."[42]

But what exactly is nature for Nietzsche? Generally speaking, it appears to him in the sense of *physis*, that is, as a dynamic principle of growth and production. In fact, in this first period, and despite distancing himself from Schopenhauer in the work on tragedy, his influence is still quite apparent. This is why in a fragment dated 1870–1871, he speaks of a "nucleus of nature" as "true being, being in itself, anonymous truth, the sphere of eternal being, the inaccessible One and Eternal, the abyss of true being."[43]

But whereas in *The Birth of Tragedy* nature is present as a great artist—who expresses herself symbolically through Dionysian dithyramb, who creates the tragic chorus, through the symbolic resources of dance, music, and language, who manifests her knowledge, the ground of herself, the ground of things and the *universal will*— nature will appear much later, in a greatly enlarged sphere of culture, aspiring to her own humanization and liberation, engendering, with the help of culture, the "philosopher," "artist," and the "saint."

Nietzsche's idea of nature will thus be restated and developed in *Schopenhauer as Educator*, a work that forms part of *Unmodern Observations*, but that, along with the other three works composing the text, clearly contrasts with the bold insights and the malleability of style characteristic of the earlier writings.

Effectively, in section 5 of *Schopenhauer as Educator*, Nietzsche fleshes out what he means by an end of nature, as well as the relation that exists between Nature and culture. In an affirmative statement, where the critique of Darwin is patently obvious, he writes:

> They are those true *men, those no-longer animals, the philosophers, artists and saints.* In their appearance and through their appearance, Nature, who makes no leaps, makes her only leap, a leap of joy! For the first time she feels that she has reached her goal (*am Ziele*), the point at which she intuits that she will have to unlearn her goals (*Ziele*), and that she has staked too much on the game of life and Becoming.[44]

It is thus culture that implements liberation, growth, and transfiguration—in brief, the fulfillment of *physis*. For: "This is the fundamental idea of *culture*, insofar as culture imposes only one duty on each of us: *to promote the production of the philosopher, the artist, and the saint, within us and in the world, and thereby to labor for the perfection of Nature.*"[45]

But nature, left to herself, is incapable of utilizing these means to arrive at an end. It wastes its energies, and dispenses its forces by "follies and blunders." Almost everywhere it fails and unceasingly spoils its work, to start over and over again. It finds itself in distress, "striving toward Man, in her pain at seeing her work once again miscarry, yet everywhere successfully producing beginnings, features, forms."[46]

But this work, like nearly all of Nietzsche's writings, raises more questions than it resolves. For, although the conception of nature and culture is revisited and extended, the relations between the two remain in the end cast in shadow. Nature is presented as an active principle of production that, nevertheless, needs culture to achieve its ends. But culture is that very *physis*, which appears worked, improved, and transfigured. This is apparent in section 5 of the abovementioned text: "And if all nature aspires to man, it is to show us that man is necessary in order to redeem nature from the curse of animal existence; and that in man existence at last owns a mirror in whose depths life no longer appears as senseless, but in its metaphysical meaning."[47] Thus, are there two principles or one? This is a question that is also posed by Nietzsche: "where does the animal end and man begin?"

Certain interpreters, Kaufmann among them, see in these two domains of *physis-culture*, as in the couple *Dionysus-Apollo*, a correspondence with *matter-form*. *Physis* is the chaos to be organized, or the matter to be informed, elevated and transfigured. Thus, the conclusion is that the young Nietzsche is a dialectician, whose thought in the later writings becomes monistic, exemplified by the will to power. For Kaufmann, the *will to power* represents the final reconciliation bridging the abyss between conflicting drives, that is, those of Dionysus and Apollo, nature and values, *physis* and culture, disorder and finality, the empirical self and the true self.[48] But these authors run up against numerous difficulties in trying to settle the question of knowing if Nietzsche is a "monist" rather than a "dualist," since either one of these responses can only be reached by an act of force. That is to say, Nietzschean thought is set constantly in a coming and going, in an "interval," in a ceaseless movement that repeats itself as difference, or as the affirmation of difference—in short, as the reality by which it expresses and shows itself and, continually, tries to evaluate itself. This explains the metaphor of the bridge, used frequently in Nietzsche's work. This metaphor reappears in the form of the "tightrope walker" in the speech Zarathustra gives when he arrives at a small village situated at the edge of the forest. After having announced the coming of the overman to the people gathered in the marketplace, he speaks about the man who wills to "go under." Indeed, it is after having come down form the mountain and crossed the forest that, at its very *edge*, Zarathustra announces the overman. Then, in an amazed tone, he exclaims:

> "Man is a rope, tied between beast and overman—a rope over an abyss. A dangerous across, a dangerous on-the-way, a dangerous looking-back, a dangerous shuddering and stopping."
> "What is great *in* man is that he is a bridge and not an end (*Zweck*): what can be loved in man is that he is an *overture* (*Übergang*) and a *going under* (*Untergang*)."[49]

Martin Buber says that:

> The problem of man is for Kant a problem of limits (*ein Grenzproblem*), that is, the problem of a being who effectively belongs to nature but not to nature alone, of a being who settles at the frontier of nature and some

other realm. For Nietzsche, the problem of man is a problem of borders (*ein Randproblem*), the problem of one being who, leaving the heart of nature, finds himself at its extreme border, at the perilous extremes of natural Being, where he does not find that, as in Kant, the ether of the spirit begins, but, rather, the vertiginous abyss of nothingness.[50]

This statement will become clearer if we consider it in the perspective of what is represented, for the Hellene, in the person of Socrates, tragic wisdom, and science.

SOCRATES, TRAGEDY, SCIENCE

A sentence in chapter 14 of *The Birth of Tragedy* both consolidates and demonstrates the principal arguments of the book, namely, the essence of tragedy and its death by Socratism:

"Optimistic dialectic drives *music* out of tragedy with the scourge of its syllogisms; that is, it destroys the essence of tragedy, which can be interpreted only as a manifestation and projection into images of Dionysian states, as the visible symbolizing of music, as the dream-world of Dionysian intoxication."[51] In his *Attempt at a Self-Criticism*, Nietzsche will add that tragedy, born of the Dionysian and of tragic myth, has died as a result of "Socratic morality," the dialectic, or the frugality and cheerfulness of the theoretical man. For, given that "the problem of science cannot be recognized in the context of science," that same science, considered for the first time "as problematic, as questionable," will be the task of this book, that is, "*to look at science in the perspective of the artist, but at art in that of life.*"[52]

In fact, as we have said in the beginning, the central and most interesting part of the work, in which Nietzsche establishes his "metaphysics of the artist," is found in chapters 7 through 15. These chapters center on the birth and death of tragedy, employing dense and difficult nuances, which are hard to grasp in their richness and, subsequently, their ambiguity. Socrates, who enters the stage in chapter 12, kills tragedy by speaking through Euripides: "Even Euripides was, in a sense, only a mask."[53]

Nietzsche associates Socratism, dialectics, and logic with science, to the extent that science advances by reasoning and maintains a finality and universal validity to the detriment of the power of illusion, intuition, appearance, and the play of fantasy that produces art and affirms life. The concept is ice cold, ossified, a symptom of an indigence rather than an ascendant and overflowing life, which justifies itself, affirms itself in its excess of force. Thus, regarding Heraclitus and Parmenides, Nietzsche will write:

> While each word of Heraclitus expresses the pride and majesty of truth, but of truth grasped in intuitions rather than attained by the rope ladder of logic, while in Sibylline rapture Heraclitus gazes but does not peer, knows but does not calculate, his contemporary Parmenides stands beside him as counter-image, likewise expressing a type of truth-teller but one formed of ice rather than fire, pouring cold piercing light all around.[54]

Calculated reasoning moves arduously; it requires solid foundations on which to step in the course of its laborious advance. But what gives philosophy the capacity to leap over great distances, to reach its objective by light and quick steps? It is an alien and illogical force called imagination. "Lifted by it, it leaps from possiblilty to possibility, using each one as a temporary resting place."[55] This is why Heraclitus appears to Nietzsche as a philosopher whose "regal possession is his extraordinary power to think intuitively," whereas "toward the other kind of thinking, the type that is accomplished in concepts and logical combinations, in other words toward reason, he shows himself cool, insensitive, in fact hostile, and seems to feel pleasure when he can contradict it with an intuitively arrived-at truth."[56] But when and how did tragedy die?

At the very beginning of chapter 11 of *The Birth of Tragedy*, Nietzsche states: "Greek tragedy met an end different from her older sister-arts: she died by suicide, in consequence of an irreconcilable conflict; she died tragically. . . ."[57] What this means, then, is that tragedy can only die tragically. And it died by the intervention of one of its greatest representatives, Euripides, the tragic poet who brought the common people onto the stage, who privileged the dialogue and its skein of arguments at the expense of music and the choir—in short, who excluded the original Dionysian element from tragedy: ". . . to reconstruct tragedy purely on the basis of an un-Dionysian art, morality, and world view. . . ."[58] What is tested, then, is the very *Apollonian clarity* that obstructs access to the Dionysian vision of the world and to the joy of beautiful appearances. It is the *Socratic aesthetic* or the dialectical optimist who, by way of his go-between Euripides, dissociates the Apollonian element from the Dionysian and kills tragedy. One could say that Socrates "is the father of the logic possessing the most pronounced characteristics of pure science.

He has destroyed the musical drama that had brought together the threads of all ancient art."[59] For dialectic, as science, is essentially optimistic, believing in cause and effect, a relation between crime and punishment, virtue and happiness. "The dialectic's arithmetic operations leave no remainder; it cancels out everything that cannot be decomposed by its concepts."[60]

Nietzsche realizes, however, that an anti-Dionysian tendency had already slipped little by little into tragedy even before Socrates, and that the predominance of dialogue and argumentation had made it more and more effective. In Sophocles, for example, one already experiences a displacement of the chorus by actors, which destroys its principal responsibility for creating the tragic effect, and thus contributes to its effacement in Euripides, Agathon and the new comedy.

If Nietzsche considers that the decline of tragedy reached its nadir with Euripides, it is compensated for by Sophocles and Aeschylus, both of whom fit the title of true tragic poets. But, in the end, it is Aeschylus who receives his nearly complete admiration. For it is Aeschylus who touched the surface of the most inexplicable and terrifying depths of myth. There is a difference between Sophocles and Aeschylus, though: in Sophocles, one is made aware of the glory of passivity; in Aeschylus, on the contrary, of the glory of activity. The hero of Sophocles's *Oedipus at Colonus* patiently endures the excesses of his agonies, thus demonstrating that it is at the extreme limits of his passivity that he accedes to supreme activity—an activity to which all of his conscious deeds and gestures of the past have not led. Inversely, Aeschylus's hero rises to titanic stature, gains culture by his own efforts and forces, and compels the gods to enter into an alliance with man, thus symbolizing the narrow and obscure link of mutual dependence that exists between men, particularly the artist, and the divine. Prometheus "found the defiant faith that he had the ability to create men and at least destroy the Olympian gods, by means of his superior wisdom which, to be sure, he had to atone for with eternal suffering."[61] This is why Nietzsche sees in the sovereign *power* of the great genius and in the stern pride of the artist the content and soul of Aeschylus's poem, while Sophocles's *Oedipus* sounds as a prelude the saint's song of triumph.

According to Nietzsche, the Promethean myth, which belongs, since its origin, to the Aryan community and evidences their gift for the profoundly tragic, has the same characteristic significance for the Aryan mentality as the myth of the fall has for the Semitic mentality. There exists between the two myths a family connection comparable to that between brother and sister. Only—and this will explain the difference between the two myths—in the Promethean legend man does not receive fire as a gift from heaven as a blazing lightning bolt or the warming rays of the sun; rather, he feels himself free and capable of mastering fire because of a sacrilege, that is, an act paid for with consequences that involve "the whole flood of sufferings and sorrows with which the offended divinities have to afflict the nobly aspiring race of men."[62]

> This is a harsh idea which, by the *dignity* it confers on sacrilege, contrasts strangely with the Semitic myth of the fall in which curiousity, mendacious deception, susceptibility to seduction, lust—in short, a series of pre-eminently feminine affects was considered the origin of evil. What distinguishes the Aryan notion is the sublime view of *active sin* as the characteristically Promethean virtue. With that, the ethical basis for pessimistic tragedy has been found: the *justification* of human evil, meaning both human guilt and the human suffering it entails.[63]

The Promethean hero, in his titanic striding to destroy the barriers of individuation and to rise up as the unique essence of the world, reveals through his acts the interconnection of two worlds: those of the human and the divine. These two worlds, taken separately, have right on their side, but confronted by one another, they are condemned to suffer for their individuation. The hero, however, must take it on himself to suffer the consequences of his rebellion and his immeasurable pride: ". . . which means he commits sacrilege and suffers. Thus the Aryans understand sacrilege as something masculine, while the Semites understand sin as feminine, just as the original sacrilege is committed by a man, the original sin by a woman."[64]

After this digression, which is necessary for Nietzsche to establish his view of the tragic, comes the question of the death of tragedy by the dialectical optimist or the Socratic aesthetic. For, according to Nietzsche, even if an anti-Dionysian tendency was in the air before Socrates, it was with him that this tendency reached an unprecedented fullness.

Indeed, in *The Birth of Tragedy* Socrates is presented as the model of the theoretical man, in whom the logical nature has developed in such an unbridled and excessive way that one can find a parallel only in the most powerful instinctive forces:

> In this utterly abnormal nature, instinctive wisdom appears only to *hinder* conscious knowledge occasionally. While in all productive men it is

instinct that is the creative-affirmative force, and consciousness acts critically and dissuasively, in Socrates it is instinct that becomes the critic, and consciousness that becomes the creator—truly a monstrosity *per defectum!*[65]

For Socrates, then, tragedy represents something unreasonable, a mere semblance of truth, "full of causes apparently without effects, and effects apparently without causes."[66] He reckoned tragedy among the flattering arts that portray only the agreeable, not the useful, and thus as something that can only be addressed to people "who are not very bright" (*Verstand*). In this Socratic universe, where tragic poetry no longer has the freedom of the city, it serves no purpose other than to revert to the new literary forms and be expressed, for example, in the forms of the Platonic dialogue:

> If tragedy had absorbed into itself all the earlier types of art, the same might also be said in an eccentric sense of the Platonic dialogue which, a mixture of all the extant styles and forms, hovers midway between narrative, lyric, and drama, between prose and poetry, and so has also broken the strict old law of the unity of linguistic form.[67]

But the question posed presently, and to which Nietzsche tries to produce a response, is that of knowing if between Socratism and art, between science and tragedy, or between theoretical and tragic man, there is *necessarily*, and simply, an antagonistic relation. And, further, if one can, in the end, conceive of an "artistic Socrates."

In fact, at the end of chapter 14 of *The Birth of Tragedy*, Nietzsche invokes passages from the *Phaedo*, where the imprisoned Socrates relates to his friends an apparition from a recurring dream that always urges: "practice music." Socrates, who up until then considered his philosophy to be the highest in the art of the muses, gives in, in the end, to the warning of a dream and starts to practice that contemptible popular music to which, however, the god urged him. Perhaps, asks Nietzsche, these words that Socrates has heard in a dream represent the only sign of a scruple or hesitation regarding the limits of logic. And in following this line of questioning, Nietzsche re-creates Socrates' own thoughts: "Perhaps—thus he must have asked himself—what is not intelligible to me is not necessarily unintelligent? Perhaps there is a realm of wisdom from which the logician is exiled? Perhaps art is even a necessary correlative of, and supplement for science?"[68] For Socrates' influence, "that has spread over posterity like a shadow that keeps growing in the evening sun,"[69] has persisted up until the present, and, it seems, will compel art to continual regeneration. What is being said here is that both the *theoretical man* and the artist bathe in the same illusion, in the tireless illusion and infinite delight in what is, of what appears, covered and uncovered, given and necessarily hidden: "Whenever the truth is uncovered, the artist will always cling with rapt gaze to what still remains covering even after such uncovering; but the theoretical man enjoys and finds satisfaction in the discarded covering and finds the highest object of his pleasure in the process of an ever happy uncovering that succeeds through his own efforts."[70] What this means is that science is optimistic and, in a certain way, naive in its endless search for the "truth," for the ground of things, their intelligibility and, subsequently, their justification. This is why Nietzsche evokes Lessing's confession, where he admits the search for truth is more important than truth itself. And it is in the person of Socrates that Nietzsche sees the prototype of the theoretical man. This is the type of man who has the unshakable faith that thought, using the thread of causality, can not only penetrate the deepest abysses and greatest expanses of being, not only attain being through consciousness, but even *correct* it. In this perspective, wisdom and knowledge acquire the virtue of a panacea and error is conceived as evil in itself.

But what is even more surprising, in that mad dash and insatiable thirst of optimistic knowledge, is the reversal operated by the forces at the very moment they reach their most extreme limits, and, thus, transform themselves into tragic resignation and into the need of art. For science, spurred on by its powerful illusions, falls short of its limits, where its optimism, concealed in the essence of logic, is totally wrecked.

> For the periphery of the circle of science has an infinite number of points; and while there is no telling how this circle could ever be surveyed completely, noble and gifted men nevertheless reach, e'er half their time and inevitably, such boundary points on the periphery from which one gazes into what defies illumination. When they see to their horror how logic coils up at these boundaries and finally bites its own tail—suddenly the new form of insight breaks through, *tragic insight* which, merely to be endured, needs art as protection and remedy.[71]

Perhaps *myth* is a necessary consequence of science. Myth may, moreover, be what science ultimately aims for, since the tragic artist, who comes to its aid at the very moment science shatters against its own limits, remains suspended in what remains in the covering, surface, epidermis, appearance, color, sound, word, and form. The artist is profound, because *superficial.* Art protects him from dying from truth: "truth in its condition of being eternally condemned to untruth."[72] In fact, "no doubt, certainty is what renders one insane. . . ."[73] Knowledge alone would thrust an artist toward dispair and annihilation. But art wills life, it saves him.

> Does he not actually live *by means of* a continual process of deception? Does nature not conceal most things from him, even the nearest things, his own body, for example, of which he has only a deceptive "consciousness?" He is locked within this consciousness and nature threw away the key. Oh, the fatal curiosity of the philosopher, who longs, just once, to peer out and down through a crack in the chamber of consciousness. Perhaps he will then suspect the extent to which man, in the indifference of his ignorance, is sustained by what is greedy, insatiable, disgusting, pitiless, and murderous—as if he were hanging in dreams on the back of a tiger.
>
> "Let him hang!" cries *art.* "Wake him up!" shouts the philosopher in the pathos of truth. Yet even while he believes himself to be shaking the sleeper, the philosopher himself is sinking into a still deeper magical slumber. Perhaps he then dreams of "ideas" or immortality. Art is more powerful than knowledge, because *it* desires life, whereas knowledge attains as its final goal only—annihilation.[74]

The above text of 1872 is related to what Nietzsche will call "the man who goes under," in Prologue 4 of *Thus Spoke Zarathustra*: "I love him who lives to know, and who wants to know so that the overman may live some day. And thus he wants to go under."[75]

In fact, after having pointed out the *overman* and *the man who goes under*, Zarathustra speaks of the most contemptible of beings, that is, *the last man*, in whom the flame of desire no longer burns, who can no longer even despise himself, and who lets himself be extinguished, slowly, dejectedly, in a nothingness of will. His bowstring has forgotten how to vibrate and he can no longer shoot the arrow of his longing beyond man. "What is love?" he asks. "What is creation?" "What is longing?" "What is a star?"[76]

But the man who *goes* under, the one who *wills his own decline*, may come to the last man's aid in order to make the overman appear. He is the arrow of longing shot toward the other river bank, the herald of the lightning bolt, the builder of the overman's abode, and he goes under, all the time heralding. Worse than the one who wills his own decline, is the one who *wills nothing at all,* not even nothingness. Worse than the theoretical man, who butts against the limits of his own logic and his thirst for knowledge, is he who perishes passively. For the theoretical man is the soil from which the artist may grow, the heavy drop falling from the dark cloud, the herald of the lightning bolt.

To the question posed by Nietzsche in chapter 14 of *The Birth of Tragedy,* namely, "if after all the birth of a 'Socratic artist' is something of a contradiction in itself," we add: Is a purely theoretical Socrates thinkable? Or, better still, can one conceive only of an absolutely theoretical being, and an absolutely artistic being?

If man is a rope stretched over the abyss between beast and overman, if he is a bridge and not an end, a passageway and a decline, moments between here and there, it is because his existence is nothing, in the last analysis, than an eternal imperfect: "And if death finally brings the forgetfulness he longs for, yet at one stroke it robs him of both the present and existence, and seals his realization that human existence is merely an uninterrupted past tense, a thing that lives by denying and consuming itself, by opposing itself."[77]

Thus man wills his own decline to call forth the overman, to engender art and other values, other judgments and other appreciations he is able to establish.

Nihilism, *Ressentiment*, "Great Pan Is Dead"

Nihilism

Although nihilism and the instinct of decadence that characterizes it did not develop fully until Nietzsche's third period—a period in which he elaborates his discoveries and insights regarding forces, their relations, and the *will to power*[78]—nonetheless, the distinctive lines of the nihilistic movement already appear in the writings of the first period, namely, those that treat the tragic, art, and culture in general.[79]

In a fragment written in fall 1887, Nietzsche defines nihilism in the following terms: "*That the highest values devaluate themselves.*"[80] This definition is preceded by several questions: "The aim is lacking; 'why?' finds no answer" "What does nihilism mean?"[81] Indeed, nihilism is a question of a movement that can neither be reduced to a psychological state, nor to a form or a historical fact, since it is—as Heidegger stresses—inherent in the very history of the West, moving through and traversing that history under all the forms in which it has been clothed:

> Nihilism is a historical movement, and not just any view or doctrine advocated by someone or other. Nihilism moves history after the manner of a fundamental ongoing event that is scarcely recognized in the destining of western peoples. Hence nihilism is also not simply one historical phenomenon among others—not simply one intellectual current that, along with others, with Christendom, with humanism, and with the Enlightenment—also comes to the fore within Western history.[82]

In other words, History cannot be thought but under the forms, under the forces and the relations of forces peculiar to nihilism. May it be, in Nietzsche's distinction, an active nihilism, insofar as it is a sign of the increased power of the spirit who prospers, increases, attacks, destroys and assigns itself new ends; or a passive and exhausted nihilism, that ceases to attack, to create and erect new ideals.

Although the complete awareness of this long-term process is only realized in the nineteenth century, its symptoms remain no less marked and recognizable under the masks, disguises, and transformations through which the different civilizations have passed up to Nietzsche's age. One of the faces and movements of nihilism is to settle into ideals, to disguise them, adorn them with shining cloaks and costumes, and with that devalue life, deny existence, illusion, appearance, and change. Another modern metamorphosis and expression of nihilism is its ability to destroy and invert its own values, previously considered the highest values, assigning to them new tasks, powers, and imperatives. For after having lost belief in the highest values, it is necessary to call forth another authority that knows absolutely how to speak, command and direct ends.

> The authority of *conscience* now steps up front (the more emancipated one is from theology, the more imperativisitic morality becomes) to compensate for the loss of *personal* authority. Or the authority of *reason*. Or the *social instinct* (the herd). Or *history* with an immanent spirit and a goal within, so one can entrust oneself to it.[83]

It is in this spirit, then, that *The Birth of Tragedy* establishes the state that has led to the Socratic culture of the nineteenth century—a state from which a mistrust of its own foundations arises and a loss of the naive confidence it had placed in the eternal validity of its presuppositions.

. . . it is a sad spectacle to see how the dance of its thought rushes long-ingly toward ever-new forms, to embrace them, and then, shudderingly, lets them go suddenly as Mephistopheles does the seductive Lamiae. It is certainly the sign of the "breach" of which everyone speaks as the fun-damental malady of "modern culture, that the theoretical man, alarmed and dissatisfied at his own consequences, no longer dares entrust him-self to the terrible icy current: he runs timidly up and down the bank. . . . Besides, he feels that a culture based on the principles of sci-ence must be destroyed when it grows to be illogical, that is, to retreat before its own consequences.[84]

But nihilism can only be defeated by itself, logic can only be over-come by its own limits, in the same way science sees itself constrained in retreating from the walls against which it butts its own optimism and its belief in an unlimited knowledge.

Nietzsche, moreover, distinguishes two types of nihilism: a *complete* and an *incomplete* nihilism. The former "is the necessary consequence of prior ideals," whereas *incomplete* nihilism assumed forms the end of the century was then fully experiencing. But what aggravates the problem, Nietzsche concludes, are the attempts to escape nihilism without reversing its values.[85] This is why he insists on another mode of pessimism, on a new road leading toward the *Yes*, the *Dionysian Yes*, that affirms the world such that it is and seeks to "understand the directions until then *denied*, not only insofar as they are necessary, but insofar as they are desirable";[86] desirable because of what they contain of strength, power, fear, and truth.

Ressentiment

Contrary to that acquiescent Dionysian, the spirit of vengeance and hatred regarding the noble strengths, exceptions and natures is revealed as largely symptoms of the herd instinct, which *denies*, depreciates, and con-demns life. In questioning the origins of nihilism, Nietzsche provides two answers, the second of which is as follows: "The lower species ('herd,' 'mass,' 'society') unlearns modesty and blows up its needs into *cosmic* and *metaphysical* values. In this way the whole of existence is *vulgarized*: in so far as the mass is dominant it bullies the *exceptions*, so they lose their faith in themselves and become *nihilists*."[87]

This is why in *History in the Service and Deservice of Life*, written in 1874, Nietzsche already lays stress on the effects that produce the masses on the development of Christianity, in the sense that Christianity's historical success, its power, tenacity, and duration would far from prove that it was due to the greatness of its founder but, on the contrary, only be evidence against it. For: "But between him and the historical success lies a very worldly layer, dark with passion, error, hunger for powers and honors, the still-active forces of the *imperium Romanum*, from which Christianity inherited that earthly taste and earthly residue which made possible its persistence in this world, and its staying power."[88] For Nietzsche, the best disciples of Christianity, that is, the most pure and authentic, have always obstructed rather than promoted its "worldly success"; they have been obstacles and naysayers to Christianity's so-called historical power and to the "process of the Christian idea."

But this does not only apply to the masses. The weak in general, the powerless and the decadents foster a constant rancor against productive and exceptional men. In this regard Nietzsche refers to the hostility that exists between the scholar (*der Gelehrte*) and the genius. The scholar is barren, whereas the genius is productive. The scholar is filled with petty instincts and trifling inclinations that are *human, all too human*, and which lead to pure knowledge, to wisdom without limits, without results, and therefore barren. This is the reason why geniuses and scholars are constantly feuding. "The scholar wants to kill nature, to dissect it and understand it; the man of genius wants to augment nature with freshly living nature . . ."[89]

But, as Nietzsche recalls in *The Birth of Tragedy*, the very optimism and belief in a unlimited knowledge on which the modern Socratic culture is based, can penetrate into the society's lowest strata and, in the end, turn against that same culture:

> Let us mark this well: the Alexandrian culture, to be able to exist permanently, requires a slave class, but with its optimistic view of life it denies the necessity of such a class, and consequently, when its beautifully seductive and tranquilizing utterances about the "dignity of man" and the "dignity of labor" are no longer effective, it gradually drifts toward a dreadful destruction. There is nothing more terrible than a class of barbaric slaves who have learned to regard their existence as an injustice, and now prepare to avenge, not only themselves, but all generations.[90]

The highest values can then also collapse, leaving a place for other values that could be filled with consequences, uncertainties, risks and new creations.

"Great Pan Is Dead"

The question of the death of God insofar as it involves a negation and devaluation of the highest values received its first explicit formulation in *The Gay Science*, Paragraph 108:

> *New struggles*—After Buddha was dead, his shadow was still shown for centuries in a cave—a tremendous, gruesome shadow. God is dead; but given the way of men, there may still be caves for thousands of years in which his shadow will be shown.—And we—we still have to vanquish his shadow, too.[91]

But the possibility that a god dies and the idea that it can have a twilight of the idols is already found in the texts leading up to *The Birth of Tragedy*. In a fragment of September 1870–January 1871, one, in fact, reads: "In the temple of Pan. 'Great Pan is dead.'"[92] This expression, already found in Plutarch and then reiterated by Pascal in the *Pensées* (thesis 695), will be repeated and elaborated by Nietzsche in *The Birth of Tragedy*, in the following terms: "Just as Greek sailors in the time of Tiberius once heard on a lonesome island the soul-shaking cry, 'Great Pan is dead,' so the Hellenic world was now pierced by the grievous lament: 'Tragedy is dead! Poetry itself has perished with her! Away with you pale, meager epigones! Away to Hades, that you may for once eat your fill of the crumbs of our former masters!'"[93]

The idea of the death of God occupies such an important place in Nietzsche's reflections, that Heidegger considers it as the beginning of the awareness of a radical inversion of values and of identifying God, insofar as he is a value, with the suprasensory world. "The suprasensory ground of the suprasensory world, taken as the efficient reality of the real, has become unreal. This is the metaphysical meaning of the word thought metaphysically: 'God is dead.'"[94]

But whether it be the Christian God, or Plato's Ideas, or the categorical imperative, what Nietzsche already denounces in the early writings, it is the moral background, the relation or the relations of forces that mutually dispute the power under the blinding glare and guise of ideals. The negative forces of life will its destruction, condemn it and flee from it. The affirmative forces of life, on the contrary, will its victory, its exuberance and its overabundance. This is why in the *Dionysiac World View*, written in 1870, one already sees Nietzsche state:

The Greek gods, in the perfection with which they already appear in Homer, are certainly not to be understood as having been born of calamity and need; it is certain that such creatures were not conceived by a heart shaken with fear; it was not to turn away from life that a genial fantasy projected their images into the blue. What speaks out of them is a religious life, not one of duty or asceticism or spirituality. All these figures breathe the triumph of existence, a luxuriant vitality that accompanies their cult. They do not make demands; all that exists is deified in them, regardless of whether it is good or evil.[95]

In a fragment of the same period (end of 1869–spring 1870) one can read something very similar: "The ascetic ways are to the greatest extent opposed to nature and are often only the consequence of an atrophied nature. Nature wills not to propagate a degenerated race. Christianity can only triumph in a decayed world."[96]

However, even defeated and overcome, nihilism still remains nihilism. Its values, although inverted, remain nevertheless values, to the extent that one can assert along with Heidegger: "But if the thinking that thinks everything in terms of values is nihilism when thought in relation to Being itself, then even Nietzsche's own experience of nihilism, i.e., that it is the devaluation of the highest values, is after all a nihilistic one."[97]

There is a difficulty here that will not escape Nietzsche, namely, nihilism can only be thought in an equivocal, paradoxical and ambiguous movement. It can in fact appear as an *active* nihilism, as an indicator of force, in the sense that "the force of spirit has been increased to such a degree that the fixed ends *up to that point* ('convictions,' articles of faith) are no longer adequate."[98] In this case other ends, other authorities and other circumstances can arise and serve as the fertile soil where such a spirit could prosper, grow and acquire the power for destruction and construction. But *active* nihilism can be also "a sign of a force insufficient to productively *assign* a new end, a why, a belief."[99] Everything is a sham, sighs the disillusioned spirit. Nothing is any longer worth the pain, better to let it die peacefully, calmly, cheerlessly, tepidly, in a nothingness of will.

But Nietzsche takes into account yet another form of nihilism. This is nihilism in its most extreme cast, where appearance, lie, and the taking-for-truth are more necessary, more profound and pure than truth itself. Then:

The most extreme form of nihilism would be: that *each* belief, each taking-for-truth, is necessarily false: because a *true world* does not exist absolutely. Thus: an *illusion of perspective* the origin of which resides in ourselves (as far as *we have a continual need* for a confined, abbreviated and simplified world).

—it is a *measure of force*, of degree, of how far we can admit to ourselves appearance, the necessity of lies, without perishing.

In this sense nihilism, insofar as it is negation of a veridical world, of a being, could be a divine way of thinking.[100]

WHAT WILLS *THE BIRTH OF TRAGEDY*?

We have mentioned at the beginning of our reflections on *The Birth of Tragedy* that the heart of the work can be found in sections 7 through 15. Here we discover the questions of the birth and death of tragedy and the relations between art and science, between art and Socratism, and the artist and the theoretical man. It is in this part that Nietzsche already discerns—although still not in the explicit, polemical, aggressive, and compressed manner of the later writings—the *relations of forces* at work in the world of art and science. For Nietzsche, art is what affirms, accepts, transforms, and transfigures life in its excesses, exuberance and overabundance. On the other hand, science, dialectic, theoretical knowledge, in short, *Socratism*, appear as the symptoms of lassitude, decadence, and twilight. They both reveal and disguise the forces that negate life, condemn, judge, and depreciate it.

Fifteen years later, in *Attempt at a Self-Criticism*, Nietzsche's genius, with all its richness of expression and analysis, will bring to light the forces and disguises employed by morality to deny existence. In this fifteen-page essay, where only an exceptionally gifted individual would have been capable of retracting his earlier view with a precision, audacity, insight, and incomparable beauty of style, Nietzsche denounces morality as the great enemy of life and as hostile to art:

> It was *against* morality that my instinct turned with this questionable book, long ago; it was an instinct that aligned itself with life and that discovered for itself a fundamentally opposite doctrine and valuation of life—purely artistic and *anti-Christian*.[101]

Why *anti-Christian*, if Nietzsche himself recognizes "the careful and hostile silence with which Christianity is treated throughout the whole book . . ."?[102] In fact, the principal enemy of art denounced in this book is not Christianity, but *Socratism*. Socrates, at least insofar as he is the model for the theoretical man and the source through whom the powers of logic and dialectic—destroyers of Dionysian art—are completed and perfected.

It is necessary, however, to take into consideration the development and changes in Nietzsche's work and thought. For, if at the time of *The Birth of Tragedy*, dialectic, logic, or science, in the person of Socrates, occupy the forefront of forces harmful to art and, consequently, to life, it will be Christianity that appears to Nietzsche in the later writings as the principal forms of nihilism and as being fundamentally, forcefully moral. Thus, in a fragment of 1888 in connection to *The Birth of Tragedy*, we read: "Art is here the only valid force that is a superior antagonist to every will to negate life: anti-Christian, anti-Buddhist, anti-nihilist par excellence . . ."[103]

Although *The Birth of Tragedy* makes explicit mention of Christianity (chapter 11) and two panegyrics to the Reformation and Luther, Nietzsche deliberately observes a "careful and hostile" silence toward Christianity. Christianity is considered neither Apollonian nor Dionysian, but as the enemy of life, art, and the only values recognized in *The Birth of Tragedy*, namely, aesthetic values. This is why, already in chapter 3, Nietzsche responds to what need, lack, or constraint has given rise to Olympus and its gods. "For there is nothing here that suggests asceticism, spirituality, or duty. We hear nothing but the accents of an exhuberant, triumphant life in which all things, whether good or evil, are deified."[104] It is deified and transfigured by an overabundance of life, where the will to appearance, lie, error, and illusion unfold as the affirmative *Yes*, the transfiguring *Yes*, the only true *Yes*, the supreme *Yes* of a state resigned to existence, "in which even sorrow, all kinds of sorrow, is made an eternally integral part, as a means of intensification: the *tragic Dionysian* state."[105]

Whereas Socrates is presented in *The Birth of Tragedy* as someone who has killed tragedy and decomposed Hellenism, art is here conceived "as the truly *metaphysical* activity of man."[106] According to Nietzsche, aesthetic values—and not moral values—are the only values by which the world and its existence can be justified.

> In truth, nothing could be more opposed to the purely aesthetic interpretation and justification of the world which are taught in this book than the Christian teaching, which is, and wants to be, *only* moral and which art, *every* art, to the realm of *lies;* with its absolute standards, beginning with the truthfulness of God, it negates, judges and damns art. Behind this mode of thought and valuation, which must be hostile

to art if it is at all genuine, I never failed to sense a *hostility to life*—a furious, vengeful antipathy to life itself: for all of life is based on semblance, art, deception, points of view, and the necessity of perspectives and error. Christianity was from the beginning, essentially and fundamentally, life's nausea and disgust with life, merely concealed behind, masked by, dressed up, as faith in "another" or "better" life. Hatred of "the world," condemnations of the passions, fear of beauty and sensuality, a beyond invented the better to slander this life, at bottom a craving for nothing, for the end, for respite, for "the sabbaths of sabbaths"—all this always struck me, no less than the unconditional will of Christianity to recognize *only* moral values, as the most dangerous and uncanny form of all possible forms of a "will to decline"—at the very least a sign of abysmal sickness, weariness, discouragement, exhaustion, and the impoverishment of life. For, confronted with morality (especially Christian, or unconditional, morality), life *must* continually and inevitably be in the wrong, because life *is* something essentially amoral—and eventually, crushed by the weight of contempt and the eternal No, life *must* then be felt to be unworthy of desire and altogether worthless.[107]

Then the question: "What wills *The Birth of Tragedy*?" could be substituted for by the question: "Who wills in *The Birth of Tragedy*?" For what is at issue here is a subject who interprets, evaluates, imposes a meaning and *wills* illusion so that truth will not kill him. "Truth is ugly: *we possess art*, lest we *perish of the truth*"[108] In other words, the value of the world lies in the interpretation of who establishes values. It is an expression of the growth or lack of growth of the power of who evaluates and names, from a particular perspective, what is "good" and "evil," "beautiful" and "ugly." This is why Nietzsche will say: "The world that *concerns us* is false, that is, it is not a matter of fact but poetic invention, a rounded off total of a meager sum of observations: it 'fluctuates,' like something in a state of becoming, like an error that is constantly shifting, which never approaches the truth: for—there is no 'truth.'"[109] There are only evaluations and interpretations from a relation or relations of forces, that affirm life, or condemn it. The interpretations are constantly and continually shifting, both as an obstacle and passageway to new interpretations and horizons for who evaluates, interprets, creates, and invents poetically.

What is beauty? What is ugliness? Nietzsche, who in *The Birth of Tragedy* conceived of beauty as a game of mirrors by which the Greeks as artists transfigured suffering, would say sixteen years later that nothing is more relative or bounded than our sense of beauty.

Nothing is beautiful. Only man is beautiful: when he embellishes the world with his own "beauty" and the reflection of his feeling of perfection. Nothing is ugly. Only man is ugly when he fills the world with his "ugliness," that is, with his weariness, degeneration, and exhaustion. This is why Nietzsche rails against the philosopher who claims the good, the beautiful, and the "true" are only one. Then he avows:

> It is the problem of the relations between art and truth that had first inspired me: now, again, I feel the same sacred indignation before their divorce. My first book was devoted to this problem; *The Birth of Tragedy* believed in art on the basis of another belief; that it is not possible to live with truth; that the "will to truth" is already a symptom of degeneration . . .[110]

But only someone like Zarathustra, who can climb to the summit of the greatest heights and descend to the deepest abysses, will be able to affirm that art is worth more than truth and say *Yes* unreservedly to life, "even to suffering, even to guilt, even to everything that is questionable and strange in existence."[111] One might say that such a thought can only be expressed *paradoxically*, since the will to power asserts itself in difference, multiplicity, becoming, change, the plenitude and overabundance of life through an unlimited *Yes*, a tragic Dionysian *Yes*, that involves both the luminescent and the terrible forces, the will to build and to destroy, the delight in becoming, which is also delight in annihilation.

2

The Interval

Human, All Too Human

> Human, all too human. One cannot meditate on morality without manifesting it and involuntarily revealing oneself morally.
>
> —*KSA* 12, p. 13

> I mistrust all systematizers and I avoid them. The will to a system is a lack of integrity.
>
> — *TI: Maxims and Arrows* (26)

Nietzsche published *Human, All Too Human* in 1878. In the following year a second volume was issued under the title: *Assorted Opinions and Maxims* and, finally, a third part, *The Voyager and His Shadow*, which appeared in 1880.

These three works, along with *Daybreak* and *The Gay Science*, are traditionally considered the intermediate works that link Nietzsche's early writings to his mature ones. Nietzsche himself, in a letter to Lou Salomé, dated July 3, 1882, saw *The Gay Science* as the result of six years of work which began with *Human, All Too Human*.

It is clear that any schema is arbitrary and insufficient when it is applied to the work of a great thinker, particularly if one takes into consideration, as is the case with Nietzsche, the enormous number of posthumous fragments attached to the completed works that Nietzsche elaborated with a view toward publication. And to those works one has to also add the letters, lectures, philological writings, and the student work.

But can one speak in a strict sense of a mature Nietzschean work? If one compares Nietzsche to Hegel from the point of view of intellectual production, the term "aging" well suits Hegel, for the Berlin lectures of the later years of his life were devoid of original ideas and were made up for the most part of old notes and works written before he came to Berlin. Nietzsche's career was different. The nineteen years of his public intellectual production, which began at Basel, in 1869, with the courses, lectures, and writings on tragedy, were marked by nuances and an intensification of ideas, discoveries, experiments, reprises, corrections, and particularly in the later years, by a dramatization, an irratability, a contraction, and at the same time, a richness of style and insights—until *his word* was finally silenced by madness.

In a somewhat pretentious scholarly introduction to Nietzsche's philosophy, Eugen Fink states à propos *Human, All Too Human*: "Like Janus, Nietzsche is a two-faced figure: both philosopher and sophist."[1] Although the author takes care to mitigate this assertion—which, at first glance, appears shocking—by claiming that Nietzsche had not cultivated sophistics as the art of debate, all the same it contains two fundamental errors. First, Nietzsche was not a two-faced figure but a thousand-faced figure. Second, the method practiced in *Human, All Too Human*, and which is one of the methods inherent in his very thought, his ethics and his vision of man and of the world, is neither that of demonstration nor persuasion. In a fragment of 1888 concerning style, he states emphatically: "Great style comes from great passion. It disdains pleasing, and forgets to convince. It commands. It *wills*."[2]

In fact, in introducing aphorisms in his work for the first time, Nietzsche not only introduced a difference regarding his earlier writings, but also an opposition to all deductive reasoning that proceeds on the basis of a concatenation of ideas derived from general principles. But the absence of logical continuity does not necessary mean the absence of meaning. This is why Nietzsche becomes indignant and poses the question of the shortsighted reader, the enemy of sentences: "*Against the shortsighted*—Do you think this work must be fragmentary because I give it to you (and have to give it to you) in fragments?"[3] In other words, the method Nietzsche proposes is that of genealogy and of dissection, a metaphor that he already uses and that will serve later on to indicate the role of the one who dissects, who analyzes, who interprets and evaluates:

> *Immoralists.*—Because they dissect morality, moralists must now be content to be upbraided as immoralists. But he who wants to dissect has to kill; yet only for the sake of better knowledge, better judgement, better living; not so that the world shall start dissecting. Unhappily, how-

ever, people still believe that every moralist has to be a model and ideal
in all he does and that others are supposed to imitate him: they confuse
him with the preacher of morals.[4]

In *Philosophy in the Tragic Age of the Greeks* (posthumous writing of
1873), Nietzsche already accords a privileged place to intuition and designates Heraclitus as the philosopher of "Sibylline rapture," as one who recognizes truth rather than deducing it or attaining it by "climbing the rope
ladder of logic."[5] And in *Human, All Too Human*, intuition and the exper-
imental method of aphorism will be used in the dissection, analysis, and
evaluation of the most hidden motivations of individuals, that is, their
excitations, their stakes, their forces, and instincts. It is Nietzsche's way of
being "objective": to reflect on the meaning of events he perceives with a
look directed toward the interior and at the same time turned toward the
distance, or, as Lou Salomé says in her beautiful book on the life and work
of the philosopher: "His defective eyesight gave his features a completely
unique kind of magic in that they only reflected whatever coursed through
his inner being rather then reflecting changing, outward impressions.
These eyes looked into the interior and, at the same time, looked far
beyond immediate objects into the distance: better put, the interior was
like a distance."[6]

Human, All Too Human represented for Nietzsche a crises, a rupture,
a victory, and a liberation from everything that was up until that point
fixed as ideal but which in the end turned out to be things only *human,
all too human*. He himself acknowledges this in *Ecce Homo*: "*Human, All
Too Human* is the monument of a crisis. It is subtitled "A Book for *Free
Spirits*": almost every sentence marks some victory—here I liberated
myself from what in my nature *did not belong* to me. Idealism, for example; the title means . . . where *you* see ideal things, *I* see what is—human,
alas, all-too-human!—I know man better."[7]

But can one speak here of a rupture in the sense of an absolute separation? When Nietzsche uses the word *Krisis*, he must very probably, in
that he is a philologist, be thinking of the Greek verb *krino*, which means,
alternately, to separate, to chose, to distinguish, to decide, to accuse, to
condemn, but also to explain and to interpret. For more than a rupture
with Wagner and with Schopenhauer's philosophy, which, moreover, continuously obsessed Nietzsche, this book is a reprise and a reevaluation of
the themes arrived at previously, such as morals, metaphysics, culture, art,
science, religion, and the State. This is why he would say, in the preface
to the second edition (September 1886):

But it has always required time, recovery, distancing, before desire awoke within me to skin, exploit, expose, "exhibit" (or whatever one wants to call it) for the sake of knowledge something I had experienced and survived, some fact or fate of my life. To this extent, all my writings, with a single though admittedly substantial exception, are to be *dated back*—they always speak of something "behind me"—[8]

But at the same time the perspective of *Human, All Too Human* extends and reevaluates the questions treated in the earlier work, it announces, prepares, and foreshadows the developments that will follow in the later works. Thus, the advice that Nietzsche gives to the readers of *Daybreak* is clearly applicable to those who try to understand *Human, All Too Human:*

This art (philology) does not so easily get anything done, it teaches to read *well*, that is to say, to read slowly, deeply, looking cautiously before and aft,[9] with reservations, with doors left open, with delicate eyes and fingers. . . . My patient friends, this book desires for itself only perfect readers and philologists: *learn* to read me well![10]

Human, All Too Human also longs for patient readers, experts in the art of ruminating over an aphorism, for it is through aphorism that Nietzsche establishes a new meaning in his work: the meaning of the fragmentary thought that thinks multiplicity, or, better, that thinks in multiplicity, becoming, difference, force, willing and relations. This is why this work is to be read and reread slowly, with a look aft and another before (*rück-und vorsichtig*).

The last paragraph of *Human, All Too Human I*, entitled "The Wanderer," is very curious, in that one engages someone who finds greater pleasure in change and passage than in the end. He advances amicably by changes, transformations, nuances, and chiaroscuro, which recall the greatest depths of night and the Daybreak, sometimes the most limpid, sometimes the most afire.

THE WORLD AS REPRESENTATION AND ERROR

Whereas in *The Birth of Tragedy* Nietzsche designates Kant's and Schopenhauer's philosophy as "*Dionysian wisdom* put into concepts" and sees in tragic art, and in music in particular, the copy of the originary One and the reproduction of the inner essence of things, *Human, All Too Human* involves an evaluation and a perspective remarkably different from the dominant ideas both in *The Birth of Tragedy* and the other writings of the first period.

Thus, neither art nor religion, nor metaphysics are capable of touching or furnishing the essence of the world or the thing-in-itself. But why the thing in itself? Does an essence of the world really exist? In fact, Nietzsche declares ironically: "Even if the existence of such a world were never so well demonstrated, it is certain that knowledge of it would be the most useless of all knowledge: more useless even than knowledge of the chemical composition of water must be to the sailor in danger of a shipwreck."[11] And in the same spirit: "Perhaps we will then recognize that the thing in itself is worthy of Homeric laughter: that it *appeared* to be so much, indeed everything, and is actually empty, that is to say empty of significance."[12]

Nietzsche does not deny that, in the age of the writing of tragedy, there can be a world where existence, with the aid of Dionysian art, could find a lasting pleasure behind the phenomenal world. What he criticizes, under the influence of Kant and Schopenhauer, is the pretension of science to a universal validity and the optimism of logic, that believes itself capable of realizing first causes and the inner essence of things. This is why he sees Kant's work as valuable, original, and innovative.

Certainly Kant has imposed limits on logic and has delimited the domains of knowledge, but he has not contested them thoroughly. Knowledge as such remains untouchable, in the sense that its limits and rights remain assured and safeguarded. Nietzsche has not yet unmasked the forces that hide behind these conceptions, and thus the relations and the will that governs them. Even in *On Truth and Lying in the Non-Moral Sense* (1873), he still hesitates. His bold insights are pared and softened by Kantian or Schopenhauerian formulas. Thus, regarding perception, the phenomenon, and the essence of things he will say:

> But generally it seems to me that the correct perception—which would mean the full and adequate expression of an object in the subject—is something contradictory and impossible; for between two absolutely different spheres, such as subject and object are, there is no causality, no correctness, no expression, but at most an *aesthetic* way of relating, by which I mean an allusive transference, a stammering translation into a quite different language. . . . The word appearance (*Erscheinung*)

contains many seductions, and for this reason I avoid using it as far as possible; for it is not true that the essence of things appears in the empirical world.[13]

To be sure, the essence of things, the thing in itself, the phenomenal world and the metaphysical world will reappear in *Human, All Too Human*, but to be considered, this time, as a sum of errors, illusions and passions created by humanity in order to deceive itself and to secure a stable, lasting, and profound happiness.

It is true, there could be a metaphysical world; the absolute possibility of it is hardly disputed. We behold things through the human head and cannot cut off this head; while the question nonetheless remains what of the world would still be there if one had cut it off. This is a purely scientific problem and one not very well calculated to bother people overmuch; but all that has hitherto made metaphysical assumptions *valuable, terrible, delightful* to them, all that has begotten these assumptions, is passion, error, self-deception; the worst of all methods of acquiring knowledge, not the best of all, have taught belief in them. When one has disclosed these methods as the foundation of all extant religions and metaphysical systems, one has refuted them![14]

In a study on Nietzsche, Ofelia Schutte observes that if a metaphysic obsessed him so intensely, it is because he also sought a beyond as the ground of values: "But his ground of values differed significantly from that of the traditional metaphysician. The metaphysical beyond to which Nietzsche objected rested on dualism, whereas he claimed a reality beyond good and evil, that is, beyond the human being's alienation from the flow of life."[15] And this is what appears in the first paragraph of *Human, All Too Human*, where Nietzsche insists on the necessity of a "Chemistry of the moral, religious and aesthetic conceptions and sensations,"[16] as well as emotions and affects related to the currents of modern civilization. In this aphorism, that in some way helps to better understand the other ideas that form the work, Nietzsche also refers to a historical philosophy, conceived not as a search for origins, for there are no pure origins, but as the effort to decompose *interminably* the phenomena and conceptions covered by the masks and disguises of metaphysics, aesthetics, and religion, in short, of morality. In this sense one can speak of a genetic search or of a genealogy, thus of a symptomatology. For that is the subject-matter of *Human, All Too Human*. To cut up and dissect an event, a fact, an idea, to interpret their metamorphoses, their irruption and disappearance, is at the same time to ask what forces have produced them, what will them, what will drives them, and which one had obeyed.

In *On Truth and Lying in the Non-Moral Sense*, cited above, Nietzsche already affirms that anyone who searches for truth, "truth in itself," the universal," is basically only seeking the metamorphosis of the world in human beings."[17] And, as in *Human, All Too Human*, Nietzsche invokes, in this work, the metaphor of the astrologer to indicate that the truth-seeker "measures all things against man, and in doing so he takes as his point of departure the erroneous belief that he has these things directly before him, as pure objects. Thus, forgetting that the original metaphors of perception where indeed metaphors, he takes them for the things themselves."[18] In other words, the "shifting mass" of metaphors becomes a solid architecture for the one who builds it, and whose memory assumes the role of forgetting: forgetting in favor of the one who searches for and discovers the "truth," who forges and builds the well ordered pyramid of logic and concepts. For such a search, discovery and conceptual structure are achieved, in the end:

> Only by forgetting this primitive world of metaphor, only by virtue of the fact that a mass of images, which originally flowed in a hot, liquid stream from the primal power of the human imagination, has become hard and rigid, only because of the invincible faith that *this* sun, *this* window, this table is a truth in itself—in short only because man forgets himself as a subject, and indeed as an *artistically creative subject*, does he live with some degree of peace, security, and consistency; if he could escape for just a moment from the prison walls of this faith, it would mean the end of his "consciousness of self."[19]

This is why, in *Human, All Too Human*, Nietzsche insists on becoming, on "historical philosophy," and the continual shifting of ideas and the faculty of knowing. Moreover, he rails against philosophers who consider man as a reality in itself, as something stable, immutable and eternal, toward which all things in the world originally converge. In fact: "All philosophers have the common failing of starting out from man as he is now and thinking they can reach their goal through an analysis of him. They involuntarily think of 'man' as an *aeterna veritas*, as something that remains constant in the midst of all flux, as a sure measure of things. . . . But everything has become, there are *no eternal facts*, just as there are no absolute truths."[20]

But man names and imposes a meaning on things and, in doing so, he believes he can attain the heart of the world and gain for himself a profound, stable, rich, and complete happiness. In this respect, he demonstrates the same arrogance one finds in astrology: "For astrology believes the starry firmament revolves around the fate of man; the moral man, however, supposes that what he has essentially at heart must also constitute the essence and heart of things."[21] In other words, the metaphysical world man creates, as well as his moral judgments, lie in the idea of the interest and utility he can draw from them: "First of all, one calls individual actions good or bad quite irrespective of their motives but solely on account of their useful or harmful consequences. Soon, however, one forgets the origin of these designations and believes that the quality "good" or "evil" is inherent in the actions themselves, irrespective of their consequences."[22] Nietzsche thus sees this capacity to forget acting at the very source of the judgment of so-called just or disinterested actions. "How little moral the world would appear without forgetfulness! A poet could say that God has placed forgetfulness as doorkeeper on the threshold of the temple of human dignity."[23]

Outside of this distinctly utilitarian treatment, the idea of the origin of moral judgments that interests Nietzsche in this period is influenced strongly by his reading of the French moralists, such as Montaigne, La Rochefoucauld, La Bruyère, Fontenelle, Vauvegargues, and Chamfort. A reevaluation will, however, come into play when he develops, particularly in the later writings, insights and elaborations around the *will to power*. Then, Nietzsche will place more stress on the relation or the relations of forces than on feeling. The questions he will pose will be thus: is it a question of an overflow of forces that affirm life and say *Yes* to its overabundance? Or of forces that deny life, condemn and judge it?

But although these discoveries only become transparently clear in the later period, *Human, All Too Human* already provides a glimpse of the relations and will grounding our representations, actions, and judgments concerning the world of metaphysics, aesthetics, religion, culture, and morality. Thus, in this work, Kant is presented as an obscurantist,[24] and Schopenhauer is praised with irony: "although all the dogmas of Christianity have long since been demolished, the whole medieval Chrisitian conception of the world and of the nature of man could in Schopenhauer's teaching celebrate a resurrection."[25] In a fragment written in 1887, Nietzsche recalls his break from both Wagner and Schopenhauer. This occured at the end of 1876, in the same period in which he reassembled his notes for what would later become *Human, All Too Human*. The critique he directs at Schopenhauerian philosophy is the most clear and incisive:

> Around the same time I realized that my instinct was after the opposite of Schopenhauer's: it aspired to a justification of life, even in its most dreadful, ambiguous and mendacious forms—for this I had ready the formula "Dionysian."
>
> (—against the view that an "in-themselves of things" must necessarily be good, blissful, true, one, Schopenhauer's interpretation of the in-itself as will was an essential step: but he didn't know haw to *deify* this will, and remained caught in the moral, Christian ideal.
>
> Schopenhauer was still so much dominated by Christian values that once the thing-in-itself' had ceased to be "God" to him, it must now be bad, stupid, absolutely reprehensible. He didn't understand there are endless ways that one can be different, ways even that one can be God.
>
> The curse of that narrow-minded duality: good and evil.[26]

Good and Evil, good and bad, just and unjust, so many evaluations transposed in the metaphysical world, so many symptoms of the forces of decadence that provide a meaning, or impose a meaning, that judge or condemn. Thus "the pessimistic condemnation of life in Schopenhauer is a *moral* transposition of the herd criteria in the metaphysical domain."[27] To move from this apparent world to a true world, from this conditional world to an unconditional one, from this contradictory world to a non-contradictory one, appears to Neitzsche as *reasoning inspired by suffering*: "fundamentally they are *desires* that such a world should exist; in the same way, to imagine another, more valuable world is an expression of hatred for a world that makes one suffer: the *ressentiment* of metaphysicians against actuality is here creative."[28]

The search for a more valuable world is equally evoked in a paragraph from *The Gay Science*. This time, however, the accent is on the need for support and stability, which is expressed among the masses as they represent the decadent forces aimed at preservation:

> Metaphysics is still needed by some; but so is that impetuous *demand for certainty* that today discharges itself among large numbers of people in a scientific-positivistic form. The demand that one *wants* by all means that something should be firm (while on account of the ardor of this demand one is easier and more negligent about the demonstration

of the certainty)—this too, is still the demand for a support, a prop, in short, that *instinct of weakness* which, to be sure, does not create religious, metaphysical systems, and convictions of all kinds but—conserves them.[29]

If one really wants to believe in something, the content and the arguments that ground it are of little importance. The necessity that something be held to be true is more imperious and more constraining than something actually being true. "The true world and the apparent world" is a formula that Nietzsche analyses from the point of view of the relation of values. Values and their modification are directly related to the increase or decrease of the power of the one who institutes them. The art of interpretation thus supposes the force of its interpretation.

> The inventive force that invented categories labored in the service of our needs, namely of our need for security, for quick understanding on the basis of signs and sounds, for means of abbreviation:—"substance," "subject," "object," "being," "becoming" have nothing to do with metaphysical truths.
> It is the powerful who made the names of things into law, and among the powerful it is the greatest artists in abstraction who created the categories.[30]

One already finds this essentially ambiguous character of metaphysics developed by the forces of decadence in *Human, All Too Human*. Here these same forces are revealed as those by which man invents, creates, labors, and builds a world at the same time more stable, varied and rich in significations. In this book, in fact, one sees a significant reevaluation of music in relation to *ideas* and thoughts. Whereas in *The Birth of Tragedy* music is presented as the mirror of universal willing and as the language most apt to reproduce the ground of nature and the ground of things, it is now given a place inferior to that of the plastic arts and knowledge:

> Music is thus *not* a universal language for all ages, as has so often been claimed for it, but accords precisely with a measure of time, warmth and sensibility that a quite distinct individual culture, limited as to area and durations, bears within it as an inner law. . . . It lies in the nature of music that the fruits of its great cultural vintages grow unpalatable more quickly and are more speedily ruined than the fruits of the plastic arts, let alone those that have ripened on the tree of knowledge: for of all the products of the human artistic sense *ideas* are most enduring and durable.[31]

No less important is the reevaluation of the figure of the genius in this transitional work. In the texts of the early period the genius was presented as someone who expressed symbolically the originary suffering of the world, and transfigured it, or as someone who, engendered by the culture of a people, sees himself on a cosmic and liberating mission, or as an exemplar of culture, in that he pushes *physis* so as to achieve it. *Human, All Too Human*, however, will completely reverse this perspective, and will present the genius as someone who *produces himself* by a laborious, patient, and common endeavor:

> Do not talk about giftedness, inborn talents! One can name great men of all kinds who were very little gifted. They *acquired* greatness, because "geniuses" (as we put it), through qualities the lack of which none who knew what they were would boast of . . . they allowed themselves time for it, because they took more pleasure in making the little, secondary things well than in the effect of a dazzling whole.[32]

The next paragraph begins in the same spirit:

> The belief in great, superior, fruitful spirits is not necessarily, yet nonetheless is very frequently associated with that religious or semi-religious superstition that these spirits are of supra-human origin and possess certain miraculous abilities by virtue of which they acquire their knowledge by quite other means than the rest of mankind. One ascribes to them, it seems, a direct view of the nature of the worlds, as it were a hole in the cloak of appearance, and believes that, by virtue of this miraculous seer's vision, they are able to communicate something conclusive and decisive about man and the world without the toil and rigorousness required by science.[33]

If this is now Nietzsche's conception vis-à-vis the genius, and if he considers "ideas" as being the most solid and durable among humanity's artistic production, one will be no less surprised to see him deploring an eventual renunciation of metaphysical perspectives; a renunciation that will involve limiting the horizon of the individual and depriving him of the impulse to build lasting institutions: "For the metaphysical outlook bestows the belief that it offers the last, ultimate foundation upon which the whole future of mankind is then invited to establish and construct itself."[34]

Thus, at the same time that metaphysics is presented in *Human, All Too Human* as the history of a great error and "the thing in itself" "worthy of Homeric laughter," it is precisely this error and this necessity for a *true*, stable world, free of contradictions and becoming that appear as what makes man master in the art of creating, inventing, thinking, lying, and contructing. Consequently, every effort to understand this history will itself be seen facing the same impasse as Nietzsche himself, that is, in a coming-and-going movement, in continual displacement, oscillating from one difficulty to another, without ever being able to settle—for here every possibility is valid and all solutions provisory. In the meanderings of reality, Nietzsche's thought tests, experiments with, and explores all the issues that it encounters on this road. That is to say, reality is already interpretation, already construction, a construction which is never completed, since it continuously begins anew. In a fragment most likely referring to *Human, All Too Human*, one in fact reads:

> One notices in my early writings a distinct will to open horizons, a certain guileful prudence before convictions, a distrust toward the traps set by conscience, and the magic tricks which lure all vigorous faith; free for everyone to see first hand the wariness of a scalded child, of a duped idealist . . . that taste which rebels against square oppositions, *desires* in things a good part of uncertainty and the suppression of oppositions, as a friend of half-tones, shadows, afternoon light, and infinite seas.[35]

This moving, fluent thought, friend of "afternoon light," is also found in the world of science, art, and religion.

SCIENCE, ART, RELIGION

To try to understand the ambiguous and paradoxical character of metaphysics, such as it is presented in *Human, All Too Human*, is at the same the time to discern it in its relations with science, art and religion. For in these three domains, Nietzsche's conceptions are all the more ambiguous, problematic, and subject to diverse interpretations as they are strewn with traps and surprises in nearly each parargraph, and sometimes in one and the same paragraph. In fact, despite the the thematic division of book I, for example, the subjects that develop in *Human, All Too Human*, such as metaphysics, science, art, religion, culture, and morality, interfere constantly with one another. They are found in the form of aphorisms, insights, and thoughts coordinated and juxtaposed rather than arranged in a logical and continuous order. Thus thinking in multiplicity, difference, and relation constitutes Nietzsche's fundamental method and objective. In *Daybreak* he will refer with irony and contempt to those who acquiesce to the spirit of a system: "Systematizers practice a kind of play-acting in as much as they want to fill out a system and round off its horizon, they have to try to present their weaker qualities in the same style as their stronger—they try to impersonate whole and uniformly strong natures."[36]

A number of commentators, however, see *Human, All Too Human* as representative of Nietzsche's "positivistic" phase or his *Aufklärung*, in the sense that he takes leave of his "metaphysics of the artist" and focuses his attention and hopes on science.[37]

Curiously, as is often the case, Nietzsche himself facilitates and prepares the ground for these interpretations when he affirms, for example: "The finest and healthiest element in science is, as in the mountains, the keen air that wafts through it.—The spiritually delicate (such as artists) avoid and slander science on account of this air."[38]

But science, in the way it is viewed in *Human, All Too Human*, is much more rich, much more flexible and nuanced than it appears at first glance. It is not situated in the sense in which it is understood by *theoretical man*, that is, as a system of logical propositions based on universal principles and connected the one to other by deduction and demonstration. Nietzsche continues to attack this means of knowledge, resulting from *Socratism* and characterized by an optimism thoroughly denounced in *The Birth of Tragedy*. He does this by referring to the "utility" that has hitherto dominated philosophy. "There has hitherto been no philosopher in whose hands philosophy has not become an apologia for knowledge; on this point at least each of them is an optimist, inasmuch as he believes that knowledge must be in the highest degree useful. They are all tyrannized over by logic; and logic is *by its nature optimism*.[39]

But Nietzsche's conception of science is neither to situate it in the framework offered by modern times, and whose principal role is to bring together data and proceed to the experimentation and introduction of these same givens in a deductive mechanism.

The science viewed by Nietzsche in *Human, All Too Human* is method, observation and analysis, a science that is not concerned to completely eliminate doubt, on the contrary: "science needs doubt and distrust for its closest allies."[40] Rather than a definitive model to rigorously follow, science is the open road of the free spirit, who does not exclude any particular science but who, at the same time, does not prefer one to the detriment of others. This will appear more clearly still in *Daybreak*, paragraph 432:

> There are no scientific methods which alone lead to knowledge! We have to tackle things experimentally, now angry with them and now kind, and successively just, passionate and cold with them. . . . We investigators are, like all conquerors, discoverers, seafarers, adventurers, of an audacious morality and must reconcile ourselves to being considered on the whole evil.[41]

Genealogy, genetics, and symptomatology are thus the methods used by Nietzsche in seeking, dissecting, analyzing, and unmasking the forces and the will that have produced our aberrations and our errors. "However credit and debit balance may stand: at its present state as a specific individual science the awakening of moral observation (*der moralischen Beobachtung*) has become necessary, and mankind can no longer be spared the cruel sight of the moral dissecting table and its knives and forceps."[42] Thus, to study the origin and evolution of moral sensations means to examine the history of their errors and misdirections, what science has, according to Nietzsche, sidestepped and neglected up until now. But the question which returns to this: Would it be possible to have happened otherwise? Doesn't Nietszche himself acknowledge that "we have for millennia made moral, aesthetic, religious demands on the world, looked upon it with blind desire, passion or fear"?[43] And that science will not eliminate these errors without disclosing some moral intention? Could they at least be eliminated?

> Rigorous science is capable of detaching us from this ideational world only to a limited extent—and more is certainly not to be desired—inasmuch as it is incapable of making any esstential inroad into the power of habits of feeling acquired in primeval times; but it can, quite gradually and step by step, illuminate the history of the genesis (*Entstehung*) of this world as an idea—and, for brief periods at any rate, lift us up out of the entire proceeding.[44]

Thus, niether the exact sciences nor the sciences in general would guarantee total freedom from our errors—"besides, it is not a desirable thing"—for these errors, with the nihilistic force of which they are the expression, are inherent in culture itself, its history, creations, ruptures, and developments.

Even given the above, there are several commentators who view *Human, All Too Human* as Nietzsche's "positivistic" phase comparable to his attachment to science. And perhaps foremost among the paragraphs and passages they use to support this point of view is the last sentence of paragraph 222 of Book I: "The scientific man is the further evolution of the artistic."[45] This affirmation, however, can mean something very different if one places it in the context in which it forms the conclusion. This is why we reproduce the entire paragraph:

What is left of art.—It is true, certain metaphysical presuppositions bestow much greater value upon art, for example when it is believed that the character is unalterable and that all characters and actions are a continual expression of the nature of the world: then the work of the artist becomes an image of the *everlastingly steadfast*, while with our conceptions the artist can bestow upon his images validity only for a time, because man as a whole has become and is changeable and even the individual man is not something firm and steadfast.—The same would be so in the case of another metaphysical presupposition: supposing our visible world were only appearance, as the metaphysicians assume, then art would come to stand quite close to the real world, for there would then be only too much similarity between the world of appearance and the illusory world of the artist; and the difference remaining would even elevate the significance of art above the significance of nature, because art would represent the uniform, the types and prototypes of nature—These presuppositions are, however, false: after this knowledge what place still remains for art? Above all, it has taught us for thousands of years to look upon life in any of its forms with interest and pleasure, and to educate our sensibilities so far that we at last cry: "Life, however it may be, is good!" This teaching imparted by art to take pleasure in life and to regard the human life as a piece of nature, as the object of regular evolution, without being too violently involved in it—this teaching has been absorbed into us, and it now reemerges as an almighty requirement of knowledge. One could give up art, but would not thereby relinquish the capacity one has learned from it: just as one has given up religion but not the enhancement of feeling and exaltations one has acquired from it. As the plastic arts and music are the measure of the wealth of feelings we have actually gained and obtained through religion, so if art disappeared the intensity and multifariousness of the joy in life it has implanted would still continue to demand satisfaction. The scientific man is the further evolution of the artistic.[46]

Already at the beginning of this passage one discovers that man is in a state of *becoming*, that is, a continual *having been*, a being who "is not something firm and steadfast." And to this idea of the essentially changing character of man, Nietzsche adds another: art teaches us to take pleasure in existence and to look at human life "as a piece of nature . . . without being too violently involved in it." In fact, one can detect a change of perspective here in relation to the "metaphysic of the artist" presented in *The Birth of Tragedy*, where art appears as that by which existence and the world are justified and transfigured. But what is important in this new conception of art is that Nietzsche continues to insist on the pleasure we receive from art, or on the capacity we get from art to enjoy what is yet to be completed: "if art disappeared the intensity and multifariousness of the joy of life it has implanted would still continue to demand satisfaction." Here, then, the accent is placed rather on the lack and on the pleasure derived than on the form or the forms under which knowledge appears, whether they be art, science, or religion. The conditional usage of the verb in the phrase (*so würde nach einem Verschwinden der Kunst*) emphasizes the idea that science is not a necessary result of art, nor the synthesis of what would be two moments: religion and art.

Nietzsche's conception of science, art, and religion remains here, and in other texts, ambiguous, fluent, and *paradoxical.* The forces that move them change and are constantly displaced, continually assuming new masks, new disguises, and new faces. This means that the different forms and expressions that clothe civilizations are inherent in their very history, as well as the different metamorphoses that civilizations traverse. This does not mean, however, that these forms and disguises unfold following an invariable and necessary course, for what they reveal and hide is precisely the ability these forces have to metamorphosize, mutate, and adapt.

Certainly, science manifests for Nietzsche the degree of maturity attained by a culture, and scientific method allows us to locate, uncover and diagnose the errors of our representations, but science—no more than art or religion—is incapable of reaching the heart of things or the "thing in itself." To Kant's statement, according to which "the understanding does not draw its laws from nature, it prescribes them to nature," Nietzsche will add that "this is wholly true with regard to the *concept of nature* that we are obliged to attach to nature (nature = world as idea, that is, as error). but which is the summation of a host of errors of the understanding.[47]

One should note, however, that these errors are neither to be condemned nor abolished. On the contrary, it is through them, through the misdirections and metamorphoses produced by religions and arts, that humanity has become more profound, more subtle, and more ingenious. "Anyone who revealed to us the nature of the world would produce for all of us the most unpleasant disappointment. It is not the world as thing in itself, it is the world as idea (as error) that is so full of significance, profound, marvelous, and bearing in its womb all happiness and unhappiness."[48] One will find resonances of this paragraph in *The Gay Science*, where it is a question of the art of dreaming, dissimulating, creating, and embellishing existence and the world through appearance, surface, and exteriority: "'The human being under the skin' is for all lovers a horror and unthinkable, a blasphemy against God and love."[49] This is why we always cry out against nature that vexes us and seems to violate our secrets of love. But we triumph over nature by the magic of dream, illusion and fantasy: ". . . we somnambulists of the day! We artists! We ignore what is natural. We are moonstruck and God-struck. We wander, still at death, unwearied, on heights that we do not see as heights but as plains, as our safety."[50] For: "An artist cannot endure reality, he looks away from it, back: he seriously believes that the value of a thing resides in that shadowy residue one derives from colors, form, sound, ideas; he believes that the more subtilized, attenuated, transient a thing or a man is, the *more valuable* it becomes; *the less real, the more valuable.*"[51]

Again in *The Gay Science*, paragraph 107, Nietzsche appears to return to his former conception of art, according to which "it is only as an *aesthetic phenomenon* that existence and the world are eternally *justified.*"[52] In fact, in this same paragraph art appears in addition as something that renders us most light, airy, and irresponsible:

> As an aesthetic phenomenon existence is still *bearable* for us, and art furnishes us with eyes and hands and above all the good conscience to be *able* to turn ourselves into such a phenomenon. At times we need a rest from ourselves by looking upon, by looking *down* upon, ourselves and, from an artistic distance, laughing *over* ourselves or weeping *over* ourselves. We must discover the *hero* no less than the *fool* in our passion for knowledge; we must occasionally find pleasure in our folly, or we cannot continue to find pleasure in our wisdom. How then could we possibly dispense with art—and with the fool? . . . And as long as you are in any way *ashamed* before yourselves, you do not belong with us.[53]

The conception of art presented in the tragic writings, that is, art as illusion and play, as the mirror of the universal will and the language

gushing from the world's foundation, will undergo successive transformations to intersect, in the later period, with this kind of perspective: art as
interpretation, as force, as the will to power, and as the will to deception:

> Knowledge-in-itself in a world of becoming is impossible; so how
> is knowledge possible? As error concerning oneself, as will to power, as
> will to deception.
> Becoming as invention, willing, self-denial, overcoming of oneself:
> no subject, but action, a positing, creative, no "causes and effects."
> Art as the will to overcome becoming, as "enternization," but
> shortsighted, depending on perspective: repeating in miniature, as it
> were, the tendency of the whole.[54]

But the vision of art as a deceptive game also appears in *Human, All
Too Human* in the form of a theme that Nietzsche has in fact never abandoned. In a paragraph entitled *Alleged "real reality,"* he employs both the
metaphor of the veil and that of the silk-weaver to present the poet as an
impostor, who behaves "as though he had been present at the weaving of
the whole nexus of the world."[55] The poet deceives *those who do not know*
(*Nichtwissenden*) and completes himself by being sincere and believing in
his own truthfulness."[56] In other words, people of sensibility wish to be
fooled; they return to the poet his own truth for, like him, they need the
poetic dream and appearances "as a beneficent relaxation and night for
head and heart."[57]

This, oddly enough, allows us to affirm that the more the appearance
is specious and false, the more it is true. All the more false, all the more
real. This is why

> Poets *conscious* of possessing this power deliberately set out to discredit
> that which is usually called reality and transform it into uncertain appar-
> ent, spurious, sinful, suffering, deceptive; they employ all the doubts that
> exist as to the limitations of knowledge, all the extravagances of scepti-
> cism, to spread a wrinkled veil of uncertainty over things: in order that
> after this darkening their sorcery and soul-magic shall be unhesitatingly
> taken for the path to "true truth," to "real reality."[58]

In referring, in paragraph 244 of *Human, All Too Human*, to the sum
of sensations, items of knowledge, and experiences that have been accumulated in European culture, Nietzsche insists on the necessity of a *new
Renaissance* as a means of diminishing the intensity of this torrent of sen-

sations that, according to him, endangers this culture's mental health. But what is the source of the force and intensity of these sensations? "We have Christianity, the philosophers, poets, musicians to thank for an abundance of profound sensations: if these are not to stifle us we must conjure up the spirit of science, which on the whole makes one somewhat colder and more skeptical and in especial cools down the fiery stream of belief in ultimate definitive truths; it is principally through Christianity that this stream has grown so turbulent."[59]

Thus, one sees here that science serves to remedy, regulate, and restrain the impetuosity of this torrent of sensations and emotions; whereas the philosophers, poets, musicians, and in particular, Christianity are considered as those principally responsible for this state of things. Now one reads in the same book, in paragraph 154, which is centered on the art of playing with life, that:

> The facility and frivolity of the Homeric fantasy was necessary for soothing the immoderately passionate disposition and over-subtle intellect of the Greeks and temporally banishing them. When their intellect speaks, how cruel and bitter life appears! They do not deceive themselves, but they deliberately and playfully embellish life with lies. Simonides advised his compatriots to take life as a game; they were only too familiar with its painful seriousness (for the misery of mankind is among the favorite themes for song among the gods), and they knew that even misery could become the source of enjoyment solely through art. As a punishment for this insight, however, they were so plagued by a delight in telling stories that it was hard for them to desist from lies and deception in the course of everyday life—just as all poetical peoples take a delight in lying, a delight that is moreover quite innocent.[60]

We have thus two paragraphs that analyze differently two situations that both maintain, nonetheless, basic resemblances: the first counsels recourse to science as a means of restraining the fiery emotions and sensations threatening modern Europe; the second affirms, inversely, that it will take the facility and frivolity of Homeric fantasy to temper the excess of passion and oversubtle intellect that reigns among the Greeks. In the first case, it is the poets and musicians, along with the philosophers and Christianity that feeds the impetuous river of fantasy and sensations dangerous to sanity; in the second, it is the poets who weave a veil of lies and fictions around life so as to make it more facile and supportable, for they know that "even misery could become a source of enjoyment solely through art."[61]

Then, do we have here, in these two cases, a contradiction or, rather, a way of thinking compelled to take account of the ambiguities, chiaroscuro, and paradoxes inherent in all interpretation and writing? This question could also apply to the entirety of *Human, All Too Human*, as well as to Nietzsche's work in general. The different analyses that develop *Human, All Too Human* around science, art and religion are and remain ambiguous. To neglect this fundamental attitude of their author, would be to ignore a way of thinking that moves and can only move in difference, multiplicity, fragmentation, and illogic.

> Among the things that can reduce a thinker to dispair is the knowledge that the illogical is a necessity for mankind, and that much good proceeds from the illogical. It is implanted so firmly in the passions, in language, in art, in religion, and in general in everything that lends value to life, that one cannot pull it out of these fair things without mortally injuring them.
> . . . Even the most rational man from time to time needs to recover nature, that is to say his *illogical original relationship with all things.*[62]

Thus only a stroke of force could make *Human, All Too Human* into a "positivisitic" work. As is well known, all positivistic reflection is based on the deductive system. This work, on the contrary, is constructed entirely out of aphorisms: it develops more by intuitions and by the lightning flashes of a fragmentary thought than by following the thread of a discursive thought.

Only by a stroke of force could one see in *Human, All Too Human* a representative of the Enlightenment thinkers. To be sure, Nietzsche dedicated this book to Voltaire as "one of the greatest liberators of the spirit"; he also insists on scientific method as a means of shedding light on the history of moral, religious, and aesthetic sensations. But this does not change the fact that he considers the idea of progress with contempt and irony, just like the discourse around reason and the French Revolution.

Nietzsche has written this book in the same spirit that he has written all the others, that is, to relax, to forget, and thus to recover from himself "in some piece of admiration or enmity or scientificality or frivolity or stupidity."[63] He has obtained this book by force and artifice, he has turned it to his advantage through falsification and poetry: "—and what else have poets ever done? and to what end does art exist in the world?"[64] For:

One lives no longer in the fetters of love and hatred, without yes, without no, near as far as one wishes, preferably slipping away, evading, fluttering off, gone again, again flying aloft, one is spoiled, as everyone is who has at some time seen a tremendous number of things *beneath* him—and one becomes the opposite of those who concern themselves with things which have nothing to do with them. Indeed, the free spirit henceforth has to do only with things—and how many things!—with which he is no longer *concerned* . . .[65]

To see an enormous chaos of diversities beneath oneself, to try to reassemble the pieces of this immense puzzle, of this backgammon game without end, is to add a signification, to interpret with courage, love and hate, with the force and the will to construct, that is also the will to destroy. Do not neglect the nuances, the tonalities, the softened light, nor the meter that beautifies, for:

Meter lays a veil over reality; it effectuates a certain artificiality of speech and unclarity of thinking; by means of the shadows it throws over thoughts it now conceals, now brings into prominence. As beautification requires shadows, so clarification requires "vagueness."—Art makes the sight of life bearable by laying over it the veil of unclear thinking.[66]

This is a thought that expresses, or that expresses itself through the play of drives, through forces, the relations of forces and the *Will to Power*.

THE RELATION OF FORCES, THE WILL TO POWER, MORALITY

From the perspective of the *Will to Power*, the study of the origin and evolution of moral sensations in *Human, All Too Human* reveals itself as the history of the errors produced by art, metaphysics, religion, and science. But this study will also show that these errors are precisely what have made humanity and the world at the same time profound, rich, terrifying, and charged with meanings. It is in this spirit that Nietzsche considers the problem of morality, when he refers to the fictions that man has woven, those fictions that have allowed him to lift himself above the animals:

The over-animal.—The beast in us wants to be lied to; morality is an official lie told so that it shall not tear us to pieces. Without the errors that repose in the asumptions of morality man would have remained animal. As it is, he has taken himself for something higher and imposed sterner laws upon himself. That is why he feels a hatred for the grades that have remained closer to animality: which is the explanation of the contempt formerly felt for the slave as a non-man, as a thing.[67]

This paragraph sums up the major questions that are treated and that occupy the center of Nietzsche's preoccupations in the later years of his productive life. These questions, that already arise in the early writings and which reappear in this period of transition as a kind of chiaroscuro, are those of *ressentiment*, nihilism, morality—in short, questions of the relations of forces and the *will to power*. That is to say, to pose the question of morality in Nietzsche is to pose the question of force, or the relation of forces that express the will to power. But what can be understood by *force* and by *will to power*? The interpretations that one can give are as diverse and ambiguous as those definitions and questionings given by Nietzsche himself regarding these two major points of his later philosophy.[68]

One could say that forces manifest the *will to power*, and that the will to power indicates, or determines forces at the same time that it is determined by these forces in their relations, their multiplicty, and becoming. But can one know a force? Is it a hypothesis or else an empirical statement? In fact, in a fragment dated fall 1885–fall 1886, Nietzsche poses the question: "Has the existence of a force ever been verified? No, only effects translated into a completely foreign language. We are so used, however, to regularity in succession that its oddity no longer *seems odd to us*."[69] In another fragment, dated spring 1888, where there is an implicit attack on Spinoza's conception of force, Nietzsche will enlarge the field of *will to power* by underscoring becoming:

> The will to accumulate force is special to the phenomena of life, to nourishment, procreation, inheritance—to society, state, custom, authority. Should we not be permitted to assume this will as a motive cause in chemistry, too?—and in the cosmic order?
> Not merely conservation of energy, but maximal economy in use, so the only reality is the will *to grow stronger of every center of force*—not self-preservation, but the will to appropriate, dominate, increase, and grow stronger.[70]

One sees here an energy dynamic spilling out across the entire organic, political, and cultural worlds, even across the entire cosmos.

Something similar is expressed in another fragment of the same period, which refers, this time, to an organic becoming and the idea of pleasure and displeasure in particular: "Let us take the simplest case, that of primitive nourishment: the protoplasm extends its pseudopedia in search of something that resists it—not from hunger but from will to power. Thereupon it attempts to overcome, appropriate, assimilate what it encounters: what one calls 'nourishment' is merely a derivative phenomenon, an application of the original will to become *stronger*."[71]

But returning to the previous fragment: there, in fact, after having criticized Spinoza's conception of force and insisted on the becoming of will to power, present in the totality of beings, Nietzsche turns his attacks against mechanism and its theory of effects:

> Is mechanism only a sign language for the *internal* factual world of struggling and conquering quanta of will? All the presuppositions of mechanistic theory—matter, atom, gravity, pressure and stress—are not "facts in themselves" but interpretations with the aid of *psychical* fictions.
>
> Life as the form of being most familiar to us, is specifically a will to accumulation of force; all the processes of life depend on this: nothing wants to preserve itself, everything wants to be added and accumulated . . . the basic innermost thing is still this will. (Mechanics is merely the semiotics of the results).[72]

Consequently, one will search in vain for a systematic analysis or a synthesis of what Nietzsche means by will to power. Thus, after having spoken of the "will to truth," the will to obey and to command, Zarathustra continues: "Where I found the living, there I found will to power; and even in the will of those who serve I found the will to be master."[73] One will again hear the echo of these words in a fragment dated fall 1885–fall 1886: "What are our evaluations and moral tables really worth? *What is the outcome of their rule?* For whom? in relation to what?—Answer: for life. But *what is life?* Here we need a new, more definitive concept of "life." My formula for it is: Life is will to power."[74] However, in a critique of Schopenhauer's concept of the *will*, Nietzsche will be quite incisive: "—this is the highest degree the case with *Schopenhauer:* what he calls 'will' is a mere empty word. It is even less a question of a 'will *to live*'; for life is merely a *special case* of the will to power;—it is quite arbitrary to assert that everything strives to enter into *this* form of the will to power."[75]

Thus, among the variety of Nietzsche's definitions of *the will to power,* such as it is expressed in the world of art, culture, the natural sciences, and knowledge in general, one will not find any answer that would be valid in all cases, any text that would be closed to or exempt from some new interpretation. But would Nietzsche proceed in any other way? Isn't any definition an interpretation that is added to another interpretation, that in turn becomes obsolete and therefore no longer has the force to impose itself? Is it not the case that all thought that attempts to capture the multiple is constrained to reinterpret, or to reinterpret *itself* out of a relation of forces, that are themselves constantly being renewed and repeated, in difference? "Interpretation,—*not* 'explanation' (in most cases a new interpretation over an old interpretation that has become incomprehensible, that is no longer itself a sign). There are no facts, everything is in flux, incomprehensible, elusive; what is relatively most enduring is—our opinions."[76]

In other words, to interpret is already to become master over something, it is to impose a new meaning, lay hold of it, appropriate it, reassembling and chosing the phenomena and facts in a continual process of reinventing, in a perpetual recreation. This is why the question "Who then interprets?" turns out to be an absurd question. For: "the interpretation itself is a form of the will to power, exists (but not as a "being" [*Sein*] but a *process*, a *becoming*) as an affect."[77] But just as interpretation can be a symptom of growth and an affirmation of life when it is made from a multiplicity of new perspectives, it can also be a symptom of decadence and exhaustion when it involves *inert* forces, that no longer question the enigmatic and disturbing character of the world. This is what is demonstrated, for example, in paragraph 99 of book I: "All evil acts are motivated by the drive to preservation (*Trieb der Erhaltung*) or, more exactly, by the individual's intention of procuring pleasure and avoiding displeasure."[78] Similarly, in paragraph 102 of the same book, one reads: "one desires pleasure or to ward off displeasure; it is always in some sense a matter of self-preservation. Socrates and Plato are right: whatever man does he aways does the good, that is to say, that which seems to him good (useful) according to the relative degree of his intellect, the measure of his rationality."[79]

Indeed, in every relation there are forces that command and forces that obey. The force that obeys is no less manifest in the will to power, for it is more difficult to obey than command, says Zarathustra. Inversely, the forces that destroy or auto-destruct, be it actively, or in a negation of the will, also express a will to power. For just as they are the forces that affirm life, they are also forces that condemn, and deny it. The slave remains no less a slave when he or she occupies the place of the master. One will find in this connection, in a series of reflections on nihilism, a suprisingly strong relationship with the paragraph of *Human, All Too Human* cited at the very beginning of this section. Thus:

> There is nothing to life that has value except the degree of power—assuming, presiscely, that life itself is the will to power. For *those who have come off badly*, morality provided protection from nihilism by confering on *each* an infinite value, a metaphysical value, and positioning him within an order that does not coincide with the worldly order of rank and power: it taught submission, meekness, etc. *If belief in this morality fell into ruin*, those who come off badly would lose their consolation—and *would be ruined too*.[80]

Thus, for Nietzsche, the degree of interpretation is measured by the degree of power, and vice versa. Where there is a *Yes* to life, there will also be a superabundance and surplus of life. Inversely, where one finds decline, lassitude, and the dimunition of force, life will also be denied, depreciated, and judged. The failures will see in the powerful their mortal enemies. Good and evil, noble and vile are categories that Nietzsche analyzes to the extent that he develops and elaborates the major lines and themes of *ressentiment*. Thus, in referring in paragraph 45 of *Human, All Too Human*, to the double prehistory of good and evil, he first considers them from the perspective of dominant tribes and castes: "He who has the power to requite, good with good, evil with evil, and also actually practices requital—is, that is to say, grateful and revengeful—is called good; he who is powerless and cannot requite counts as bad (*schlecht*). . . . The good are a caste, the bad a mass like grains of sand." In coming to the subjected and powerless: "Here every *other* man, whether he be noble or base, counts as inimical, ruthless, cruel, cunning, ready to take advantage." This question will be developed and better clarified when Nietzsche analyzes, in *On the Genealogy of Morals* (first essay), the origin of the qualitative "good" from the perspective of the powerful themselves, that is, of those who, being different from the commoners, the failures, the powerless, arrogate the right to name themselves and their acts "good."

In *Human, All Too Human* the influence of the French moralists of the sixteenth, seventeenth, and eighteenth centuries appears on nearly every page. Consequently, when Nietzsche examines and evaluates human behavior, the accent is placed rather on the causes, motives, love proper, and the instinct of self-preservation. This can be seen, for example, in paragraph 99 of volume 1: "All "evil" acts are motivated by the drive for preservation (*Trieb der Erhaltung*) or, more exactly, by the individual's intention of procuring pleasure and avoiding displeasure." In paragraph 102 of the same book, one reads equally: "one desires pleasure or to ward off displeasure; it is always in some sense a matter of self-preservation. Socrates and Plato are right: whatever man does he always does the good, that is to say: that which seems to him good (useful) according to the relative degree of his intellect, the measure of his rationality."

Now this evaluation, which already begins to change with *Daybreak* and further evolves in *The Gay Science*,[81] will be completely reversed ten years later, when pleasure and displeasure are no longer considered from the point of view of the *instinct of self-preservation*, but from the *will to power*.

> Man does *not* seek pleasure and does *not* avoid displeasure: one will realize which famous prejudice I am contradicting. Pleasure and displeasure are mere consequences, mere epiphenomena—what man wants, what every smallest part of a living organism wants, is an increase of power. Pleasure and displeasure follow from the striving after that; driven by that will it seeks resistance, it needs something that opposes it—Displeasure, as an obstacle to its will to power, is therefore a normal fact, the normal ingredient of every organic event; man does not avoid it, he is rather in continual need of it; every victory, every feeling of pleasure, every event, presupposes a resistance to overcome.[82]

In other words, the delight derived from power is inconceivable without displeasure. For "Displeasure does not merely not have to result in a *diminution of our feeling of power*, but in the average case it actually stimulates this feeling of power—the obstacle is the *stimulus* of this will to power."[83] The will to power, then, comprises both pleasure and displeasure, creation and destruction, the will to construct and the will to destroy, for one takes delight in what serves as an obstacle, resists, persists, and remains interminably to be overcome, without attacing to any end or object. To ask what aims the will to power, is to pose an absurd question, for what the will to power strives for is the intensification of power itself. This is why Nietzsche rails against those who seek or find an end for power: "And Helvétius demonstrates to us that men strive after power so as to possess the enjoyments available to the powerful: he understands this striving for power as will to enjoyment! as hedonism!"[84] The will of which Nietzsche speaks *does not will power*, since it is aleady will *to* power; it does aim to delight, because it is already delight, already rapture, a continual rapture, but one which is always begun anew, always renewed, in suffering and joyfulness, in the will to build and the will to destroy. This is not an instinct of preservation, but rather a will-ing-to-become-greater, willing-to-become-master, willing-to-become-more.[85] The more a will detects a decisive principle in the instinct of self-preservation, the more the world appears limited, confined, and truncated. Inversely, the more the will seeks greater power, the more the world will manifest its diversity of meanings, forms, perspectives, and resistances. "Rather has the world become 'infinite' for us all over again, inasmuch as we cannot reject the possiblilty that *it may include infinite interpretations.*"[86]

This allows us to affirm that it is always unproductive to arbitrarily judge Nietzsche's work without taking account of the changes of his thought, as well as his changing, inconstant, Protean character, which expresses itself through forces in their overabundance, their excesses and enormity. Such a thought can only lead to confusion:

> We are misidentified—because we ourselves keep growing, keep chang-ing, we shed our old bark, we shed our skins every spring, we keep becoming younger, fuller of future, taller, stronger, we push our roots ever more powerfully into the depths—into evil—while at the same time we embrace the heavens ever more lovingly, more broadly, imbib-ing their light ever more thirstily with all our twigs and leaves. Like trees we grow—this is hard to understand, as is all of life—not in one place only but everywhere, not in one direction but equally upward and out-ward and inward and downward; our energy is at work simultaneously in the trunk, branches, and roots; we are no longer free to do only one particular thing, to *be* only one particular thing.
>
> This is our fate, as I have said: we grow in *height*; and even if this should be our fatality—for we dwell ever closer to the lightning—well, we do not on that account honor it less; it remains that which we do not wish to share, to make public—the fatality of heights, *our* fatality.[87]

This swarm of forces deployed in *The Gay Science* through the tree metaphor is already expressed in certain passages of *Human, All Too Human*, even if in this work the accent is placed, not upon the *will*, but on *sensation*: sensations of power, sensations of vengeance, or of superi-ority. This does not, however, deter Nietzsche from using the tree metaphor in *Human, All Too Human*, where it serves to make manifest the different forces and indicate that the same soil and roots can bear good and evil, good and bad, vices and virtues: "But all these motives, whatever exalted names we may give them, have grown up out of the same roots as those we believe evilly poisoned; between good and evil actions there is no difference in kind, but at the most one of degree. Good actions are sublimated evil ones; evil actions are coarsened, brutalized good ones."[88]

One cannot deny that out of this blossom, that is, the errors, the wild deviations in moral judgments, a more varied world has grown, more marvelous, terrifying, and much richer in new interpretations. Thus, *goodness* and *wickedness* in judgments are neither terms of praise nor blame, for they essentially belong to them. This is why Nietzsche maintains: "He who wants to become wise will profit greatly from at some time having harbored the idea that mankind is fundamentally evil and corrupt: it is a false idea, as is its opposite; but it enjoyed dominance throughout whole ages of history, and its roots have branched out even into ourselves and our world."[89] In other words, there are no sins in the metaphysical sense, but neither are there, in the same sense, virtues, "that this whole domain of moral ideas is in a state of constant fluctuation, that there exist higher and deeper conceptions of good and evil, of moral and immoral."[90]

These considerations allow us to conclude that the role of morality is and remains paradoxical, for at the very same time it arrogates the right to judge or depreciate the world and life, it engenders, simultaneously, a multiplicty of meanings, knowledges, and discoveries in the different domains of art, religion, science, and metaphysics. "*Morality* a useful error; more clearly in the case of the greatest and least prejudiced of its advocates, a lie that is considered necessary."[91] Moreover, the figure of the ascetic, that Nietzsche already presents in *Human, All Too Human* and which will be taken up again and developed in the texts that treat nihilism and the will to power,[92] is typical of the inventiveness and the capacity possessed by the forces of decadence to transmutate and to assume new disguises. In a fragment of spring 1888 that refers to supreme values, Nietzsche will ask:

> *What* here determines the supreme value? *What* is morality, really?—The instinct of decadence; it is the exhausted and disinherited who *take revenge* in this fashion. *Historical* proof: philosophers are always decadents—in the service of the *nihilistic* religions.
> The instinct of decadence which appears as *will to power*. Proof: the absolute *immorality* of *means* throughout the entire history of morality.[93]

The history of morality is, in this perspective, the history of philosophy, and vice versa, for all philosophers are expert masters in the art of creating new tables, inventing and erecting new values. Thus, despite the privileged position the Pre-Socratics enjoy in the early writings,[94] and the considerations sometimes invoked regarding the Sophists, the texts of the later period present, more often than not, all philosophers as part of a great line of moral decadents: "Since Plato, philosophy has been dominated by morality. Even in his predecessors, moral interpretations play a decisive role (with Anaximander, the perishing of all things as punishment for their emancipation from pure being; with Heraclitus, the regularity of phenomena as witness to the moral-legal character of the whole world of becoming)."[95] In other words, the history of philosophy is this constant parade of masks which, successively, used by the forces of morality in their ability to disguise and continually change. In Greece: "These great philosophers represent one after the other the *typical* forms of decadence: the moral-religious idiosyncracy, anarchism, nihilism (*adiaphora*), cynicsim, obduracy, hedonism, reaction."[96]

But these same forces will be found throughout the history of philosophy, in that they both reveal and hide the instinct of decadence, *the will to annihilation, which is also will to power.* Modern dogmatists deck themselves out in philosopher's clothing: "Fichte, Schelling, Hegel, Feuerbach, Strauss—all of them stink from the odor of theologians and the Church Fathers."[97] The nihilistic forces serving morality are at work in all of them. Kant is no exception: "this nihilist with his Christian dogmatic entrails," this "catastrophic spider," who knew all too well how to weave a cobweb of dogmas, "considered pleasure an *objection.*"[98] But Kant's success was only that of a theologian. In him the repressed dogmatist ran directly into the blasé skeptic:

> inferior in his psychology and knowledge of human nature; way off when it comes to great historical values (French Revolution); a moral fanatic à la Rousseau; a subterranean Christianity in his values; a dogmatist through and through, but ponderously sick of his inclination, to such an extent that he wished to tyrannize it, but also weary right away of skepticism; not yet touched by the slightest breath of cosmopolitan taste and the beauty of antiquity—a *delayer* and *mediator*, nothing original . . .[99]

If one compares Nietzsche's attacks on Kant in the later years of his productive life with the virtually unreserved deference he gave him in the very early writings, and if one now considers these two periods in the perspective of *Human, All Too Human,* Kant will appear in this transitional work in a special light, that is, in a chiaroscuro, an interval. Here, in fact, Nietzsche tests, examines and dissects the forces at work in morality, without for all that arriving at the remarkable clarity of the analyses and conclusions present in the later philosophy. A text that confirms this idea can be found precisely in a paragraph entitled *Obscurantists,* where he tries to unmask the forces of decadence that hide not only in Kantian metaphysics, but in all critical metaphysics:

> Ingenious metaphysicians who prepare the way for skepticism, and through their excessive acuteness invite mistrust of acuteness, are excellent instruments in the hands of a more refined obscurantism.—Is it possible that even Kant can be used to this end? that he himself, indeed, according to his own notorious declaration, *desired* something of the kind, at any rate for a time: to open a path for *faith* by showing *knowledge* its limitations?—which, to be sure, he failed to do, just as little as did his successors on the wolf- and fox-paths of this most refined obscurantism: the most dangerous of all, indeed, for her the black art appears in a veil of light.[100]

This distrust that Nietzsche nurtures with regard to all pretentiously critical and skeptical metaphysics will only be stressed to the extent that he proceeds to cut up, analyze, and diagnose the nihilistic forces, characteristic of the history of thought. Through this history, it is the instinct of decadence, clothed in the flashy attire of skepticism and critique, that hides itself, it is the spirit of vengeance and hate toward all overflowing life, all plenitude, all excess that is continually at work. This *No* to life, in service of decreasing the forces of *ressentiment,* will be summarized ten years later by Nietzsche in the formulation: "In physiological terms, the *Critique of Pure Reason* is already a latent form of cretinism: and Spinoza's system is a phenomenology of consumption."[101]

But one must be content for the moment to observe these forces— that the inversion of all values will bore right through—under a pale glimmer of light which the considerations carried on causes, motives, and sensations render sometimes intense, sometimes diluted under nuances and tonalities rich in forewarnings. In the paragraph on obscurantism cited above, Nietzsche insists further on the play of light and shadow through which images of "black magic," "obscurantism," and "a veil of light" are alternated and exchanged, leaving one to divine something more than a simple recourse to literature. In fact, a more attentive reading of *Human,*

All Too Human in general, and of the posthumous fragments of 1878–1879 in particular, will reveal a fundamental attitude that dominates the philosopher's spirit in this period.

"DESCENT INTO HADES"

The abovementioned fragments, along with the information that fills his letters, are an inestimable source for understanding the state of profound solitude in which Nietzsche found himself during the period in which he wrote the two latter parts of *Human, All Too Human*: the poor state of health that compelled him to give up university activities, the headaches and the bad eyesight that hindered reading, going to the theater, visiting close friends, or forced him to hike for hours on end seeking fresh air, alone with his shadow. It is in this setting that he completed *Assorted Opinions and Maxims*, of which the last aphorism carries this significant section's title:

> *Descent into Hades,*—I too have been in the underworld, like Odysseus, and will often be there again; and I have not sacrificed only rams to be able to talk with the dead, but have not spared my blood as well. There have been four pairs who did not refuse themselves to me, the sacrificer: Epicurus and Montaigne, Goethe and Spinoza, Plato and Rousseau, Pascal and Schopenhauer. With these I have had to come to terms when I have wandered long alone, from them will I accept judgment, to them I will listen when in doing so they judge one another. Whatever I say, resolve, cogitate for myself and others: upon these eight I fix my eyes and see theirs fixed upon me.—May the living forgive me if *they* sometimes appear to me as shades, so pale and ill-humored, so restless and, alas! so lusting after life; whereas those others then seem to me so alive, as though now, *after* death, they could never again grow weary of life. *Eternal liveliness,* however, is what counts: what do "eternal life," or life at all, matter to us![102]

This aphorism bears witness not only to the state of the author's soul, but also, as G. Colli has observed, to "a dark" and silent philosophy, where objects and the world are displayed ephemerally, fleetingly, and from where the living emerge and disappear like shades, "so pale and ill-humored, so restless and, alas! so lusting for life."[103]

This vision continues in three fragments of the same period, where Nietzsche plays equally with shadow and light, suffering and the emphemeral: "The truth, like the sun, cannot be too bright, otherwise men would flee in the night and dusk."[104] "One should know how *to die* (*scheiden*) in a determined phase of life, like the sun reaches its extreme shine, even if one does not want to be reborn (*aufgehen*)."[105] "It is marvelous how I continue to believe myself away from the philosopher, and I moved forward with my nostalgia completely befogged. Suddenly."[106]

Descent into Hades often advances the arguments of those who wish to find or establish the influences and preferences that have marked Nietzsche's thought. But this task is always exceedingly difficult in that the same philosophers appear, in mentions elsewhere, sometimes elevated, sometimes denigrated, some of them even ignored completely in passages that evoke possible influences. In this aphorism, oddly enough, neither the Pre-Socratics nor Socrates himself are invoked. Absent also is Voltaire, to whom Nietzsche dedicated *Human, All Too Human*, and who is considered, in paragraph 463, as superior to Rousseau: "It is not *Voltaire's* moderate nature, inclined as it was to ordering, purifying, and reconstructing, but *Rousseau's* passionate follies and half-lies that called forth the optimistic spirit of the Revolution against which I cry: '*Ecrasez l'infame!*'"[107]

In another text, where the names of ancient "educators" appear, Nietzsche will recognize the Pre-Socratics, while the philosophers mentioned in the above aphorism are ignored, and denigrated with contempt: "The great philosophers are rarely successful. What are finally these Kant, Hegel, Schopenhauer, Spinoza?! So impoverished, so narrow! One understands that an artist may attribute more importance to himself than to them. The knowledge imparted by the great Greeks has educated me: there is in Heraclitus, Empedocles, Parmenides, Anaxagoras, Democritus more to admire, they are *more complete*."[108]

But it is Heraclitus who will appear as the only possible predeccesor for Nietzsche through the homage the philosopher pays to him in *Ecce Homo*, one of his last writings:

> Before me this transposition of the Dionysian into a philosophical pathos did not exist: *tragic wisdom* was lacking; I have looked in vain for signs of it even among the *great* Greeks in philosophy, those of the two centuries *before* Socrates. I retained some doubt in the case of *Heraclitus*, in whose proximity I feel altogether warmer and better than anywhere else, The affirmation of passing away *and destroying*, which is the decisive feature of a Dionysian philosophy; saying Yes to opposition and

war; *becoming*, along with a radical repudiation of the very concept of *being*—all this is clearly more closely related to me than anything thought to date.[109]

One will also find this *Yes* to impermanence and annihilation, to everything that passes and becomes, in the *Descent into Hades*, where those dwell who seem full of life, so full that "as though now, *after* death, they could never again grow weary of life."[110] But one can discover this same supreme *Yes*, the same mobility and capacity to always return to one-self, always more affirmative, always more overflowing and, at the same time, more lively and lighter, throughout the reflections Nietzsche raises from the depths of his most complete solitude. In the section of *Ecce Homo* devoted to *Human, All Too Human*, he will say in effect:

> That nethermost self which had, as it were, been buried and grown silent under the continual pressure of *having to* listen to other selves (and that is after all what reading means) awakened slowly, shyly, dubiously—but eventually it spoke again. Never have I felt happier with myself than in the sickest and most painful periods of my life: one only needs look at *Daybreak* or perhaps *The Wanderer and His Shadow* to comprehend what this "return to myself" meant—a supreme kind of recovery . . .[111]

But a "supreme form of recovery" is also a form of supreme affirmation, of saying *Yes* to contradiction and warfare, to becoming and destruction. The play of light and shadow that animates the period of *Human, All Too Human* is an expression of this multiple and Protean thought, that tends to suggest more than it actually gives. But the peculiarity of such thought is to express itself only through "vagueness," through nuances and light that are constantly modified, transformed, modularized and repeated, in difference. The *Wanderer* says to his *Shadow*:

> *The Wanderer: How* we talked together? Heaven defend me from long-spun-out literary conversations! If Plato had taken less pleasure in spin-ning-out his readers would take more pleasure in Plato. A consversation that gives delight in reality is, if transformed into writing and read, a painting with nothing but false perspectives: everything is too long or too short.—But should I perhaps be permitted to tell *what* it was we were in accord over?
>
> *The Shadow:* That I am content with; for they will all recognize in it only your opinions: no one will think of the shadow.

The Wanderer: Perhaps you are wrong, my friend! Up to now people have perceived in my opinions more shadow than me.

The Shadow: More shadow than light! Is it possible?[112]

Human, All Too Human, then, is a work of chiaroscuro and transition, where Nietzsche reevaluates his older ideas and foreshadows other reevaluations and conceptions that later works will develop, illuminate, and, in their turn, supersede. To try and undertand this move requires rediscovering it in his other writings, that is, in the pathways that bring us back insensibly, continually, sinuously to new horizons, to dangerous, unknown, and promising terrains.

3

Thinking and Writing as Artifice

> One does not only wish to be understood when one writes; one wishes just as
> surely not to be understood.
>
> —*GS* (381)

> There are many different kinds of eyes. The Sphinx also has eyes: there is in
> consequence many kinds of "truths," thus there is no truth.
>
> —*KSA* 34 (320), XI, p. 498

If *Human, All Too Human* appears to us as a transitional work, where
Nietzsche reevaluates his older conceptions and previews developments to
come, *Daybreak*, and particularly *The Gay Science*, are already inscribed,
to our thinking, in what will be the philosopher's last productive period.

To be sure, the influence of the French moralists is still quite visible
in *Daybreak*. The notions of the appreciation of values, sensation, pleasure
and displeasure, utility and love are dominant in this work as well. Even
so, the insights and reflections on what will much later become the ideas
of nihilism, the spirit of decadence and the will to power are more or less
clear and precise. Nietzsche already refers here to another kind of pleasure, that is, the pleasure caused by resistance and, in paragraph 271, one
will find an extremely interesting analysis of the game between the acqui-
sition and loss of power, and the joy that ensues from it.

In *Ecce Homo*, he opens the section devoted to *Daybreak* with this
statement: "With this book my campaign against morality begins." This
assertion is not entirely accurate if one considers Nietzsche's hostility

toward morality to be already present in writings prior to *Daybreak.* But the assertion is true to the extent that, the analyses concerning the relations between society and the individual, with the ethical consequences and signifcations resulting from these relations, do appear in this book. This work also contains the basic configuration of the critiques against modern civilization and a more definitive arrangement of the notions of decadence and the herd instinct.[1] All of these themes will be revisited, deeply and more precisely analyzed in *The Gay Science,* where one will, in fact, find the "herd instinct," the "death of God," "nihilism," as well as the elaborations centered on the will to power and the first statement of the Eternal Return.[2]

But can one speak of development in Nietzsche's work while maintaining that his thought is multiform, paradoxical, and ambiguous? Besides, certain insights and discoveries that do appear in the very first works stand in contrast, by their audacity and their richness, with works published immediately after. We consider, however, that to overlook all development in Nietzsche's work is as arbitrary as submitting it to a logical development carried to a grand synthesis, where all manifestations of a dualistic nature would be ultimately resolved. Moreover, Nietzsche himself constantly refers, in his prefaces, letters, notes, and in the body of the works themselves, to his earlier books, to the common questions which animate them, as well as to the writings he has immediately in view. In a letter of April 7, 1884, addressed to Overbeck, he states: "On reading *Daybreak* and *The Gay Science,* I happened to find that hardly a line there does not serve as an introduction, preparation, and commentary to the aforesaid *Zarathustra.*"[3] And in the preface to *On the Genealogy of Morals,* written in 1887, one finds in paragraph 2: "My ideas on the *origin* of our moral prejudices—for this is the subject of this polemic—received their first, brief, and provisional expression in the collection of aphorisms that bears the title *Human, All Too Human. A Book for Free Spirits.*"[4] Again, one will read on the title page of *The Genealogy:* "To complete and clarify *Beyond Good and Evil,* published recently.*"

Nietzsche, nonetheless, is and remains a *paradoxical* thinker. To move through his works, is to risk traveling through labyrinths or pathways that lead ceaselessly to new horizons, new creations, to a construction-destruction that continuously recommences and renews itself, in both repetition and difference. One could well apply to the Nietzschean text the metaphor of the road to Galta chosen by Octavio Paz as the point of departure of his book *El Mono Gramático*:

To the extent that I write, the road to Galta fades away and I am led astray into its ravines. Here and there I am compelled to return to the point of departure. Instead of advancing, the text pivots around itself. And at each turn it redoubles in another text, which is both its translation and transposition: an endless spiral of repetitions and reiterations that are resolved in the negation of writing as a road. I see my text going nowhere, save to meet itself. I have realized then that the repetitions were metaphors, and the reiterations, analogies: a system of mirrors that reveal little by little another text.[5]

Perhaps Nietzsche is his own metaphor, his own text, the road or roads leading him to himself, or, to use the metaphor of the old castle fortress that he once confided to Lou Salomé:

I resemble an old, weather-proof fortress which contains many hidden cellars and deeper hiding places; in my dark journeys, I have not yet crawled down into my subterranean chambers. Don't they form the foundation of everything? Should I not climb up from my depths to all the surfaces of the earth? After every journey, should not one return to oneself?[6]

In this chapter, we will try to stress Nietzsche's paradox or paradoxes, always insisting on his writing or on his text, a text we consider as splayed, as what resists and hides from the grip of discourse as such. This is why it is far from our intention to present a systematic and sustained account of precisely *what* will be paradox in Nietzsche. This would betray his very thought, a thought that gives itself only to the extent that it is masked and stripped of all restraint, all mastery, every interpretation. But doesn't every interpretation already hide another interpretation?

The hermit does not believe that any philosopher—assuming that every philosopher was first of all a hermit—ever expressed his real ultimate opinions in books: does one not write books precisely to conceal what one harbors? Indeed, he will doubt whether a philosopher could *possibly* have "ultimate and real" opinions, whether behind every one of his caves there is not, must not be, another deeper cave—a more comprehensive, stranger, richer world beyond the surface, an abysmally deep ground behind every ground, under every attempt to furnish "grounds." Every philosophy is foreground philosophy—that is a hermit's judgment. Every philosophy *conceals* a philosophy; every opinion is also a hideout, every word also a mask.[7]

OF STYLE AND MASKS

Nietzsche's more traditional commentators, such as Karl Jaspers, Walter Kauffman, and Jean Wahl, are unanimous in admitting that his work contains "contradictions" and ambiguities. The differences in these points of view only appear at the very moment the causes and reasons for these "contradictions" are determined. Most often, they identify them as "apparent contradictions," in the sense that they will form, ostensibly unknown to Nietzsche, a logical thread leading his texts toward a coherent and continuous unity. Another approach, that resembles the first, consists in affirming that Nietzsche is not aware of the "contradictions." This is characteristic of Karl Jaspers method in his classic study, *Nietzsche: An Introduction to the Understanding of His Philosophical Activity*, where, in reality, he tends to cast more light on his own "philosophizing." He makes the following interesting remark: "All statements seem to be annulled by other statements. *Self-contradiction* is the fundamental ingredient in Nietzsche's thought. For nearly every single one of Nietzsche's judgments, one can also find an opposite. He gives the impression of having two opinions about everything."[8]

But for Jaspers these oppositions resolve themselves on the condition that one situates them in the context from which they have been drawn and where they are integral in a logical movement, or, to use his own expression, in a "whole." "A *whole* emerges, not one already attained but one that impels us to persevere by raising the increasingly incisive question concerning the central axis of Nietzsche's entire thinking in all of its phases."[9] In other words, Nietzsche moves directly toward the whole, toward a reconciliation of all reality in the whole, but without realizing it: "He thereby loses sight of the cleavage between a conceivable whole in which all contradictions are resolved and the finiteness of *Existenz* that must choose between contradictories. *Without realizing it*, he is for a while stranded on the ancient idea of reconciliation within the whole."[10]

It is curious to note that these same authors who affirm the presence of a unity, a synthesis or an underlying order in Nietzsche's "contradictions," create, through this claim, two autonomous principles and thus fall into the very dualism they wish to avoid. It is not then a question of merely restoring to their context the citations which make Nietzsche sometimes a monist, sometimes a dualist, sometimes a dialectician, since in one and the same paragraph we can find multiple difficulties, where one runs into a thought that can only be expressed in a fragmentary, plural, or *paradoxical* manner. In this case, only forceful strokes can cut through it. This is why Kaufmann has become renown in the English-speaking world as the individual who, finally, cleansed Nietzsche of any blemish of antisemitism. Now the inverse result can also be obtained—and it has already been—on condition that one centers on those patently antisemetic passages in Nietzsche's work.

The old adage that one cannot dissociate an author from his or her style gains considerable force if one considers the variety of styles, genres, and tropes that serve Nietzsche as a means of expressing a thought that is itself multiform and paradoxical. He has effectively cultivated poetry, aphorism, *autobiography*, dialogues, philosophical treatises, maxims, parables, and proverbs.

> This is also the point for a general remark about my *art of style*. To com-*municate* a state, an inward tension of pathos, by means of signs, includ-ing the tempo of these signs—that is the meaning of every style; and considering that the multiplicity of inward states is exceptionally large in my case, I have many stylistic possibilities—the most multifarious art of style that has ever been at the disposal of one man. *Good* is any style that really communicates an inward state.
>
> Good style *in itself*—a pure folly, mere "idealism," on a level with the "beautiful *in itself*," "the good *in itself*," "the thing *in itself*."[11]

Thus, it is Nietzsche himself who includes and enhances the importance of *tempo* in the art of communicating by signs, for, as Eric Blondel recalls:

> One often stresses the polysemic charge in Nietzsche's texts, but one never speaks of rhythm (texts short or long, interrupted phrases, ana-coluthia, long dashes or blank spaces between the aphorisms, syncopa-tion, etc.), of melody (the concatenation of metaphors, hiatuses and movements of phrase, *Leitmotif*, alliterations, for example, in *Zarathus-tra*), of harmony (different levels of writing, allusions, citations of par-ody, a hierarchy of drives, etc.).[12]

It is thus the plurality of styles, genres, tropes and rhythms that essen-tially constitute communication in Nietzsche. He himself refers to his own diversity of states and, consequently, to the possibilities of expressing them and linking them together. Writing functions and unfolds as the means which, succeeding to the extent that it fails, tries interminably to bring about the connection and the passage between the different forces and meanings. But there is only meaning where there is resistance, and thus great delight. Zarathustra enjoys the chattering of his animals and reassures them by saying:

> —O my animals, replied Zarathustra, chatter on like this and let me listen. It is so refreshing for me to hear you chattering: where there is chattering, there the world lies before me like a garden. How lovely it is that there are words and sounds! Are not words and sounds rainbows and illusive bridges between things which are eternally apart?
> Precisely between what is most similar, illusion lies most beautifully; for the smallest cleft is the hardest to bridge.[13]

If speech is thus misleading when it is spoken, it will be even moreso when it is written, for writing is the art of falsifying, of turning to one's advantage what fulfills one's needs. In a fragment of 1884, Nietzsche reproduces Stendahl's citation of Napoleon's words: "An almost instinctive faith with me that every powerful man lies when he speaks and the more when he writes."[14] That is to say, writing is reading, imposing a meaning and grasping it, what presupposes the force of interpretation: "that previous evaluations have been perspective valuations by virtue of which we can survive life, i.e., in the will to power, for the growth of power; that every *elevation of man* brings with it the overcoming of narrower interpretations; that every strengthening and increase of power opens up new perspectives and means, believing in new horizons—this idea permeates my writings."[15]

In this perspective, there is *no single* interpretation, no *single* meaning, no *single* road. What one finds, or, better, what one creates, what one brings forth, are new evaluations, new horizons: "We set up a word at the point at which our ignorance begins, at which we can see no further, e.g., the word 'I,' the word 'do,' the word 'suffer':—these are perhaps the horizon of our knowledge, but not 'truths.'"[16]

Does Nietzsche thus reject all truth? Are there no truths? If he continuously affirms that there are neither "truths" nor "facts," will he then be prepared to admit that what he affirms is false, or at least not absolutely true? To be sure, in paragraph 43 of *Beyond Good and Evil*, he attacks the supporters of Truth, but at the same time he wagers on the philosophers of the future and on those who would keep *their* truths to *themselves*.

> Are these coming philosophers new friends of "truth?" That is probable enough, for all philosophers so far have loved their truths. But they will certainly not be dogmatists. It must offend their pride, also their taste,

if their truth is supposed to be a truth for everyman—which has so far been the secret wish and hidden meaning of all dogmatic aspirations. "My judgment is *my* judgment": no one else is easily entitled to it—that is what such a philosopher of the future may perhaps say to himself.[17]

The philosopher of the future, then, would have the power to name, to create and appropriate a meaning: "my judgment is *my* judgment." A truth thus remains truth insofar as other relations of forces do not reverse it in order to produce another truth, another meaning and another perspective appear in its place. If Nietzsche's thought, as we suggest, moves in and from a relation of forces, it follows that every interpretation is provisional and that his style changes according to the appearance of new perspectives that tend to condition it, and are conditioned by it. If Nietzsche always employed the same style for different perspectives, one can assume that they are not entirely autonomous and that they can only be expressed through that style. But, observes Alexander Nehamas:

> It may be objected to this claim that, in fact, if the same idea is presented in a variety of styles, it may well appear that this idea can be presented in any style, that it is thus independent of style, and that it is therefore absolutely true. But it seems to me that we cannot easily describe Nietzsche's various writings as each presenting the same idea in a different mode. Though there are naturally connections and repetitions, each work makes its own contribution to Nietzsche's literary and philosophical production.[18]

Nehamas is correct, but in our estimation he neglects this capital point: the same ideas neither become independent nor absolutely true precisely because they are expressed in a different way. Or, better, the *same* ideas are *reread* and *reinterpreted* at each instant, in repetition and difference, in a continual renewal and a continual *re-creation*. What is important is not what one says, but *how* one says it. In this sense, we will only be able to create when we know how to name what everyone *sees* and knows already. Consequently, all in all, there are no original individuals: "What is originality? To *see* something that has no name as yet and hence cannot be mentioned although it stares us all in the face. The way men usually are, it takes a name to make something visible for them,—Those with originality have for the most part also assigned names."[19]

But these same names, once spun out and written, become a picture filled with truths that quickly freeze. This is why thoughts must be constantly *retold*, rewritten, *re-read*, and reinvented; otherwise they will lose their morning freshness.

> Alas, what are you after all, my written and painted thoughts! It was not long ago that you were still so colorful, young, and malicious, full of thorns and secret spices—you made me sneeze and laugh—and now? You have already taken off your novelty, and some of you are ready, I fear, to become truths: they already look so immortal, so pathetically decent, so dull!
> . . . We immortalize what cannot live and fly much longer—only weary and mellow things![20]

Like his style, Nietzsche's thoughts are circuitous. Continually shifting, they move, transform, slip away, dissemble in order to reappear younger, more vivacious, more malicious and more artful. Their route is filled with unforseeable detours. Sometimes the pace is slower, becoming more hesitant, as if it wanted to mislead or distract the reader regarding the mask or the disguise it is about to adopt. It follows this cadence like "rivers with many meanderings and secluded hermitages; there are places in their course where the river plays hide-and-seek with itself and creates for itself a brief idyll, with islands, trees, grottos and waterfalls: and then it goes on again, past rocky cliffs and breaking its way through the hardest stone."[21]

If Nietzsche's thought is crossed by diverse transformations, if he often changes his style in the sense that he employs, for each occasion, figures, tropes, and different rhythms, it is because he has cultivated and managed to its limit, and even beyond its limit, the art of disguise. This art takes on, particularly from the point of *Zarathustra*, a subtlety and an elaboration such that Nietzsche assumes the right—perhaps to better mislead the reader—to confound personages while playing on the need for yet a second mask. This is what happens, for example, in the dialogue with the wanderer, paragraph 278 of *Beyond Good and Evil*: "And whoever you may be: what do you like now? what do you need for recreation? Name it: whatever I have I offer to you! Recreation? Recreation? You are inquisitive! What are you saying! But give me, please—' What? What? Say it! Another mask! A second mask!"[22]

The above dialogue begins with the metaphor of the sounding lead: "Wanderer, who are you? I see you walking on your way without scorn, without love, with unfathomable eyes: moist and sad like a sounding lead that has returned to the light, unsated, from every depth—what did it seek down there?"[23] One will find this same idea of "depth" in paragraph 289 of the same book, but this time enriched by metaphors of the cave, labyrinth, and the gold mine:

> When a man has been sitting alone with his soul in a confidential discord and discourse, year in and year out, day and night; when in his cave—it may be a labyrinth or a gold mine—he has become a cave bear or treasure digger or a treasure guard and dragon; then even his concepts eventually acquire a peculiar twilight color, and odor just as much of depth as of mold [sic], something incommunicable and recalcitrant that blows at every passerby like a chill.[24]

Beyond Good and Evil was published in 1886. In that same year Nietzsche wrote the prefaces for the reedition of *The Birth of Tragedy, Human, All Too Human, Daybreak, The Gay Science*, as well as book V of the latter. These prefaces, along with everything that had been written since *Daybreak*, are rich in metaphors such as veils, surface, nudity, skin, abyss, and everything related to subsoil. Thus, already at the beginning of the preface to *Daybreak* the ideas of undermining, darkness, and silence reemerge:

> In this book you will discover a "subterranean man" at work, one who tunnels and mines and undermines. You will see him—presupposing you have eyes capable of seeing his work in the depths—going forward slowly, cautiously, gently inexorable, without betraying very much of the distress which any protracted deprivation of light and air must entail; you might even call him contented, working there in the dark. Does it not seem as though some faith were leading him on, some consolation offering him compensation? As though he perhaps desires this prolonged obscurity, desires to be incomprehensible, concealed, enigmatic, because he knows what he will thereby also acquire: his own morning, his own redemption, his own *daybreak?* . . . He will return, that is certain: do not ask him what he is looking for down there, he will tell you himself of his own accord, this seeming Trophonius and subterranean, as soon as he has "become a man" again. Being silent is something one completely unlearns if, like him, one has been for so long a solitary mole—[25]

The passage most often evoked to confirm Nietzsche's basic affinity for masks is that which opens paragraph 40 of *Beyond Good and Evil*:

"Whatever is profound loves masks." But this passage can mislead the reader who is not aware of the exaggerated apology in favor of masks developing within the paragraph itself. This ostentation can be, moreover, another of Nietzsche's masks, for he on occasion knowingly laughs and mocks at any confidence and assurance too quickly accorded to his writings. Thus, the criticism he levels at Socrates could well be applied to himself: "Everything is exaggerated, eccentric, caricature, in Socrates, a *buffo* with the instincts of Voltaire."[26] However, in a letter addressed to Ferdinand Avenarius, December 10, 1888, Nietzsche admits to being a buffoon: "This year, where I am under the strain of having to reevaluate all values and that I, to speak literally, must bear the destiny of all men, it is incumbent on me to prove that I am, that I can be a buffoon, satyr or, if you prefer, a "serial writer," as I have been in *The Case of Wagner.*" In *Ecce Homo*, it is rather the desire to be a satyr that Nietzsche expresses: "I am, for example, by no means a bogey, or a moralistic monster—I am actually the very opposite of the type of man who so far has been revered as virtuous. Between ourselves, it seems to me that precisely this is part of my pride. I am a disciple of the philosopher Dionysus; I should prefer to be even a satyr to being a saint."[27] Again in *Ecce Homo*, we read a statement that is difficult to access: "I am one thing, my writings are another matter.—Before I discuss them, one by one, let me touch on the question of their being understood or *not* understood."[28]

Returning now to paragraph 40 of *Beyond Good and Evil*, one will find some passages where the mask, shame and profundity go together: Thus, already at the beginning: "Whatever is profound loves masks; what is most profound even hates image and parable. Might not nothing less than the *opposite* be the proper disguise for the shame (*die Scham*) of a god?"[29] Later on, it is the shame of human being in general to which Nietzsche refers: "It is not the worst things that cause the worst shame: there is not only guile (*Arglist*) behind a mask—there is so much graciousness in cunning (*List*)."[30]

These passages form very curious relations with Nietzsche's other texts in which the themes of shame, surface, and profundity also appear. But whereas the above paragraph speaks of the shame of a god or human being in general (*Mensch*), in the other texts it is rather woman (*das Weib*) who occupies front stage. This is why in a fragment of summer 1887, he will say:

> Woman (*das Weib*), conscious of man's (*der Mann*) feelings concerning women, *assists his efforts at idealization* by adorning herself, walking

beautifully, dancing, expressing delicate thoughts: in the same way, *she practices modesty*, reserve, distance—realizing instinctively that in this way the idealizing capacity of man will *grow* (—Given the tremendous subtlety of woman's instinct, modesty remains by no means conscious hypocrisy: she divines that it is precisely an *actual naive modesty* that most seduces a man and impels him to overestimate her. Therefore woman is naive—from the subtlety of her instinct, which advises her of the utility of innocence. A deliberate *closing of one's eyes to oneself*—Wherever dissembling produces the stronger effect when it is unconscious, it *becomes* unconscious.)[31]

In this same series of reflections, Nietzsche had affirmed a bit above that: "*truth, the will to truth* will in fact be something quite different and even a simple *disguise.*" Consequently, to disguise in order to show better, to hide depth under a mask, a veil, a surface, a skin, for the human being is surely something hideous under the skin. The more truth is concealed, the more seductive it becomes. The Greeks knew how to live, for they knew how to stop at the surface, they were able "to adore appearance, to believe in forms, tones, words, in the whole Olympus of appearance. Those Greeks were superficial—*out of profundity.*"[32]

In paragraph 339 of *The Gay Science*, Nietzsche revives the *Leitmotiv* of art as veil, lie, and game of deception, but, this time, he enriches it with the metaphor of woman (*Weib*) and transforms life itself into an artwork: "But perhaps this is the most powerful magic of life: it is covered by a veil interwoven with gold, a veil of beautiful possibilities, sparking with promise, resistance, bashfulness, mockery, pity, and seduction. Yes, life is a woman."[33]

These words resonate intensely in the Preface to the second edition of *The Gay Science*, mentioned above, where Nietzsche asks: "Perhaps truth is a woman who has reasons for not letting us see her reasons?" For truth is unbearable to look at: "No, this bad taste, this will to truth, to 'truth at any price,' this youthful madness in the love of truth, have lost their charm for us: for that we are too experienced, too serious, too gay, too burned, too *deep*! We no longer believe that truth is truth when the veils are withdrawn—we have lived enough not to believe this."[34] This is why he added two years later, when he would reproduce the same text in *Nietzsche contra Wagner*: "*Tout* comprendre—c'est tout mépriser . . ."[35]

Art is then the veil of lies and fictions that prevents us from dying from the truth. It is only insofar as one is an artist that one creates, destroys, and increases one's power. What is important in this case is to know how to and, above all, *be able to name* things and not to lift the mantle of appearances with which little by little things were enveloped and *became* what they are, that is, *things*, *realities*, and *essences*. Besides, one could not do without the masquerade of morality, morality "as symptom, as mask, as tartufferie, as illness, as misunderstanding."[36] In paragraph 352 of *The Gay Science*, Nietzsche recounts a tragi-comic parable to demonstrate what grounds the disguise of "moral men."

> A naked human being is generally a shameful sight. I am speaking of us Europeans (and not even of female Europeans!). Suppose that, owing to some magician's malice, the most cheerful company at table suddenly saw itself disrobed and undressed; I believe that not only their cheerfulness would vanish and that the strongest appetite would be discouraged—it seems that we Europeans simply cannot dispense with that masquerade which one calls clothes.
>
> Now consider the way "moral man" is dressed up. How he is veiled behind moral formulas and concepts of decency—the way our actions are benevolently concealed by the concepts of duty, virtue, sense of community, honorableness, self-denial—should the reasons for all this not be equally good? I am not suggesting that all this is meant to mask human malice and villainy—the wild animal in us; my idea is, on the contrary, that is precisely as *tame animals* that we are a shameful sight and in need of the moral disguise, that the "inner man" in Europe is not a long shot bad enough to show himself without shame (or to be *beautiful*).[37]

Nietzsche, then, sees morality's masquerade as a necessary lie and as both a symptom of decadence and an expression of the herd instinct. But the mask can also be a symptom of the growth of power, of the will to power, of the will to deceive and to be taken in. In other words, nihilism is fundamentally ambiguous, in the sense that it cannot be expressed, insofar as it is a relation of forces, other than paradoxically. In the *Journal of the Nihilist* one reads in fact:

> *Disaster:* What if lie where something divine? . . .
> What if the value of all things did consist in the fact that they are false? . . .
> What if despair would be nothing other than a consequence of belief in the *divinity of truth*?
> What if *lie* and *falsification* (converting into falsity), the introduction of a meaning, are not precisely a value, a meaning, an end
> What if one did believe in God not because he is not true (*but because he is false*—?).[38]

True and false are the judgments Nietzsche analyses from the point of view of the relation of forces. The most extreme form of nihilism consists, for him, in considering each belief, each considering-something-true as necessarily false, for *"there simply is no true world."*[39] But the will to illusion, the will that something be *held* to be true is more powerful, more constraining and more imperious than the "truth" itself. Thus, all considered, despair would be the consequence of a belief in the divinity of "truth." For only a madman would suffer absolute certainty. But perhaps even the madman would like to doubt, resist and be adverse to truth:

> Even if we were mad enough to consider all our opinions true, we should still not want them alone to exist—: I cannot see why it would be desirable that truth alone should rule and be omnipotent; it is enough for me that it should possess *great power.* But it must be able to *struggle* and have opponents, and one must be able to *find relief* from it from time to time in untruth—[40]

Tracy B. Strong draws a curious parallel between Nietzsche's conception of knowledge and the old Calvinist doctrine concerning the finitude of human knowledge.[41] For him, the two conceptions have, paradoxically, points in common. In fact, in the First Book of *Institutes of the Christian Religion*, Calvin states:

> For, since man is subject to a world of miseries, and has been spoiled of his divine array, this melancholy exposure discovers an immense mass of deformity: every one, therefore, must be so impressed with a consciousness of his own infelicity, as to arrive at some knowledge of God. Thus a sense of ignorance, vanity, poverty, infirmity, depravity, and corruption, leads us to perceive and acknowledge that in the Lord alone are to be found true wisdom, solid strength, perfect goodness, and unspotted righteousness; and so, by our imperfections, we are excited to a consideration of perfections of God.[42]

Strong does not refer, at least directly, to the text that we have cited above, and the parallel he makes between Nietzsche's conception of knowledge and that of Calvinism concerns rather the limits of the human capacity to know the world such that it is. Moreover, the author stresses that from 1872—the publication date of *The Birth of Tragedy*—Nietzsche insisted explicitly on the incompatibility between truth and life and on the necessity of new "horizons," bearers of meaning.[43]

We are well aware that at the beginning of January 1889 Nietzsche collapsed in a street in Turin and that from that point onward he was consumed by total dementia until his death on the 25th of August 1900. Some days immediately before and immediately after his collapse, he wrote letters and short notes signed in the name of Dionysus, or the Crucified or just Nietzsche. The question of knowing what is "normal" and what is "morbid" in Nietzsche's work remains for us an idle and futile one. Curiously, it is Nietzsche himself who asserts in a fragment of 1880: "Mad," a frontier as uncertain as good and beautiful! or "ridiculous" and "shameful."[44]

One thing we can be certain of is that his thinking and writing grew in intensity in the last five years of his productive life. The first person became more and more possessive and his style, particularly in the course of the last year, witnessed a contraction, tension, and a beauty never attained previously, while the art of disguise reached its summit. The mobility with which Nietzsche changes masks becomes all the more subtle the more often it escapes notice.

Some letters written in the period of crisis that preceded the eleven years of inactivity and progressive paralysis throw quite a bit of light on the last stage of Nietzsche's thought. Thus:

To Catulle Mendès, (dedication)

Turin, Jan. 1, 1889

Since I have proven to humanity that I am limitless, I will present them with my dithyrambs.
I put them in the hands of the poet of Isoline, the greatest and foremost satyr living today—and not only today . . .

Dionysus[45]

To Cosima Wagner

Turin, Jan. 3, 1889

I was told that a certain divine buffoon has lately completed his Dionysian dithyrambs . . .

(unsigned)[46]

To Meta von Salis

Turin, Jan. 3, 1889

Miss von Salis
The world is transfigured, for God is on earth. Can't you see all the heavens rejoicing? I have come to take possession of my property; I will throw the Pope in prison and I will execute Wilhelm, Bismark and Stöcker.

The Crucified[47]

To Heinrich Köselitz

Turin, Jan. 4, 1889

To My Maestro Pietro

Sing me a new song: the world is transfigured and all the heavens rejoice.

The Crucified[48]

To Jakob Burkhardt

Turin, Jan. 6, 1889

Dear Professor

Actually I would much rather be a Basel professor than God; but I have not ventured to carry my private egoism so far as to omit creating the world on his account. You see, one must make sacrifices, however, and wherever one may be living . . .

The unpleasant thing, and one that nags my modesty, is that at root every name in history is I; also as regards the children I have brung into the world, it is a case of considering with some distrust whether all of those who enter the "Kingdom of God" do not also come *out of* God.

Nietzsche[49]

Nietzsche is henceforth installed on the throne of God, whence he contemplates the unfolding of all history; or, more precisely, he *is* each name of history, since all barriers have been removed. There no longer exists either a high or low, a "beyond," nor an "on this side of." Zarathustra has already made sure of this:

But whoever is of my kind cannot escape such an hour—the hour which says to him:
"Only now are you going your way to greatness! Peak and abyss—they are now joined together . . .
But you, O Zarathustra, wanted to see the ground and background of all things; hence you must climb over yourself—upward, up until even your stars are *under* you.
Indeed, to look down upon myself and even upon my stars, that alone I should call my *peak*; that has remained for me my *ultimate* peak.[50]

Nietzsche has exceeded all limits. Meaning is no longer a problem, for *Vollendung* (completion) has reached its end. Thought now lives out of itself; in itself it consumes itself, gorges on itself, ceaselessly replenishing itself. "But I live in my own light; I drink back into myself the flames that break out of me," says Zarathustra in *The Night Song*.[51]

Madness and forgetting are two terms that continually reappear in Nietzsche's writings. Thus, in referring to the sighs of solitary and agitated minds: "Ah, give me madness, you heavenly powers! Madness, that I may at last believe in myself! . . . I am consumed by doubt, I have killed the law, the law anguishes me as a corpse does a living man: if I am not *more* than the law I am the vilest of all men."[52]

We will hear the echo of this complaint in paragraph 39 of *Beyond Good and Evil,* where it is a question of the death that can result from absolute certainty and knowledge: "Indeed, it might be a basic characteristic of existence that those who would know it completely would perish, in which case the strength of the spirit should be measured according to how much of the 'truth' one could still barely endure—or to put it more clearly, to what degree one would *require* it to be thinned down, shrouded, sweetened, blunted, falsified."[53]

Nietzsche often associates the madman with the fool, a comparison that appears in paragraph 107 of the *Gay Science:*

> At times we need a rest from ourselves by looking upon, by looking *down* upon, ourselves and, from an artistic distance, laughing *over* ourselves or weeping *over* ourselves. We must discover the *hero* no less than the *fool* in our passion for knowledge; we must occasionally find pleasure in our folly, or we cannot continue to find pleasure in our wisdom. . . . How then could we possibly dispense with art—and with the fool?—And as long as you are in any way *ashamed* before yourselves, you do not belong with us.[54]

Artists and fools are beings endowed with the privilege of being unable to adapt, to know how to dissimulate, falsify, and turn their needs to their own advantage. "We artists! We ignore what is natural. We are moonstruck and God struck. We wander, still as death, unwearied, on heights that we do not see as heights but as plains, as our safety."[55]

But it is not only on the heights that art plays its game of losing, hiding and forgetting; it also descends to the deepest abysses: "My melancholy wants to rest in hiding places and abysses of *perfection:* that is why I need music."[56] Music, abyss, forgetting, and solitude become synonymous under Nietzsche's pen. In other words, in order to enjoy art one must be alone, for the theater levels, flattens, and impedes art from exfoliating: "No one brings along the finest senses of his art to the theater, nor does the artist who works for the theater. There one is common people, audience, herd, female, Pharisee, voting cattle, democrat, neighbor, fellow man."⁵⁷ In this sense, anything perfect cannot be witnessed. The artist must flee the masses, forget the world, forget himself or herself:

> I do not know of any more profound difference in the whole orientation of an artist than this, whether he looks at his work in progress (at "himself") from the point of view of the witness, or whether he "has forgotten the world," which is the essential feature of all monological art; it is based *on forgetting*, it is the music of forgetting.⁵⁸

In a fragment of spring 1888, we read anew: "The word "Dionysian" means: an urge to unity, a reaching out beyond personality, the everyday, society, reality, across the abyss of transitoriness, a passionate-painful over-flowing into darker, fuller, more floating states."⁵⁹ On July 18 of the same year, Nietzsche writes a letter to Carl Fuchs that ends in these words:

> I have given to humanity a more profound book than it has ever possessed, my Zarathustra: a book that confers such a great distinction that one can state: "I have understood six phrases from it, that is, I have lived them," may belong to a superior order of mortals. But what he has to atone for this, what a price to pay for this! this nearly spoils the character! the chasm has become too wide.
> Your friend
>
> Nietzsche⁶⁰

Silence is close at hand, the chasm will soon be filled, doubt will no longer exist, for *Vollendung* will have reached its end. Nietzsche will be master of history: of the present, past, and the future. All the names will march before him and all the masks will be offered to him and they will all fit perfectly. Lou Salomé ends her very beautiful book on Nietzsche with this sentence: "We, too, are greeted by a shattering double-sound from his laughter, the laughter of a strayer—and the laughter of a conqueror."⁶¹

To be sure, *Vollendung* is forever concluded, but Nietzsche continues to smile. In *Beyond Good and Evil* he even says: "and occasionally even foolishness is the mask for an unblessed all-too-certain knowledge."⁶²

Perhaps foolishness was the last rampart behind which Nietzsche could entrench to better laugh at the world, to better laugh at himself . . .

SUFFERING, WRITING, TRANSFIGURATIONS

We have been able to establish that, in Nietzsche, style and masks change to the extent that new interpretations appear, and that these different interpretations reveal the impossiblity of even seeing thought stop at a single perspective, since it can only think in and from relations. In other words, there is interpretation only where there is, simultaneously, inclusion, overcoming and passage. One finds the same movements in the displacements that Nietzsche uses between the various states of health: sickness and health are for him lines of perspective or possibilities of reading and writing that allow passage from one state to the other, enveloping and repeating them, in difference.

> Looking from the perspective of the sick toward *healthier* concepts and values and, conversely, looking again from the fullness and self assurance of a *rich* life down into the secret work of the instinct of decadence—in this I have had the longest training, my truest experience. . . . Now I know how, have the know-how, to *reverse perspectives*: the first reason why a "revaluation of values" is perhaps possible for me alone.[63]

At the end of the 1870s, Nietzsche's health reached one of its lowest points. Constrained to give up university teaching in 1879, and given a pension that allowed him to live in modest furnished rooms, he led from that point onward an errant life between Sils-Maria, Nice, and a few Italian cities. The letters, notes, and fragments he wrote during that period are an invaluable source for understanding his state and his thought. Thus, in a letter addressed from Naumberg to Dr. Otto Eiser at the beginning of January 1880, one reads:

> On the whole, I have never been more happy in my life: and yet! Continual suffering, several hours during the day a feeling very close to sea sickness, a kind of semi-paralysis, which makes it difficult for me to speak clearly, in alternation with violent attacks (in the last one I vomited for three days and three nights, I wanted to die). It is impossible to read! I write very rarely! Impossible to see people! To listen to music! I must remain alone, take walks, breathe the mountain air and maintain a diet based on milk and eggs. All the internal sedatives turn out to be ineffective. I no longer have need of anything. The cold pains me greatly. . . . While walking, I scribble here and there on a few lose pages,

I never write on my desk, my friends decipher my scribblings. . . . I have already had several prolonged fainting spells. . . . Since the last examination, my eyesight has again gotten considerably worse . . .[64]

On March 30, 1881, when he was putting the finishing touches on the manuscript of *Daybreak*, he addressed a letter to Peter Gast complaining of the same symptoms: "My eyes are in a very bad state; at this moment, for example, after the work I did this winter, I must allow numerous days to pass without reading nor writing a word; and I hardly know how I was able to finish this manuscript."[65]

And still, seven years later, *Ecce Homo* will evoke with recognition:

The following winter, my first one in Genoa, that sweetening and spiritualizing which is almost inseparably connected with an extreme poverty of blood and muscle, produced *Daybreak*. The perfect brightness and cheerfulness, even exuberance of the spirit, reflected in this work, is compatible in my case not only with the most profound physiological weakness, but even with an excess of pain. In the midst of the torments that go with an uninterrupted three-day migraine, accompanied by laborious vomiting and phlegm, I possessed a dialectician's clarity *par excellence* and thought through with very cold blood matters for which under healthier circumstances I am not mountain-climber, not subtle, not *cold* enough. My readers know perhaps in what way I consider dialectic as a symptom of decadence; for example in the most famous case, the case of Socrates.[66]

It would no doubt be absurd to maintain that a causal link exists between sickness and artwork. But Nietzsche gives us reason to believe that art can only be produced under the conditions of failure and lack. In a fragment of 1888, he in fact claims: "These are exceptional states that condition the artist: all those who are profoundly related and tightly linked to morbid phenomena: so that it does not seem possible to be an artist without being sick."[67] We know that Dostoevsky was epileptic. Homer was blind, Beethoven was deaf, and Byron had a club foot. Nietzsche often examines the suffering that can be contained in an artwork; he always sees it as an effort directed at compensation, overcoming, and transfiguration on the part of the producer of the artwork. Thus with regard to Homer: ". . . do you not feel the pessimist and hypersensitive person who, because of his sufferings, invents in his poems the bountiful accomplishments of the Olympian gods!"[68] And in another fragment of the same period: "Beethoven—a great poor man, deaf, loving, misunderstood, philosopher, whose music is full of monumental or sad dreams."[69] It is, in the end, all the geniuses who have need to create, invent, and refashion the world and existence: "Plato's irony, which allows of an excessive delicacy of feeling and sensation, of a vulnerability of the heart to protect it or at least to hide it, the Olympian nature of Goethe, who wrote verses on his suffering in order to be delivered from it, as was also the case with Stendahl and Mérimée."[70]

But the artist is not the characters he places into the world, otherwise he would not have to create them: "A Homer would not have created an Achilles nor a Goethe a Faust if Homer had been an Achilles or Goethe a Faust."[71] And, one could add: Mozart would not have created Don Giovanni, nor da Vinci the Mona Lisa, nor Shakespeare Hamlet, no more than Nietzsche would not have borne Zarathustra if he were what he represented. The artist is "after all, only the precondition of his work, the womb, the soil, sometimes the dung and manure on which, out of which, it grows. . . ."[72] But once the artwork enters the world, it is necessary to forget it if one wishes to continue to take delight in it. In a letter of May 7, 1885, addressed to his sister, Nietzsche makes explicit the relation between the artist and his work, while underscoring the difference that separates them: "Do not believe that my son Zarathustra expresses my thoughts. He is one of my prologues, one of my interludes." This idea will reappear in *Ecce Homo*, when Nietzsche will take a further step and ask at what point the artist can maintain certainty:

> The great poet dips *only* from his own reality—up to the point where afterward he cannot endure his work any longer . . .
>
> I know no more heart-rending reading than Shakespeare: what must a man have suffered to have such a need of being a buffoon!
>
> Is Hamlet *understood*? Not doubt, *certainty* is what drives one insane.—But one must be profound, an abyss, a philosopher to feel that way.—We are all *afraid* of truth.[73]

But art prevents us from perishing of the truth. That is to say, through creation the artist transfigures, continually, what resists him and what remains in appearance, surface, sound, color, and form. Inevitably, however, the question arises: Why in Nietzsche does everything come to such a bad end? In fact, and to judge it from a purely empirical standpoint, the same question could also be applied to the premature death of the consumptive poet Keats, to Kleist's suicide, and the precocious and progressive dementia of Hölderlin.

Walter Kaufmann observes correctly that these facts do not invalidate that other fact—namely, the capacity—until its last resources—these geniuses demonstrated as they triumphed over their suffering.[74] But in our view, Kaufmann, as well as Deleuze, approach the problem only on a strictly empirical plane. The question remains one of knowing,—as we have tried to show in the preceding section—if art is not itself ultimately proved incapable of overcoming suffering, *if it is not itself turned back at the very moment it reaches its extreme limit,* thus obliging Nietzsche to leap the divide. Perhaps the ingenuity he employs in making and changing masks has, after all, given way to a supreme wisdom, even if it must hereafter take on the traits of death. In a fragment of 1885, we in fact read: "It would be necessary for us, and for good reasons, to be loners, and even to wear masks:—we will thus be unaccustomed to seek out those who are our fellow-creatures. We live alone and undoubtedly know the martyr of all seven solitudes."[75]

Sickness and health are two states that Nietzsche analyses from the perspective of those who are typically healthy (*im Grunde gesund*) and those who, inversely, are fundamentally sick, that is, exhausted, weak, decadent.

A typically morbid being cannot become healthy, much less make itself healthy. For a typically healthy person, conversely, being sick can even become an energetic *stimulus* for life, for living *more . . .*

For it should be noted: it was during the years of my lowest vitality that I *ceased* to be a pessimist; the instinct of self-restoration *forbade* me a philosophy of poverty and discouragement.

What is it, fundamentally, that allows us to recognize *who has turned out well?* That a well-turned-out person pleases our senses, that he is carved from wood that is hard, delicate, and at the same time smells good.[76]

The act of philosophizing becomes thus for Nietzsche and occasion to carry out a victory over the different stages and states that inflict illness on him. This means that the sick person travels through himself: groping across abysses, recesses, and hiding places, endlessly seeking the sun and the blue sky above. His eyesight becomes more acute, his step lighter and his ear catches and delights in a music that no one has ever heard before. One divines, one is compelled to divine the misdirections, the detours, the labyrinths, and the egresses in which, across which thought has carried every suffering philosopher. And it is only because they have a *sick body* that they let themselves attract and seduce. "The unconscious disguise of physiological needs under the cloaks of the objective, ideal, purely spiritual goes to frightening lengths—and often I have asked myself whether, taking a large view, philosophy has not been merely an interpretation of the body and a *misunderstanding of the body*."⁷⁷ In this sense, the questions and answers advanced by metaphysics on the *value* of existence are just so many symptoms, so many translations of the dispositions and physical constitutions of an individual, a social class or even entire civilizations. But the importance of these symptoms resides precisely in the knowledge they provide as to the general constitution of the body, "as hints or symptoms of the body, of its success or failure, its plenitude, power, or autocracy in history, or of its frustrations, weariness, impoverishment, its premonitions of the end, its will to the end."⁷⁸ Thus, for Nietzsche, philosophy presents itself not only as description, but also as the transfiguration, through art, of what goes on in the body and soul of the philosopher: "we have to give birth to our thoughts out of our pure pain and, like mothers, endow them with all we have of blood, heart, fire, pleasure, passion, agony, conscience, fate, and catastrophe."⁷⁹ Consequently, only *great pain* compels the philosopher to descend into his ultimate depths and to put aside everything mild, all trust, and any half-way solution: "I doubt that such pain makes us "better"; but I know that it makes us more *profound*."⁸⁰

One can understand why Nietzsche can consider himself as decadent while insisting at one and the same time on the difference that separates him from a decadent spirit:

> Apart from the fact than I am a decadent, I am also the opposite. My proof for this is, among other things, that I have always instinctively chosen the *right* means against wretched states; while the decadent typically chooses means that are disadvantageous for him. As *summa summarum*, I was healthy; as an angle, as specialty, I was decadent.⁸¹

But here, again, it is necessary to know how to distinguish between health and *great* health. The healthy person reveals himself or herself, naturally, through the thriving of the body, through joy, courage, and *élan vital.* Moreover, the fundamentally healthy person will know, in addition, how to assume, integrate, and overcome the morbid elements that might befall him or her. "What destroys more delicate men forms part of the stimulants to *great* health."⁸² This is why it is necessary not to set sickness in direct opposition to health. Where we see oppositions, Nietzsche sees only degrees and differences from one state to the other.

Health and *sickness* are not essentially different, as the ancient physicians and some practitioners even today suppose. One must not make of them distinct principles and entities that fight over the living organism and turn it into their arena. That is silly nonsense and chatter that is no good any longer. In fact there are only differences of degree between these two kinds of existence: the exaggeration, the disproportion, the non-harmony of the normal phenomena constitute a pathological state.[83]

This same idea will be reiterated and enlarged when Nietzsche distinguishes artists from morbid natures: in the first case, the richness of states continue to reign even if the artist has abused the overabundance of sap and the forces that characterize it; in the others, inversely, there is an extreme impoverishment that follows from all the excitations and nervous eccentricities that consume them.

I set down here a list of psychological states as signs of a full and flourishing life that one is accustomed today to condemn as *morbid*. For by now we have learned better than to speak of healthy and sick as of an antithesis: it is a question of degrees. My claim in this matter is that what is today called "healthy" represents a lower level than that which under favorable circumstances *would* be healthy—that we are relatively sick— . . . . The artist belongs to a still stronger race. What would be harmful and morbid in us, in him is nature—[84]

Health, joy, and affirmation of life go together in Nietzsche's work. Those rare individuals who are accomplished and in thoroughly good health are characterized by an overflowing of forces, by a kind of "divinization of the body," and everything related to the will-to-live, to fecundity, to fertility, and, therefore, to the delight of becoming. The weak, on the contrary, the miscarried and the failures, need to condemn life and find it guilty. In this sense, we can gauge the strength of a civilization by the degree of its capacity to endure suffering, to surmount it and transfigure it, through art. This is why Nietzsche already sets himself apart from Schopenhauer in *The Birth of Tragedy*, where he sees the Greek in no way subject to a resignation or a Buddhistic negation of the will, but constrained, by the Apollonian drive toward beauty, to create Olympus and its pantheon of gods. "The same impulse that calls art into being, as the complement and consummation of existence, seducing one to a continuation of life, was also the cause of the Olympian world which the Hellenic 'will' made use of as a transfiguring mirror."[85] Curiously, at the very end of the last chapter of this work, the same idea returns newly enriched by reflections on the birth, life, and death of tragedy: "how much did this people have to suffer to be able to become so beautiful!"[86] In this perspective tragic wisdom presents itself as art, or as the game of destruction-construction by which existence and the world are continually created and reinvented.

Nietzsche will pursue, reinforce, and rework this conception of tragedy and art in general throughout the later texts. Thus, in a fragment of Fall 1887, we read equally:

> And everything that is of the ugly, hard, terrible that represents art? Will art turn us away from suffering life? dispose us toward resignation? as Schopenhauer understands it?—But the artist communicates before all his *states* taking into account this fearful aspect of life: this same state is a *desirability*, whoever lives it, venerates it in a supreme fashion and communicates it, providing that he is a communicative being, that is, an artist.[87]

To create or appreciate the beautiful, then, restores a sense of power, or the will to power or of an abundance of accumulated forces, that allow the strong and successful to pronounce the judgment "beautiful" even before those things and conditions that the weak regard only as hateful and frightful.

> It is the *heroic* spirits who say Yes to themselves in tragic cruelty: they are hard enough to experience suffering with *pleasure*. . . . Supposing, on the other hand, that the *weak* desire to enjoy art that is not meant for them; what would they do to make tragedy palatable for themselves? They would interpret *their own value feelings* into it; e.g., the "triumph of the moral world-order" or the doctrine of the "worthlessness of existence" or the invitation of "resignation" (—or half-medicinal, half-moral discharges of affects à la Aristotle).[88]

But why is it precisely the weak that wind up prevailing? In fact, in a series of reflections directly mirroring the title, *Why the Weak Conquer*, Nietzsche advances the following explanation:

> *In summa:* the sick and weak have more *sympathy*, are "more humane"—the sick and weak have more *spirit*, are more changeable, various, entertaining—more malicious: it was the sick who invented *malice*. *Esprit:* quality of late races: Jews, Frenchmen, Chinese. (The

anti-Semites do not forgive the Jews for possessing "spirit"—and money. Anti-Semites—another name for the "underprivileged.") . . . the fool and the saint—the two most interesting types of human—closely related to them, the "genius." The great "adventurers and criminals." . . . The sick and the weak have had *fascination* on their side: they are more *interesting* than the healthy.[89]

Pierre Klossowski attributes this change of perspective—that is, the rehabilitation of the weak in relation to the accomplished—to a certain influence of Dostoevsky on Nietzsche:

> Such revisionism, in Nietzsche, was due in large part to his discovery of Dostoevsky. For even if they derived opposite conclusions from their analogous visions of the human soul, Nietzsche could not help but experience, through his contact with Dostoevsky's *demons* and the *underground man*, and infinite and incessant solicitation, recognizing himself in many of the remarks the Russian novelist put in his characters' mouths.[90]

Klossowski's observation is pertinent, only he neglects or simply does not know certain of Nietzsche's texts that appeared prior to his discovery of Dostoevsky, and which are demonstrably aware of the aspects of humanity's sicknesses and morbidities. These aspects have, paradoxically, the capacity to enrich man, to endow him with a delicate sense of touch, a variety of perspectives, and, therefore, of contradictions. In a fragment of 1884, when Nietzsche had not as yet read Dostoevsky, one finds a reflection on the role *sickness* plays in forgetting as part of the human capacity for knowledge.[91] Precisely because one *forgets* that there is only evaluation according to a particular perspective, the judgments pronounced by man are ceaselessly enriched by a multitude of drives and evaluations which, continually, contradict and exceed themselves: "This is the *expression of the diseased condition of man,* in contrast to the animals in which all existing instincts answer to quite definite tasks."

> This contradictory creature has in his nature, however, a great method of acquiring *knowledge:* he feels many pros and cons, he raises himself *to justice*—to comprehension *beyond esteeming things good and evil.*
> The wisest man would be the one *richest in contradictions,* who has, as it were, antennae for all types of men—as well as his great moments of *grand harmony*—a rare *accident* even in us! A sort of planetary motion.[92]

Chance—which we will return to later—as well as necessity consti-tute an essential part of Nietzsche's work. But *necessity*, along with the *Eternal Return* and the *will to power* form the stumbling block that more than one commentator has preferred to avoid. We will now treat these three themes.

THE ETERNAL RETURN, WILL TO POWER, *AMOR FATI*

Nietzsche attributes so much importance to the doctrine of the Eternal Return that he does not hesitate to consider it the principal conception of *Thus Spoke Zarathustra*:

> Now I shall relate the history of *Zarathustra*. The fundamental concep-tion of this work, the *idea of eternal recurrence*, this highest formula of affirmation that is at all attainable, belongs in August 1881: it was penned on a sheet with the notation underneath, "6000 feet beyond man and time." That day I was walking through the woods along the lake of Silvaplana; at a powerful pyramidal rock not far from the Surlei I stopped. It was then that this idea came to me.[93]

But Nietzsche wants to keep this thought as a secret for the moment. This is why he will write to his friend Peter Gast on the fourteenth of August of the same year: "Thoughts have loomed into view on my hori-zon, such that I have never seen before. I will not breathe a word of them, and I will try to keep myself in a resolute calm. I must undoubtedly live *some* more years." It will be in the following year, in *The Gay Science*, para-graph 341, that he will for the first time announce his discovery, without, nevertheless, mentioning the term *Eternal Return*.

> What, if some day or night a demon were to steal after you into your loneliest loneliness and say to you: "This life as you now live it and have lived it, you will have to live once more and innumerable times more; and there will be nothing new in it, but every pain and every joy and every thought and sigh and everything unutterably small or great in your life will have to return to you, all in the same succes-sion and sequence—even this spider and this moonlight between the trees, and even this moment and I myself. The eternal hourglass of existence is turned upside down again and again, and you with it, speck of dust!"[94]

No doubt Nietzsche alludes to the idea of an *eternal return* in other paragraphs of the same book. Besides, the same idea already appears in writings prior to *The Gay Science*. But it is only in Zarathustra that he actually explains it and makes it public, and he does this through so many ceremonies, so much preparation and secrecy that the reader ends up somewhat weary of it. It is thus in the third part (*On the Vision and the Riddle*) that he will finally decide to recount to a group of sailors the discovery that has weighed him down.

Oddly enough, Nietzsche will no longer speak, at least explicitly, of the *Eternal Return* in the books published following it: *Beyond Good and Evil, On the Genealogy of Morals,* and *The Case of Wagner.* He will wait until *Twilight of the Idols* and *Ecce Homo* (posthumous work) to newly enhance, but in brief passages, the importance of this doctrine. Moreover, the accent he puts on *his* discovery is all the more surprising when one knows he is aware of the religions of India and the Near East, just as he had a familiarity with Greek philosophy during his youthful studies. It is furthermore Nietzsche himself who admits, without committing himself: "The doctrine of the "eternal recurrence," that is, of the unconditional and infinitely repeated circular course of all things—this doctrine of Zarathustra *might* in the end have been taught already by Heraclitus. At least the Stoa has traces of it, and the Stoics inherited almost all of their principal notions from Heraclitus."[95]

If the *will to power* gives rise to different interpretations, precisely by virtue even of its very conception, that is, the impossibility of thought halting before any definitive solution, since thought thinks in and from relations of force, there will be no less difficulty in trying to understand the *Eternal Return.* Here, again, Nietzsche sees himself incapable of settling the question once and for all: he will sometimes have recourse to science, sometimes to metaphor. But neither metaphor nor particularly science will be sufficient to furnish that vision to which perhaps Nietzsche would himself aspire. Jaspers has clearly stated this difficulty, in observing: "Hence we should not overlook the wavering of this idea of recurrence. It may appear as a precise doctrine with definite content, only to become an indeterminate symbol of faith; or it may first be presented as scientifically demonstrable, only to reappear as something giving noncognitive meaning to *Existenz.*"[96]

In fact, in a series of reflections on the *eternal return,* which is also an attack against the teleological conception of mechanistic theory, Nietzsche advances this explanation:

If the world *may* be thought of as a certain definite quantity of force and as a certain definite number of centers of force—and every other representation remains indefinite and therefore *useless*—it follows that, in the great dice game of existence, it must pass through a calculable number of combinations. In infinite time, every possible combination would at some time or another be realized; more: it would be realized an infinite number of times. And since between every "combination" and its next "recurrence" all other possible combinations would have to take place, and each of these combinations conditions the entire sequence of combinations in the same series, a circular movement of absolutely identical series is thus demonstrated: the world as a circular movement that has already repeated itself infinitely often and plays its game *in infinitum.*[97]

As is clearly demonstrated at the beginning of this text, Nietzsche starts off with a presupposition: "If the world *may* be thought of as a certain definite quantity . . . and if every other representation remains indefinite and therefore *useless.*" He also postulates the finite nature of force to conclude that the world is neither unlimited nor eternally renewable: "the world, as force, may not be thought as unlimited, for it *cannot* be so thought of; we forbid ourselves the concept of the an infinite force *as incompatible with the concept "force."* Thus—the world also lacks the capacity for eternal novelty."[98] Therefore, if the world had been created and if it had an end, an intention or a *télos* it would have frozen long ago. But the world "has never begun to become and will never cease from passing away—it *maintains* itself in both.—It lives on itself: its excrements are its food."[99]

In Nietzsche's view, the hypotheses about creation depend most often on a theological ulterior motive. Similarly, questions like "if becoming *can* emerge in being or in nothingness," are, most of the time, determined by religious ulterior motives. This means that the world has neither beginning nor end. It subsists. It passes on endlessly, repeats itself and plays its game *in infinitum.* "This conception is not simply a mechanistic conception; for if it were that, it would not condition an infinite recurrence of identical cases, but a final state. *Because* the world has not reached this, mechanistic theory must be considered an imperfect and merely provisional hypothesis."[100]

But how does it come that the world *repeats* itself in difference and in *newness?* To be sure, the forces are rock solid, but because they are finite and mobile they can be rearranged and repeated an infinite number of times, without for all that the world losing its *novelty.* "That 'force' and 'rest,' 'remaining the same,' contradict one another. The measure of force (as magnitude) as fixed, but its essence in flux."[101] Force cannot therefore, according to Nietzsche, remain immobile, for "changing" constitutes part of its essence. The momentary state of force provides the condition for a new distribution of forces and the relations of forces that it contains.

We have simplified in the extreme the attempts made by Nietzsche to explain scientifically the idea of *eternal return*. But these attempts already reveal the difficulty that poses the question; they show that Nietzsche himself is not at ease with the presuppositions, data, and *proofs* he lays out. This is why he displaces, enlarges, and shortens them and tries new proofs. Perhaps metaphor is the only means of throwing light on this disturbing discovery, of which Zarathustra is the herald. This may also account for the richness of symbols and poetry that characterizes the sections: *On the Vision and the Riddle, The Convalescent,* and *The Seven Seals (Or: The Yes and Amen Song) (Zarathustra,* Third Part).

For Fink, the Third Part of *Zarathustra* forms both the nucleus and the apex of the work, which develops as follows: First, Zarathustra proclaims the overman to the crowd assembled in the market place; then, he teaches the *death of God* and the *will to power* to his disciples; finally, on the way to his cave in the mountain, he relates to a group of sailors a formidable vision that has weighed heavily on him (*On the Vision and the Riddle*).[102] But, as Fink observes, the narrative rather resembles a monologue, or a dialogue Zarathustra has with himself than a proclamation or instruction. It is then in these terms that the narration begins:

Not long ago I walked gloomily through the deadly pallor of dusk—gloomy and hard, with lips pressed together. Not only one sun had set for me. A path that ascended defiantly through stones, malicious, lonely, not cheered by herb or shrub—a mountain path crunched under the defiance of my foot.

. . . O Zarathustra, "you philosopher's stone, you slingstone, you star-crusher! You threw yourself up so high; but every stone that is thrown must fall.

"Behold this gateway, dwarf!" I continued. "It has two faces. Two paths meet here. The long lane stretches back for an eternity. And the long lane out there, that another eternity. They contradict each other, these paths: they offend each other face to face; and it is here at this gateway that they come together. The name of the gateway is inscribed above: 'Moment.' But whoever would follow one of them, on and on, farther and farther—do you believe, dwarf, that these paths contradict each other eternally?"

"All that is straight lies," the dwarf murmured contemptuously. "All truth is crooked; time itself is a circle."

"You spirit of gravity," I said angrily, "do not make things too easy for yourself! Or I shall let you crouch where you are crouching, lamefoot; and it was I that carried you to this *height*.

"Behold," I continued, "this moment! For the gateway, Moment, a long, eternal lane leads *backward*: behind us lies an eternity. Must not whatever *can* walk have walked on this lane before? Must not whatever *can* happen have happened, have been done, have passed by before? And if everything has been there before—what do you think, dwarf, of this moment? Must not this gateway too have been there before? And are not all things knotted together so firmly that this moment draws after it all that is to come? *Therefore*—itself too? For whatever *can* walk—in this long lane out there too, it *must* walk once more.

"And this slow spider, which crawls in the moonlight, and this moonlight itself, and I and you in the gateway, whispering together, whispering eternal things—must not all of us have been there before? And return and walk in that other lane, out there, before us, in this long dreadful lane—must we not eternally return?"[103]

The narrative continues, but what is important for our purposes is to know that, by the metaphor of the gateway, Nietzsche introduces here an essential difference regarding the usual conception of time. Indeed, to the mind of the dwarf, all that is straight lies: "time itself is a circle." But Zarathustra refuses the *human, all too human* way of thinking, which conceives of time as a serpent swallowing its own tail. To be sure, Zarathustra is himself tempted to think of time in the same way as the dwarf, that is, as a circuit unrolling moments, "nows, and "presents." That is why—Fink recalls—he has recourse to hyperbole and extrapolates the circularity of the intramundane moments by the metaphor of the "ring of rings." In *The Seven Seals*, in fact, Zarathustra will establish the break between the return of intramundane facticity and the circular movement of the entire position of the cosmos. "Oh, how should I not lust after eternity and after the nuptial ring of rings, the ring of recurrence?"[104]

This section, which is the last of *Zarathustra* III, begins with a metaphor similar to that of the gateway:

If I am a soothsayer and full of that soothsaying spirit which wanders on a high ridge between two seas, wandering like a heavy cloud between past and future, and enemy of all sultry plains and all that is weary and cannot either die or live . . .[105]

One recalls that Zarathustra, after having arrived at the *edge* of the forest, instructs the crowd assembled in the market place about the overman. The crowd was preparing to take part in the spectacle of a tightrope walker. It is at this point that Zarathustra teaches the overman. Jeered at, however, he looked upon the people and was amazed and continued his speech, while the tightrope walker began his performance:

> "Man is a rope tied between beast and overman—a rope over an abyss.
> "What is great in man is that he is a bridge and not an end: what can be loved in man is that he is an *overture* and a *going under* . . .
> "I love all those who are as heavy drops, falling one by one out of the dark cloud that hangs over men: they herald the advent of lightning, and, as heralds, they perish.[106]

Zarathustra now wanders on a *high* ridge between two seas. He moves like a heavy dark cloud pregnant with metamorphoses, suspended between past and future. Zarathustra is not the man who wants to perish, and nonetheless he heralds the lightning. He can encompass the past and the future, and nonetheless he is an *overture* and a *going under*, treading along the high ridge while all the time heralding.

The setting where Zarathustra first teaches the *will to power* opens in these terms: "When Zarathustra crossed over the great bridge one day the cripples and beggars surrounded him, and a hunchback spoke to him thus. . . ."[107] Zarathustra speaks to the people assembled and, further, he stresses: "A seer, a willer, a creator, a future himself and a bridge to the future—and alas, also, as it were, a crippled at this bridge: all this is Zarathustra."[108]

Zarathustra wanders in the midst of the people like among the fragments of the future that he contemplates. Willing liberates, he asserts, but what is it that puts even the liberator in chains? "It was,"—that is the name of the will's gnashing of teeth and most secret affliction.[109] Zarathustra continues:

> "All 'it was' is a fragment, a riddle, a dreadful accident—until the creative will says to it, 'But thus I willed it.' Until the creative will says to it, 'But thus I will it; thus shall I will it.'
> "And who taught him reconciliation with time and something higher than any reconciliation? For that will which is the will to power must will something higher than any reconciliation; but how shall this be brought about? Who could teach him also to will backwards?"[110]

But at this point Zarathustra's speech is abruptly interrupted and he takes on the air of extreme shock. With a frightful eye he looked at his disciples as if with arrows piercing through their thoughts and even their hidden thoughts. However, after a little while, he laughed again and, appeased, he said: "It is difficult to live with people because silence is so difficult. Especially for one who is garrulous."[111]

This interruption in Zarathustra's speech is usually attributed to his fear of retreating before the announcement of the *Eternal Return*. For our part, we suggest that the principal reason for this is to be found rather in the relation which is established between the will to overcome and time and the limits imposed by the impossibility of stepping backward. No doubt the *will to power* is characterized by a continual overcoming and a becoming more, but it is seen no less in the necessity to affirm, and the future, and the past. Is there thus a reconciliation possible? Will not the *will* be a *will to power* only to the extent that it affirms the past and future? To will what imposes itself necessarily implies the affirmation of the awareness of freedom. But in that respect, Zarathustra's speech does not go much further than the doctrine of freedom as it is understood in the tradition of Augustine, Luther, and Kant.

It is necessary nonetheless to understand the will taught by Zarathustra as the will to overcome all reconciliation and all *too human* solutions. In other words, Zarathustra *creates his own* truth wandering in the midst of the fragments of the future that he contemplates, that he binds and rebinds anew when he fails. For this is how he progresses: in his wandering across the ice fields and deserts, in the lonely climb up a difficult footpath, grinding under the defiance of his step.

The *will to power* has no real end, but it can be thought only where there is an obstacle, resistance, and thus delight: delight of creation, which is also delight of destruction. Zarathustra interrupts his speech with a surprised and questioning air. He cannot settle on anything, but he throws up bridges, he shoots arrows. To affirm becoming is his real secret. The will that creates, destroys and takes delight in its overflowing, its excess and its surplus is the same will that considers "it is part of this state to perceive not merely the *necessity* of those sides of existence hitherto denied, but their desirability; and not their desirability merely in relation to the sides hitherto affirmed (perhaps as their complement or precondition), but for their own sake, as the more powerful, more fruitful, *truer* sides of existence, in which its will finds clearer expression."[112]

The expression *Amor Fati* is already used by Nietzsche in *The Gay Science* (Section 276), and he will employ it again to indicate his fundamental attitude and affirmation vis-à-vis the world:

> Such an experimental philosophy as I live anticipates experimentally even the possibilities of the most fundamental nihilism; but this does not mean that it must halt at a negation, a No, a will to negation. It wants rather to cross over to the opposite of this—to a *Dionysian affirmation* of the world as it is, without subtraction, exception, or selection—it wants the eternal circulation:—the same things, the same logic and illogic of entanglements. The highest state a philosopher can attain: to stand in a Dionysian relationship to existence—my formula for this is *amor fati.*[113]

This same expression will appear in *Ecce Homo*, where Nietzsche will reaffirm: "My formula for greatness in a human being is *amor fati*: that one wants nothing to be different, not forward, or backward, not in all eternity. Not merely bear what is necessary, still less conceal it—all idealism is mendaciousness in the face of what is necessary—but *love* it."[114]

It is essential, however, to keep sight of the fact that there is no logical tie necessarily joining the *Eternal Return*, the *Will to Power* and *amor fati*, the latter being, moreover, the formula Nietzsche applies elsewhere to the Dionysian attitude toward life, in its necessity. The *Eternal Return* and the *Will to Power* are not derived logically the one from the other; but this is not to say that they exclude each other purely and simply, for the universe of forces in which Nietzsche's thought moves is multiform, labile, fluent, and unceasing in its inclusions, connections, ruptures, and *passages*. What is certain, nevertheless, is that the plans and test frameworks where the two themes appear do not allow us to infer a dependence between the two concepts nor—as Heidegger believes—a decision on Nietzsche's part to derive the *Will to Power* from the *Eternal Return*. However, it is not overstating the case that Nietzsche himself favors these interpretations. In fact, it would often happen that one and the same text would give birth to the most diverse readings, as well as the most opposed points of view. This is why we reproduce, in its entirety, the posthumous fragment of June–July 1885:

> And do you know what "the world" is to me? Shall I show it to you in my mirror? This world: a monster of energy, without beginning or end; a firm, iron magnitude of force that does not grow bigger or smaller,

that does not expend itself but only transforms itself; as a whole, of unalterable size, a household without expenses or losses, but likewise without increase or income; enclosed by "nothingness" as by a boundary; not something blurry or wasted, not something endlessly extended, but set in a definite space as definite force, and not a space that might be "empty" here or there, but rather as force throughout, as a play of forces and waves of forces, at the same time one and many, increasing here and at the same time decreasing there; a sea of forces flowing and rushing together, eternally changing, eternally flooding back, with tremendous years of recurrence, with an ebb and a flood of its forms; out of the simplest forms striving toward the most complex, out of the stillest, most rigid, coldest forms toward the hottest, most turbulent, most self-contradictory, and then again returning home to the simple out of this abundance, out of the play of contradictions back to the joy of concord, still affirming itself in the uniformity of its courses and its years, blessing itself as that which must return eternally, as a becoming that knows no satiety, no disgust, no weariness; this, my *Dionysian* world of the eternally self-creating, the eternally self-destroying, this mystery of the world of the twofold voluptuous delight, my "beyond good and evil," without goal, unless the joy of the circle is itself a goal; without will, unless a ring feels good will toward itself—do you want a *name* for this world? A *solution* for all its riddles? A *light* for you, too, you best-concealed, strongest, most intrepid, most midnightly men?— *This world is the will to power—and nothing besides!* And you yourselves are also this will to power—and nothing besides![115]

But does not this universe Nietzsche describes reveal itself, to him as well, as being in the end another interpretation or another fiction? Referring precisely, in another text, to the ineffective modes of interpretation used by the defenders of "Laws of nature," he concludes:

And somebody might come along who, with opposite intentions and modes of interpretation, could read out of the same "nature," and with regard to the same phenomena, rather the tyrannically inconsiderate and relentless enforcement of claims of power—an interpreter who would picture the unexceptional and unconditional aspects of all "will to power" so vividly that almost every word, even "tyranny" itself, would eventually seem unsuitable, or a weakening and attenuating metaphor—being too human—but he might, nevertheless, end by asserting the same about this world as you do, namely, that it has a "necessary" and "calculable" course, *not* because laws obtain in it, but because they are absolutely *lacking*, and every power draws its ultimate consequences at every moment. Supposing that this also is only interpretation—and you will be eager enough to make this objection?—well, so much the better.[116]

It follows that one will have difficulty finding a unique and definitive interpretation for that world of relations and going-beyonds that is the *Will to Power*—for this swarm of forces and continual rearrangements that is this universe that creates and destroys itself by a constant play of contrasts and self-contradictions, harmony, and regularity. One will search in vain for a logical continuity between *Will to Power* and the *Eternal Return*, between creation and necessity, no more than one will be able to deny all connection and all relation. In fact, to support the idea of return, Nietzsche insists, it is necessary to pursue:

> . . . the *enjoyment* of all kinds of uncertainty, experimentalism, as a counterweight to this extreme fatalism; abolition of the concept of necessity; abolition of the "will"; abolition of "knowledge-in-itself."
> *Greatest elevation of the consciousness of strength in man*, as he creates the overman.[117]

Thus, this is the way Nietzsche's work unfolds, this is the will of his *writing* and of the delight that flows from it; this delight is experienced in the uncertainties and the surprises, in the meandering paths and in the labyrinths of a thought itself sinuous that connects and reconnects, builds and destroys, in the *paradoxical* game of failure and continuous creation.

4

Nietzsche and Christianity

God suffocated by theology, and morals by morality (*an der Moralität*).

Up until now we have examined Nietzsche's paradoxes as he presents them in art, science, religion, metaphysics, morality, as well as in his writing in general. Henceforth, special attention will be given to Christianity and morality, in hope of better indicating and making explicit the diverse forces and different relations of forces characteristic of nihilism and the will to power.

This chapter will treat Christianity in the sense that it appears, in Nietzsche's view, as one of the most important movements of European nihilism and as the site where the forces of decadence have worked in a most secret, artful, and destructive way.

If Nietzsche's position vis-à-vis Socrates, Schopenhauer, and Wagner is ambiguous and paradoxical, it will be even moreso with regard to the person of Christ, who Nietzsche considers, in *Human, All Too Human*, as "the noblest human being," and in another paragraph of the same book, as someone who "promoted the stupidifying of man, placed himself on the side of the poor in spirit and retarded the production of the supreme intellect."[1]

The Antichrist is the book that in a certain way summarizes and condenses Nietzsche's vision of morality, religion in general, and Christianity in particular. This book, which is one of the last of Nietzsche's productive life, and was not published until 1895, when Nietzsche was deep in his dementia, has been cut in several places by the philosopher's sister and by his initial editors. It contains a preface, a conclusion and sixty-two paragraphs or sections, the last of which constitutes, in a certain way, a resume of the entire work[2]—a resume similar to the final secton of Nietzsche's first work, *The Birth of Tragedy*. Consisting of about a hundred pages, it extols all aspects of the ascendant life, while combating equally the Aristotelian vision of tragedy as catharsis, and it dispenses with all the pomp of erudition. In other words, Nietzsche deliberately avoids making *The Antichrist* into a work of exegesis; it is Nietzsche himself who admits this in paragraph 28:

> The time is long past when I too, like every young scholar, slowly drew out the savor of the work of the incomparable Strauss, with the shrewdness of a refined philologist. I was twenty years old then: now I am too serious for that. What do I care about the contradictions in the "tradition"? How can one call saints' legends "tradition" in the first place? The biographies of the saints are the most ambiguous kind of literature there is: to apply scientific methods to them, *in the absence of any other documents*, strikes me as doomed to failure from the start—mere scholarly idleness.[3]

The core of this work can be found in paragraphs 27 and 47, where Nietzsche examines the origins of Christianity and sets the scene for Christ, the apostle Paul, and the masses, or the *tschandala*, who are "all the failures, all the rebellious-minded, all the less favored, the whole scum and refuse of humanity. . . ."[4] Moreover, the reception and vulgarization of Christianity by the masses is well illustrated in a letter to Overbeck, dated March 31, 1885, and where he anticipates in several ways what *The Antichrist* will develop regarding the subject:

> I have been reading, as relaxation, St. Augustine's *Confessions*, much regretting that you were not with me. O this old rhetorician! What falseness, what rolling of the eyes! How I laughed! (for example, concerning the "theft" of his youth, basically an undergraduate story). What psychological falsity! (for example, when he talks about the death of his best friend, with whom he shared a *single soul*, he "resolved to go on living, so that in this way his friend would not wholly die." Such things are revoltingly dishonest). Philosophical value zero! *vulgarized Platonism*—that is to say, a way of thinking which was invented by the highest aristocracy of soul, and which he adjusted to slave natures. Moreover, one sees into the guts of Christianity in this book. I make my observations with the curiosity of a radical physician and physiologist.[5]

But the essence of Christianity already exists, albeit in a latent form, in Plato's philosophy. It appears there under the form of a Redeemer who must justify evil in the world and redeem the degenerate masses of its share of evil. Plato has thus already invented him: "The naïveté of Plato and Christianity: they have believed they could know what is "good." They have found the man of the *herd*—but *not* the creative artist. With Plato, a "Savior" was already invented, the one who descends to the level of the *wretched* and the *evil-doers*. He cannot see *reasonable character* and *the necessity of evil.*"[6]

But, in the end, it is the Apostle Paul who is, in Nietzsche's view, the true founder of Christianity. It is he who, "with the cynical logic of a rabbi," has turned the death on the cross into an instrument of vengeance and has brought to its conclusion a process of degradation that had begun with the death of Christ.

SAINT PAUL, THE JEWISH PASCAL

In fact, already in *Daybreak*, published in 1881, Nietzsche attributes to Paul the responsibility of having founded Christianity and of having imparted the direction that would guide and characterize it throughout its long history. It is at the very beginning of paragraph 68 of this book, after having spoken ironically about the "literary productions of the 'Holy-Spirit'" contained in the Bible, Nietzsche continues: "That it also contains the history of one of the most ambitious and importunate souls, of a mind as superstitious as it was cunning, the history of the apostle Paul—who, apart from a few scholars, knows that? But without this remarkable history, without the storms and confusions of such a mind, of such a soul, there would be no Christianity: we would hardly have heard of a little Jewish sect whose master died on the cross." If this history had been understood at the right time, if the writings of Paul had been read not as the revelations of the "Holy Spirit," but with a free and honest exercise of one's own spirit and without thinking all the time of our own personal needs—*really read*, that is to say (but for fifteen hundred years there were no such readers)—Christianity would long since have ceased to exist: "for these pages of the Jewish Pascal expose the origin of Christianity as thoroughly as the pages of the French Pascal expose its destiny and that by which it will perish.[7]

Nietzsche sees a curious reversal at work in that figure avid for distinction. Paul was fascinated by the prohibitions of Jewish Law: the spell it exercised on him was that transgression of the Law was all the more powerful as the Law had to be destroyed. "Is it really 'carnality' which again and again makes him a transgressor? And not rather, as he later suspected, behind it the law itself, which *must* continually prove itself unfulfillable and with irresistible magic lures on to transgression?"[8] But these thoughts did not appear so clearly to him at the moment, though doubts about the fulfillment of the Law, as well as the unbearable burdens of its demands continuted to torture him from time to time.

Nietzsche assumes that Luther also had these feelings appear when, fifteen centuries later, in his monastery he desired to become the model and exemplar of the spiritual ideal: "and similarly to Luther, who one day began to hate the spiritual ideal and the Pope and the saints and the whole clergy with a hatred the more deadly the less he dared to admit it to himself—a similar thing happened to Paul. The law was the cross to which he felt himself nailed: how he hated it! how he had to drag himself along! how he sought about for a means of *destroying* it—"[9]

But suddenly all this becomes clear on the road to Damascus. In a flash of vision—"as was bound to happen in the case of an epileptic"—the apostle found the key to the enigma: Why thus persecute precisely this Jesus, *the destroyer of the Law?* It is thus that "sick with the most tormented pride, at a stroke he feels himself recovered, the moral despair is as if blown away, destroyed—that is to say, *fulfilled*, there on the Cross!"[10] From this point onward all fault will be remitted, indeed *annihilated*, for the Law is dead. To die with Christ, is to die to the Law; to live according to the flesh, is to live according to the Law.

> With that, the intoxication of Paul is at its height, and likewise the importunity of the soul—with the idea of becoming one with Christ all shame, all subordination, all bounds are taken from it, and the intractable lust for power reveals itself as an anticipatory reveling in *divine* glories.—This is the *first Christian*, the inventor of Christianness! Before him there were only a few Jewish sectarians.[11]

But this movement can only arise from Jewish soil; Christianity is to be understood not as a reaction, but as a consequence and an inevitable result of the instinct of decadence which, reaching the farthest limits of its course, mutates into new forces and borrows new masks and new disguises. This is why Nietzsche will say in *The Antichrist*:

> The Christian church cannot make the slightest claim to originality when compared to the "holy people." That precisely is why the Jews are

the *most catastrophic* people of world history: by their aftereffect they have made mankind so thoroughly false that even today the Christian can feel anti-Jewish without realizing that he himself is *the ultimate Jewish consequence.*[12]

Thus, the zeal with which Paul tried to carry out and defend the Law was redoubled in intensity not so much toward the Law, but toward the *destroyer* of the Law. Similarly, the Jewish priest will disguise himself as a philosopher, as the Greek priest had already done before him.

> As soon as the cleft between the Jews and the Jewish Christians opened, no choice whatever remained to the latter but to apply against the Jews themselves the same procedures of self-preservation that the Jewish instinct recommended, whereas hitherto the Jews had applied them only against everything *non*-Jewish. The Christian is merely a Jew of "more liberal" ("freieren" *Bekenntnisses*) persuasion.[13]

It is in this sense that one will be able to understand Nietzsche's assertion according to which German philosophy is corrupted and vitiated by theologian's blood. "The Protestant parson is the grandfather of German philosophy; Protestantism itself, is *peccatum originale*" (original sin).[14] We are well aware that Nietzsche himself was the son and grandson of Protestant pastors. But it is not only Reformation philosophy that is altered and spoiled by the unwarrantable interference of the priest; it is its entire history and its development: "the *lie* of the "moral world order" runs through the whole development of modern philosophy."[15]

Two important moments stand out in the process of degradation that begins already, according to Nietzsche, with the death on the cross. In The *Antichrist*, Jesus is presented as the herald of the "glad tidings," becoming reality, of the Kingdom which is already there and eternal life, true life, which one has no need to seek, for it is found in our midst and in us: "it is not promised, it is here, it is *in you*; as a living in love without subtraction and exclusion, without regard to station. Everyone is the child of God—Jesus definitely presumes nothing for himself alone—and as a child of God everyone is equal to everyone."[16] In this perspective, Jesus breaks with the Jewish doctrine of repentance and reconciliation, for only practice counts: "What was *disposed of* with the evangel was the Judaism of the concepts of 'sin,' 'forgiveness of sin,' 'faith,' 'redemption through faith'—the whole Jewish *ecclesiastical* doctrine was negated in the 'glad tidings.'"[17]

Jesus takes on an air of a simple, good-natured man in *The Antichrist*. Nietzsche even uses the adjective "idiot," in the Dostoevskian sense.[18] He suffers with those who make him suffer, he prays, he loves *with* and *in* those who have done him wrong. He wants to die, and even facilitates his own judgment: "He does not resist, he does not defend his right, he takes no step which might ward off the worst; on the contrary, he *provokes* it."[19]

But what does Nietzsche use to ground this certitude, if he expressly declares himself hostile to the introduction of any scientific method in the reading and analysis of this personality, the "Savior"?[20] It will consist of correcting the mistaken idea of wishing to find, of seeking in the diverse sources of the New Testament, what emerges of the historical Jesus and what is revealed of the Christ of faith. Nietzsche, of course, has something quite different in mind:

> What concerns *me* is the psychological type of the Redeemer. After all, this *could* be contained in the Gospels despite the Gospels, however mutilated and overloaded with alien features: as Francis of Assisi is preserved in legends, despite his legends. *Not* the truth concerning what he did, what he said, how he really died; but the question *whether* his type can still be exhibited at all, whether it has been "transmitted."—The attempts I know to read the *history* of a "soul" out of the Gospels seem to me proof of a contemptible psychological frivolity.[21]

Nietzsche thus admits that it is still possible to glimpse and analyze Jesus's psychological traits, however perverted and falsified they might appear in the Gospels. To do so, he must count on his perspicacity as a physiolologist and psychologist, as well as on the methods of dissection, genealogy and symptomatology, already used in *Human, All Too Human*.[22] To be sure, he does not employ explicitly these methods in *The Antichrist*, but the metaphors that express them appear frequently enough in this third period, of which *The Antichrist* forms one of the latest works. It is thus equipped with these resources that he tries, in this work, to capture and restore "the psychological type of the Savior," as well as to indicate the two moments that effectively mark the birth of Christianity. What are these two moments?

The death on the cross is presented, in *The Antichrist*, as the end of what was the "good tidings" announced by the Savior. This is affirmed at the beginning of paragraph 39: ". . . in truth, there was only *one* Christian, and he died on the cross. The "evangel" *died* on the cross. What has been called "evangel" from that moment was actually the opposite of that which *he* had lived: "*ill* tidings," a *dysangel*."[23]

However, it is necessary above all to resist seeing in these claims a kind of nostalgia for origins on Nietzsche's part, as if he regretted that *true* Christianity was found, from its beginning, irretrievably lost. On the contrary, he insists on the idea that original Christianity is and always will be possible, provided that faith gives way to *practice*. "*Not* a faith, but a doing: above all, a *not* doing of many things, another state of *being*."[24] Do not resist, but enjoy the felicity found in peace, in tenderness, in love, and in the inability to be an enemy. For the Kingdom is already there, the true life is found in your midst, in you, in your hearts. Such was the practice taught and lived by the herald of the "good tidings," who was the "most interesting of all decadents."[25]

But the "good tidings" was nailed to and died on the cross, the kind of death reserved for the likes of the *rabble* (*canaille*) For Nietzsche, then, the principal attitude of the small community of disciples was to question: *who* in the end was this, and *why* precisely this ignominious judgment? "Only now the cleft opened up: '*Who* killed him? *Who* was his natural enemy?' This question leaped forth like lightning. Answer: *ruling* Jewry, its highest class. From this moment, one felt oneself in rebellion *against* the existing order, and in retrospect one understood Jesus to have been in *rebellion against the existing order*."[26]

The result of this is that the populace's long wait for a Messiah, who would come one day and pass judgment against his enemies, had reached fruition. And all the bitterness and contempt sustained by the Evangels against the Pharisees and the theologians was henceforth attributed to the Master. The disciples had thus effaced the equal rights taught by Christ, according to which each individual was considered a child of God. That is to say, "it was their revenge to *elevate* Jesus extravagantly, to sever him from themselves—precisely as the Jews had formerly, out of revenge against their enemies, severed their God from themselves and elevated him. The one God and the Son of God—both products of *ressentiment*."[27]

But a further step would be needed to achieve definitively the process of corruption that was born with the death on the cross. And this moment would in fact arrive when the apostle Paul entered the scene. To the question: *who*, in the end, was this and *why* precisely this kind of death? follows another: "How *could* God permit this?" The answer, however, was not long in coming. The deranged small community explained this enigma as follows: "God gave his son for the remission of sins, as a *sacrifice*. In one stroke, it was all over with the evangel!"[28]

Nietzsche assumes that from this moment on the doctrines of the last Judgment and *parousia*, death as a sacrificial death, and the resurrection, progressively constitute the Savior type. The resurrection, in particular, represents for him the crucial conception that conjures away the only and true reality of the Gospel, namely, blessedness. "Paul, with that rabbinical impudence which distinguishes him in all things, logicalized this conception, this *obscenity* of a conception, in this way: '*If* Christ was not resurrected from the dead, then our faith is vain.'"[29] It is then by this final blow delivered to the "good tidings" that Paul completes the process that had already begun in the small community of disciples: "What Paul later carried to its conclusion, with the logician's cynicism of a rabbi, was nevertheless nothing other than the process of decay which had begun with the death of the Redeemer."[30]

The apostle Paul, then, plays, in Nietzsche's view, a double role: he definitively kills the "good tidings" and at the same time founds Christianity, which, for Nietzsche, constitutes one of the major movements of nihilism. In this perspective, Paul reproduces once more the type of the Jewish priest: he expresses the domination, vengeance, rancor, and *ressentiment* proper to the will to power, which is also the will to nothingness.

> Paul wanted the end, *consequently* he also wanted the means. What he himself did not believe, the idiots among whom he threw his doctrine believed. *His* need was for *power*; in Paul the priest wanted power once again—he could use only concepts, doctrines, symbols with which one tyrannizes the masses and forms herds.[31]

If already in *Daybreak* Saint Paul is presented as invested with an "implacable will to domination," the analyses that Nietzsche will develop concerning nihilism and the will to power show that he was, in the end, "the greatest of all apostles of vengeance."[32] In other words, *The Antichrist* recaptures, sums up, and at the same time, clarifies the analyses and scrutinies that had been operated before on the forces and their relations, on their functions, and on their genealogies and metamorphoses.

We bring all this up to stress once again that the *paradox* and *ambiguity* at the origins of Christianity consist precisely in what Christianity could only grow out of Jewish soil. Its roots plunge deep into the ground of the history of Israel. The priest's desire for power is not a reaction but rather a transformation of nihilist forces that, hurled against their own limits, cast off their old masks, and assume new disguises.

Psychologically considered, the Jewish people are a people endowed with the toughest vital energy, who, placed in impossible circumstance, voluntarily and out of the most profound prudence of self-preservation, take sides with all the instincts of decadence—*not* as mastered by them, but because they divined a power in these instincts with which one could prevail *against* "the world." The Jews are the antithesis of all decadents: they have had to *represent* decadents to the point of illusion; with a *non plus ultra* of histrionic genius they have known how to place themselves at the head of all movements of decadence (as the Christianity of *Paul*), in order to create something out of them which is stronger than any *Yes-saying* party of life. Decadence is only a *means* for the type of man who demands power in Judaism and Christianity, the *priestly* type: this type of man has a life interest in making mankind *sick* and in so twisting concepts of good and evil, true and false, as to imperil life and slander the world.[33]

It remains nothing less than the instinct of decadence that arises in this movement. Moreover, the forces at work in this movement express this instinct to the extent that they say *No* to life, to its abundance, to its surplus and excess. In this sense one can state: the more powerful and self-believing a people, the more their gods are shown to be powerful, belligerent, and affirmative. Inversely, the more a people decline, the more their gods exhibit the traits of exhaustion, of the negation of life, and of the will to end it.

SUCH PEOPLE, SUCH GODS

Nietzsche sees the age of kingship as the most productive, most prosperous and powerful period in the history of Israel. Only a powerful and *just* god could exist in the midst of such a people and under these specific conditions.

Its Yahweh was the expression of a consciousness of power, of joy in oneself, of hope for oneself: through him victory and welfare were expected; through him nature was trusted to give what the people needed—above all, rain. Yahweh is the god of Israel and *therefore* the god of justice: the logic of every people that is in power and has a good conscience.[34]

This period, however, must come to an end—an end that Nietzsche attributes to three historical factors: anarchy within, the Assyrians without, and the accession to power of the priestly class. It is in this way that Yah-weh, who was an expression of the self-confidence of the people and acted in unison with Israel, becomes a God under certain conditions. The idea that one has of him is little by little transformed and denatured, and another interpretation takes its place: all happiness becomes henceforth a retribution on the part of Yahweh, and all unhappiness is seen as a pun-ishment for disobeying his command, that is, for "sin" toward God: ". . . in the hands of the Jewish priests the *great* age in the history of Israel became an age of decay; the Exile, the long misfortune, was transformed into an eternal *punishment* for the great age—an age in which the priest was still a nobody."[35]

Gods thus serve to measure the greatness or the decay of a people, and vice versa. Everywhere that power spreads, these gods carry the marks of war, conquest, and nationalism. On the other hand, one can easily rec-ognize the "good" and the failing gods by what they reveal of the traits of vengeance, hatred, punition, and ressentiment toward everything that affirms, transfigures, and uplifts life and says *Yes* even to its most terrible and destructive aspects. But the God of vengeance can also appear as the God of *peace* and *love*.

> To be sure, when a people is perishing, when it feels how its faith in the future and its hope of freedom are waning irrevocably, when submission begins to appear to it as the prime necessity and it becomes aware of the virtues of the subjugated as the conditions of self-preservation, then its god *has to* change too. Now he becomes a sneak, timid and modest; he counsels "peace of the soul," hate-no-more, forbearance, even "love" of friend and enemy. He moralizes constantly. . . . Formerly, he repre-sented a people, the strength of a people, everything aggressive and power-thirsty in the soul of a people: now he is merely a good god.[36]

This idea, according to which gods reflect the aspirations, the strength or the weakness of a people, was of value to Nietzsche well before its final elaboration in the last two years of his productive life. Thus in *Daybreak*, paragraph 424, after having underscored "that truth, *as a whole* and interconnectedly, exists only for souls which are at once powerful and harmless, and full of joyfulness and peace," and not for the weak and sickly, he concludes: "This is why others take so little real pleasure in sci-ence, and make of the coldness, dryness, and inhumanity of science a reproach to it: it is the sick passing judgment on the games of the healthy.—The Greek gods, too, were unable to offer consolation, when

Greek mankind at last one and all grew sick, this was a reason for the abolition of such gods."[37] In *Human, All Too Human*, Nietzsche quite explicitly demonstrates this again when he compares the Greek gods and Judeo-Christian God and sets in relief the game of sovereignty and decay that reveals itself in the relations between Olympus and humanity:

> The Greeks did not see the Homeric gods as set above them as masters, or themselves set beneath the gods as servants, as the Jews did. They saw as it were only the reflection of the most successful exemplars of their own caste, that is to say an ideal, not an antithesis of their own nature. . . . Where the Olympian gods failed to dominate, Greek life too was gloomier and more filled with anxiety—Christianity, on the other hand, crushed and shattered man completely and buried him as though in mud: into a feeling of total depravity it then suddenly shone a beam of divine mercy, so that, surprised and stupefied by this act of grace, man gave vent to a cry of rapture and for a moment believed he bore all heaven within him. It is upon this pathological excess of feeling, upon the profound corruption of the head and heart that was required for it, that all the psychological sensations of Christianity operate: it desires to destroy, shatter, stupefy, intoxicate, the one thing it does not desire is *measure* and that is why it is in the profoundest sense barbaric, Asiatic, ignoble, un-Hellenic.[38]

But the nobility and sovereignty do not exclude the terrifying and cruel aspects of power. On the contrary, nothing is more remote to Nietzsche's conception of power than the vision of pity, of suffering-with, of *empathy*. This is why he insists in the *Antichrist*:

> The evil god is needed no less than the good god: after all, we do not owe our own existence to tolerance and humanitarianism. . . . What would be the point of a god who knew nothing of wrath, revenge, envy, scorn, cunning, and violence? who had perhaps never experienced the delightful *ardeurs* of victory or annihilation?[39]

Curiously, one will find similar ideas in his very first writings, where Nietzsche examines the violence, cruelty and force that are at the base of Greek civilization and the Greek State:

> For it is not to be forgotten that the same cruelty, which we found in the essence of every Culture, lies also in the essence of every powerful religion and in general in the essence of *power* (*Macht*) which is always

evil (*böse*); so that we shall understand it just as well when a Culture is shattering, with a cry for liberty or at least justice, a too highly piled bulwark of religious claims.[40]

In maintaining that power, exuberance or decay of the gods expresses for Nietzsche ideas that are man-made, one cannot avoid evoking the insights and analyses of Feuerbach, according to which religion is the reflection or projection of humanity's hidden aspirations, desires and dreams. In a language in which no translation can capture the plasticity, poetry, and beauty typical of Feuerbach, one reads in effect:

> Such as are a man's thoughts and dispositions, such is his God; so much worth as a man has, so much and no more has his God. *Consciousness of God is self-consciousness, knowledge of God is self-knowledge.* By his God thou knowest man, and by man his God; the two are identical. . . . God is the *manifested* inward nature, the *expressed* self of man—religion the solemn unveiling of man's hidden treasures, the revelation of his intimate thoughts, *the open confession of his love-secrets.*[41]

But whereas Nietzsche moves in a universe of forces, and considers man, particularly in his later period, in and from the relations of force, Feuerbach remains attached to an "essentialist" world, where man converses with *himself*, speaks to himself, and talks with his genus, with his essence and his humanity. Religion is thus presented in *The Essence of Christianity* as a dialogue (or monologue) of human with human, but only as a generic human or essence:

> Religion, at least the Christian, is the relation of man to himself, or more correctly to his own nature (i.e., his subjective nature); but a relation to it, viewed as a nature apart from his own. The divine being, or, rather, the *human nature* purified, freed form the limits of the individual man, made objective—i.e., *contemplated and reversed as another, a distinct being.* All the attributes of the divine nature are, therefore, attributes of the human nature.[42]

No doubt Feuerbach centers his analyses on a particular religion, Christianity, and he sees in religion the reflection or revelation of a lack, to the extent that humans project on the divinity his or her needs, wishes, most precious aspirations. But, in spite of this, the forces and the will that produce this pantheon are not questioned. They only take its place. That is to say, the qualities and attributes man possessed before he occupied the place of God remain the same, for the forces and relations of forces have not changed. There is no *inversion of values*, there is no radical reevaluation of them. On this, Deleuze observes quite correctly:

> Feuerbach says that man has changed, that he has become God; God has changed, the essence of God has become the essence of man. But he who is Man has not changed; the reactive man, the slave, who does not cease to be slavish by presenting himself as God, always the slave, a machine for manufacturing the divine. What God is has not changed either; always the divine, the supreme Being, a machine for manufacturing the slave. What has changed, or rather, what has exchanged its determinations, is the intermediate concept, the middle term which can be either subject or predicate of each other: God or Man.[43]

The question that Nietzsche poses, then, is not one of knowing *what* man is, or what is the essence of religion, but rather: What is the will that evaluates? What are the forces and relations that are in play? Is it a question of forces that affirm life, that enrich and transfigure it, or else of forces that render existence guilty and reduce it to equations: lack = punishment, obedience = reward? This is why the religious manifestations of a people, civilization, and culture are just so many symptoms that Nietzsche tests, dissects, analyses and that allow him to diagnose the power, efflorescence, or decline of the will that has produced them. A decadent people can only create gods of vengeance and *ressentiment*. A blossoming people, on the contrary, can only create and venerate strong, powerful, cruel, affirmative, and overflowing gods. In this perspective, the Yahweh of ancient times, and particularly of the era of kingship, was an expression of the Hebrew people's awareness of its power, courage, joy, and self-confidence. But with the process of corruption underway, the priest would progressively grab power and, consequently, the interpretation given to Yahweh. Much later, the small community of disciples would appropriate the "glad tidings," the falsification of which would be completed and definitively achieved by the apostle Paul, "genius in hatred, in the vision of hatred, in the inexorable logic of hatred."[44] It is, moreover, Paul who creates the occasion for the mass-production of this type of priest, and who carries within the instinct of decadence, the will to nothingness and the will to an end.

From these considerations, it is easy to understand why Nietzsche is hostile vis-à-vis the Gospels and the New Testament in general. "One should read the Gospels as books of seduction by means of *morality*: these petty people reserve morality for themselves—they know all about morality! With morality it is easiest to lead mankind around *by the nose*."[45]

However, his vision of the Old Testament is quite different:

> The *Old* testament—that is something else again: All honor to the Old Testament! I find in it great human beings, a heroic landscape, and something of the very rarest quality in the world, the incomparable naïveté of the *strong heart*; what is more, I find a people. In the New one, on the other hand, I find nothing but petty sectarianism, mere rococo of the soul, mere involutions, nooks, queer things, the air of conventicle, not to forget an occasional whiff of bucolic mawkishness that belongs to the epoch (*and* to the Roman province) and is not so much Jewish as Hellenistic. Humility and self-importance cheek-by-jowl; a garrulousness of feeling that almost stupefies; impassioned vehemence, not passion; embarrassing gesticulation; it is plain that there is no trace of good breeding.[46]

One can easily grasp what Nietzsche blames here. The Old Testament appears in his view as a book expressing the great epoch of a people—a strong, blossoming, abundant and self-confident people. The God that it depicts can also only be a strong, powerful, affirmative, and Just God. The New Testament is, inversely, the book of decadence, of small people, of small souls, and of all those who await reward or punishment. Consequently, the God that it presents can be only the God of petty affairs, the God of precaution, demands, duty, in brief, of *morality*.

> *Morality*—no longer the expression of the conditions of the life and growth of a people, no longer its most basic instinct of life, but become abstract, become the antithesis of life—morality as the systematic degradation of the imagination, as the "evil eye" for all things. *What* is Jewish, *what* is Christian, morality? Chance done out of its innocence; misfortune besmirched with the concept of "sin" . . .[47]

A morality through which God renders judgment, reward, punishment, and imperatives is, and can only be, nearing an end: a symptom of exhaustion, decay, and the will to nothingness. Such a God is in fact the God of the "universal moral order," the God of decadence, the God of Providence.

PROVIDENCE, BEAUTIFUL CHAOS, AND SUBLIME CHANCE

When the will to power of a people declines and the conditions for a blossoming of an *ascendant life* disappear, the ideas one has of a strong, bold, dominating, and proud God transmute into those of a "God of the humble," a "God of sinners," of the weak, sick, just and *good*. One evokes, then, a divine will that commands what one ought or ought not do. The criterion allowing for the judgment of individuals and entire peoples would be their submission to this will that "manifests itself . . . as the *ruling factor*, that is to say, as punishing and rewarding according to the degree of obedience."[48]

This idea appears already in a fragment of 1885–1886, where Nietzsche maintains: "In itself, religion has nothing to do with morality: but both descendants of the Jewish religion are *essentially* moralistic religions—such as offer precepts about how one *ought* to live, and create a hearing for their demands by rewards and punishments."[49]

In this sense, the "universal moral order" invented by the philosophers is in fact only another name for what is already masked and disguised, namely, Providence. This concept is developed in greater detail in a text of fall 1887, where Nietzsche probes, analyzes, and brings to light the different metamorphoses and vicissitudes by which one recognizes the nihilist forces that up to the present have been hidden:

> *To consider:* to what extent the fateful belief in *divine providence*—the *most paralyzing* belief for hand and reason there has ever been—still exists; to what extent Christian presuppositions and interpretations still live on under the formulas "nature," "progress," "perfectibility," "Darwinism," under the superstitious belief in a certain relationship between happiness and virtue, unhappiness and guilt. That absurd *trust* in the course of things, in "life," in the "instinct of life," that comfortable resignation that comes from the faith that if everyone only does his duty *all* will be well—this kind of thing is meaningful only supposing a direction of things *sub specie boni*. Even *fatalism*, the form philosophical sensibility assumes with us today, is a consequence of this *long* belief in divine dispensation, an unconscious consequence: as if what happens were no responsibility of ours.[50]

Now, as the above text demonstrates, nihilist forces are continually changing, metamorphosing and borrowing new names such as "divine

dispensation," "nature," "progress," "perfection," "Darwinism," fatalism. . . . Morality is at work, the instinct of decadence appears in glittering clothing—"noble," "divine," flashy cloaks. The Jewish priest forges
the "divine will" as a means of assuring and maintaining his power; later,
the philosopher will come to his aid: "And the church was seconded by
the philosophers: the *lie* of the 'moral world order' runs through the
whole development of modern philosophy."[51]

Thus, one will not be surprised to see Nietzsche consider also the
doctrine of "free will" from the point of view of the relation of forces.
Already in his intermediate period, he explains the origins of this doctrine
by a position of power, from which man can consider himself free, while,
in fact, his feeling of freedom depends on the very intensity of the *feeling
of living*, that is, on what man feels in passion, duty, knowledge, and
capricious impulses. Hence the conclusion: "The theory of freedom of
will is an invention of the *ruling* classes (*herrschender Stände*)."[52]

It is, however, in the late period that the analyses around forces and
the relations of forces will be progressively developed, specified and
enriched; that Nietzsche will master those two great discoveries: *nihilism*
and the *will to power*. This is why "free will" will appear in *Twilight of the
Idols*, a later self-published book, as the art of dominating, judging, con-
demning, and finding guilty:

> Today we no longer have any pity for the concept of "free will": we
> know only too well what it really is—the foulest of all theologians' arti-
> fices, aimed at making mankind "responsible" in their sense, that is,
> *dependent upon them*. . . . The entire old psychology, the psychology of
> will, was conditioned by the fact that its originators, the priests at the
> head of ancient communities wanted to create for themselves the *right*
> to punish—or wanted to create the right for God. . . . Today as we have
> entered into the *reverse* movement and we immoralists are trying with
> all our strength to take the concept of guilt and the concept of punish-
> ment out of the world again, and to cleanse psychology, history, nature,
> and social institutions and sanctions of them, there is in our eyes no
> more radical opposition than that of the theologians, who continue
> with the concept of a "moral world order" to infect the innocence of
> becoming by means of "punishment" and "guilt." Christianity is a
> metaphysics of the hangman.[53]

But if Providence is for Nietzsche an invention of the instinct of decadence, a craftiness of nihilist forces to better dominate, guide, and assure

power, and if "free will" also presents itself as a concept of increase, a mask for the increase of the will to domination, and not as something that either hinders or questions the concept of Providence, then what, in the end, is freedom? How can we recognize the free individual?

In fact, throughout his work, Nietzsche constantly stresses the essentially *creative* role of the artist, the artist as someone who transforms and transfigures existence through the continual play of *creation*, fiction, lie, illusion, and the will to take in and to let oneself be taken in. But there is no creation without destruction, without resistance and overcoming. In other words, the more resistance there is, the more enjoyment. This is why the so-called liberal institutions are deemed worthy of the greatest contempt and the greatest irony on Nietzsche's part: "Liberal institutions cease to be liberal as soon as they are attained: later on, there are no worse and no more thorough injurers of freedom than liberal institutions. . . . Liberalism: in other words, *herd-animalization*. . . . These same institutions produce quite different effects while they are still being fought for; then they really promote freedom in a powerful way."[54] One will understand why war, too, is "a school of freedom." In fact:

> How is freedom measured in individuals and peoples? According to resistance which must be overcome, according to the exertion required, to remain *on top*. The highest type of free men should be sought where the highest resistance is constantly overcome: five steps from tyranny, close to the threshold of the danger of servitude. . . . Those large hothouses for the strong—for the strongest kind of human being that has so far been known—the aristocratic commonwealths of the type of Rome or Venice, understood freedom exactly in the sense which I understand it: as something one has or *does not* have, something one *wants*, something one *conquers*.[55]

To conquer freedom through the game of creation, which involves continual destruction and going beyond, thus expresses the joy of overcoming, of failing and of the will to more. Freedom is a war. "The human being who has *become free*—and how much more the *spirit* who has become free—spits on the contemptible type of well-being dreamed of by shopkeepers, Christians, cows, females, Englishmen, and other democrats."[56]

In claiming that man constructs and conquers his own freedom, Nietzsche does not in any way pretend to eliminate *chance*. On the contrary, in all his work chance, as well as necessity, plays a major role.[57] In a fragment of 1884, cited above, one in fact reads: "The wisest man would be one of the *richest in contradictions*, who has, as it were, antennae for all types of men—as well as his great moments of *grand harmony*—a rare *chance* even in us! . . . A sort of planetary motion—"[58]

This idea is already found in *The Gay Science*, paragraph 277, where Nietzsche introduces and links together providence, chaos, and chance. This text, which carries the significant title of *Personal providence*, begins thus: "There is a certain high point in life: once we have reached that, we are, for all our freedom, once more in the greatest danger of spiritual unfreedom, and no matter how much we have faced up to the beautiful chaos of existence and denied it all providential reason and goodness, we still have to pass our hardest test."[59] The hardest test is that of establishing that all things that happen to us, whether good or bad, "always turn out for the best." Thus regarding the most simple everyday events of existence, we ought to admit that they cannot but occur and that they are all, without exception, good or not so good, of profound significance and use *for us*. This leads Nietzsche to conclude:

> Nor should we conceive too high an opinion of this dexterity of our wisdom when at times we are excessively surprised by the wonderful harmony created by the playing of our instrument—a harmony that sounds too good for us to dare to give the credit to ourselves. Indeed, now and then someone plays *with* us—good old chance; now and then chance guides our hand, and the wisest providence could not think up a more beautiful music than that which our foolish hand produces then.[60]

One will find this same idea restated in a fragment of 1884. This time, however, Nietzsche turns his critical attack explicitly against the conceptions of a divine intention and finality in history. After having established that one starts, thanks to the most recent studies of animal evolution, to take account of the total absence of a plan in history and to realize that chance determines, in a general way, the course of events, Nietzsche will state in conclusion: "*However intentional an action may be*, the portion of chance, of absence of utility or awareness of utility it contains is largely predominant, comparable to the useless heat radiated by the sun: what *has* a meaning tends toward the infinitesimal."[61]

But it is even more surprising to see *The Antichrist*, as well as the fragments connected to it, attribute to chance the advent of certain types of superior and exceptional human beings, whose natures are the most successful and best accomplished. Nietzsche calls these exceptions "over-men." They constitute one of his most ambiguous and variously inter-preted discoveries.

> "The Overman"
> The problem I pose is *not* what shall succeed mankind in the sequence of living beings: but what type of man shall be worthier of being cho-sen, willed, *bred*...
>
> Mankind *does not* represent a development toward something bet-ter, or stronger, or higher, in the sense accepted today. . . . The Euro-pean of the 19th century is vastly inferior in value to the European of the Renaissance. Further development is not at all connected with a necessity, elevation, intensification, or strengthening.
>
> In another sense, *success* in individual cases is constantly encoun-tered in the most widely different places and cultures: here, in fact, a *higher type is found,* something which is, in relation to mankind as a whole, a kind of "overman." Such fortunate accidents of great success have always been possible and *will* perhaps will always be possible. And even whole tribes, generations and peoples may occasionally represent such a *bull's-eye* . . .[62]

The superior individual, the strong and powerful man presents him-self not only as the product of chance, but also as someone who can turn a profit. He can turn favorable strokes of luck, as well as the rich chaos of diversities, to his own advantage through force, artifice, falsification, cre-ation, and poetry. For he constantly tries to refashion, embellish, and over-come them. By this alone, that is, by affirmation and consent, by going beyond, and by the eternal advent of reconstruction, Nietzsche will be able to recognized the free men, the successes, the *truly liberated,* the "*Godless.*"

"WE GODLESS OTHERS"

When, in effect, Nietzsche refers to himself as an "atheist," the term he most often uses is "*wir Gottlosen,*" namely, we godless others, we other free spir-its, the liberated, the unencumbered of God. This will, of course, be mis-leading for those who wish to find in Nietzsche's work a concern for the old conceptual dispute surrounding the existence or nonexistence of God. Niet-zsche has only contempt and irony for the architecture of such concepts and notions as Being, the Good, the Absolute, the True, Perfection, the idea of

"God" or of an *ens realissimum* ("perfect being"), "Why did mankind have to take seriously the brain afflictions of sick web-spinners? They have paid dearly for it!"[63] The God of metaphysics represents for Nietzsche everything hostile to an ascendant life, that is, to what has affirmed and exceeded life, what is powerful and superior. The God of nihilist forces that shapes metaphysics and morality is the God of lassitude, decadence, ressentiment, in short, of the end of ends. Such a God is a good argument for not believing in him:

> That we find no God—either in history or in nature or behind nature—is not what differentiates *us*, but that we experience what has been revered as God, not as "godlike" but as miserable, as absurd, as harmful, not merely as an error but as a *crime against life*. We deny God as God. If one were to *prove* this God of the Christians to us, we should be even less able to believe in him.[64]

Already in *The Birth of Tragedy*, Nietzsche insists on what sets apart the Olympian religion, a religion characterized by the over abundance of life and, thus, by the absence of any trace of asceticism, of any sense of duty, as well as any calculation regarding reward and punishment.

> Whoever approaches these Olympians with another religion in his heart, searching among them for moral elevation, even for sanctity, the disincarnate spirituality, for charity and benevolence, will soon be forced to turn his back on them, discouraged and disappointed. For there is nothing here that suggests asceticism, spirituality, or duty. We hear nothing but the accents of an exuberant, triumphant life in which things, whether good or evil, are deified.[65]

Nothing is more antidivine, in Nietzsche's view, than a religion whose morality teaches the extirpation and liquidation of instincts; nothing is more repugnant to the Nietzschean perspective than contempt for and degradation of the body: "a *measure of urgency* set by natures who do not know how to measure and who have no other choice than to become depraved and swine or ascetics."[66] These natures have found in Christianity, as well as in Buddhism, a way of thinking that, according to Nietzsche, is typical of sick people, of small people, in short, of all those who feel like failed individuals: "we can forgive their denigrating a world in which they have been ill provided for.—But we must judge these religions and doctrines as asylums and prisons."[67]

These assertions are to be understood in the context of Nietzsche's hostility toward moral transpositions that operate in the world of metaphysics, art, science, and religion. This is why the fragments of 1881, the year in which he drafted *The Gay Science*, assert stridently a "dehumanization" of nature and a "naturalization" of humanity. In other words, peoples continually project in nature, and in existence in general, their insubstantial ways of thinking and seeing. But Nietzsche also claims a de-deification of nature for, there again, the *human, all too human* categories, evaluations and ways of judging are transposed into the domain of nature. From this point of view, the attributes we lend to nature are just so many characteristics created, conceived, and developed from nihilistic forces, from the will to deny, depreciate, and condemn life. Thus, paragraph 109 of *The Gay Science* sets forth a series of precautions aimed precisely in this direction and bordering directly on these questions: "When will all these shadows of God cease to darken our minds? When will we complete our de-deification of nature? When may we begin to '*naturalize*' humanity in terms of a pure, newly discovered, newly redeemed nature?"[68]

The above questions resonate in a fragment of fall 1887: "In place of *moral values*, purely *naturalistic* values. Naturalization of morality."[69] But what does Nietzsche understand by naturalization of morality? Is there a pure concept of nature? a nature that would be exempt from all moral judgment, from all evaluation, and all need to be reevaluated afresh, re-created anew? What would allow us to recognize a newly discovered and newly liberated nature?

A text also dated 1887, which will be reprised, modified, and used in *Twilight of the Idols*, will help to better answer these questions. It is, in fact, in an attack against Rousseau that Nietzsche will also assert a "return to nature," but this "return" and this "nature" are situated in a perspective and level far different than those of the celebrated Genevan:

> Rousseau, this first modern man, idealist and rabble in one person— one who needed moral "dignity" to be able to stand his own sight, sick with unbridled vanity and unbridled self-contempt. This miscarriage, couched on the threshold of modern times, also wanted to "return to nature"; to ask this once more, to what did Rousseau want to return?
>
> I too speak of a "return to nature," although it is really not a going back but an *ascent*—up into the high, free, even terrible nature and naturalness where great tasks are something one plays with, one *may* play with.[70]

What is small concerns the small people, the rabble, the outcasts, and all those who find repugnant the vision of strong, accomplished, successful, and overflowing types. This is why Nietzsche refers not to a "return," but to an "*ascent*—into the high, free, even terrible nature and naturalness," the naturalness which fulfills itself in the play and delight of eternally recommenced and eternally reevaluated construction-destruction. From this, one will understand the fundamental difference separating these two religious types: Dionysus and the Crucified. In the first case:

> It is *not* a difference in regard to their martyrdom—it is a difference in the meaning of it. Life itself, its eternal fruitfulness and recurrence, creates torment, destruction, the will to annihilation. In the other case, suffering—the "Crucified as the innocent one"—counts as an objection to this life, as a formula for its condemnation.— . . . The Christian denies even the happiest lot on earth: he is sufficiently weak, poor, disinherited to suffer from life in whatever form he meets it.[71]

Life denied, impoverished, depreciated thus becomes the cause of malediction and of the need to escape to the beyond. It is not powerful, terrible and natural enough to be justified by itself. Thus, the question posed by Nietzsche is that of the meaning of suffering: The Christian meaning or the tragic meaning. The tragic man acquiesces to a tremendous amount of suffering: he affirms it, transfigures it, and "deifies" it. The Christian, on the contrary, curses that very life. He is not strong enough, full enough, nor divinizing enough to transform suffering into a work of art. In other words:

> The "God on the cross" is a curse on life, a signpost to seek redemption from life: Dionysus cut to pieces is a *promise* of life: it will be eternally reborn and return again from destruction.[72]

These texts can easily lead to the conclusion that in the final reckoning, Dionysus, the eternal return, and nature are only other names or other avatars of the old God of metaphysics and morality fallen today into discredit.[73] To these conclusions one could add no new creation, could get rid of any value or any prejudice. Moreover, if one muses on Nietzsche's problematic assertion according to which "only the moral God is overcome," then his "atheism" would be abolished completely.

Now, it does not mean that Nietzsche does not continue to find life any less enigmatic, and that he considers a reversal or inversion of values involve both a way of thinking and a singular mentality. That is to say, all knowledge of the world in an individual incapable of overturning the entirety of values is, in the end, futile and inconsequential. For: "Life is supremely enigmatic: thus far all the great philosophers believed that a solution lies in the resolute *reversal* of perspective and values—All equally believed that for inferior minds a substitute will continue to be imposed, for example, morality, belief in God, in immortality, etc."[74]

But what is particularly striking about Nietzsche's relation to "atheism," is the complete absence of productive argumentation supplied to the age-old debates on the existence or nonexistence of God. Such an attitude only appears to him laughable, futile, and deserving of the greatest contempt. In fact, he even admits that there can be gods:

> And how many new gods are still possible! As for myself, in whom the religious, that is to say god-*forming*, instinct occasionally becomes active at impossible times—how differently, how variously the divine has revealed itself to me each time! . . . I should not doubt that there are many kinds of gods. There are some one cannot imagine without a certain halcyon and frivolous quality in their make-up.—Perhaps light feet are even an integral part of the concept "god"—Is it necessary to elaborate that a god prefers to stay beyond everything bourgeois and rational? and, between ourselves, also beyond good and evil?[75]

The airy spirit and light steps, these are the attributes of gods who know how to situate themselves beyond good and evil, who know how to travel all the great stretches and orbs, the open and overflowing soul of a sweet madness, of the life-will and the will to become. The gods are dancers.

One can easily envision through Nietzsche's hostility vis-à-vis the heaviness of spirit, the spirit of negation, of *ressentiment*, vengeance, and hatred, in short, of morality and all the values that it considers supreme. But these values had already begun to cave in, at least for a few. Nietzsche announces the inversion under the effects of a magnificent act, to which he unsparingly applies the tints, colors, lights, and the great mobility of his genius as a writer and artist. It is thus that he opens paragraph 343 of *The Gay Science*: "The greatest recent event—that 'God is dead,' that the belief in the Christian god has become unbelievable—is already beginning to cast its first shadows over Europe."[76]

But this succession of destructions, upheavals, ruptures, twilights, and declines is no less the bearer of a new daybreak, a daybreak filled with light, felicity, cheerfulness, and consolation:

Indeed, we philosophers and "free spirits" feel, when we hear the news that "the old god is dead," as if a new dawn shone on us; our heart overflows with gratitude, amazement, premonitions, expectations. At long last the horizon appears free to us again, even if it should not be bright; at long last our ships may venture out again, venture out to face the danger; all the daring of the lover of knowledge is permitted again; the sea, *our* sea, lies open again; perhaps there has never yet been such an "open sea."—[77]

In his book, *The Destiny of Man*, Nicolas Berdyaev makes this interesting remark: "Nietzsche has never known nor understood authentic Christianity. He has looked into the face of a degenerated Christian society, in which the heroic spirit has died out, and he rises up passionately and vigorously against this decadent and petit-bourgeois Christianity."[78] But how could Nietzsche have known any other form of Christianity if this is the only extant form that he penetrates and illuminates its nihilist forces, which are inherent in the very movement of Western history and civilization? This is why it is crucial that Christianity, so important in his view, is not to be confused with the total movement of nihilism, which, by the plasticity, mobility and metamorphoses that characterize its forces, moves, and crosses all Western history. That is to say, nihilism plunges its roots deeply into European civilization, and even beyond this civilization, since Nietzsche considers Judaism, as well as Buddhism, as religions involved in the total movement of the forces of decadence. In this perspective, we Westerners, we still live the faith that has sustained Plato and the entire Christian tradition:

> . . . that even we seekers after knowledge today, we godless anti-metaphysicians still take *our* fire, too, from the flame lit by a faith that is thousands of years old, that Christian faith which was also the faith of Plato, that God is the truth, that truth is divine.—But what if this should become more and more incredible, if nothing should prove to be divine any more unless it were error, blindness, the lie—if God himself should prove to be our most enduring lie?—[79]

To be sure, Nietzsche can designate himself by the names of "*Gottlos*" (Godless), free spirit, the liberated, and unencumbered of God. But he can do this only because he, himself, springs from a universe and movement that he endlessly, *paradoxically*, reevaluates, reinterprets, and, as a result, overcomes. How would one recognize it otherwise?

"Who Are We Anyway?"

This is precisely the question Nietzsche poses at the beginning of paragraph 346 of *The Gay Science*:

> But you do not understand this? Indeed, people will have trouble understanding us. We are looking for words; perhaps we are also looking for ears. Who are we anyway? If we simply called ourselves, using the old expression, godless, or unbelievers, or perhaps, immoralists, we do not believe that this would even come close to designating us: We are all three in such an advanced stage that one—that *you*, my curious friends—could never comprehend how we feel at this point.[80]

Thus, the attacks launched by Nietzsche against Christianity and Christian morality are to be understood only in and from this very Christianity, that is, in and from the relations of forces that he analyses, dissects and brings to light, because it is too near him, too apparent to him: "Likewise, we are no longer Christians: we've outgrown Christianity, not because we've lived too far from it but too near, and more than that because we've grown *out of* it—our stricter and more fastidious peity itself is what today *forbids* us to remain Christians."[81]

We can better understand then why, in *Daybreak*, Nietzsche already sees the origins of free thought in France in the very overcoming movement that the Christian values have, themselves, achieved.

> One cannot deny that the French have been the *most Christian* nation on earth: not because the faith of the masses has been greater in France than elsewhere, but because the most difficult of Christian ideals have there been transformed into men and not remained merely ideas, beginnings, falterings. . . . And now say why this nation's possessing these perfect types of Christianness was bound also to produce perfect counter-types of unchristian free-spiritedness![82]

Do not draw assumptions about these claims too quickly, for it often happens that Nietzsche overestimates a thought or value to the sole end of attacking others. In this paragraph, for example, after having stressed the importance of the deeds and intellectual production of Christian culture in France, he moves on to what he finally has in view, that is, to criticize the lack of finesse and efflorescence of the German spirit. ". . .—while the depths of a great German are usually kept enclosed in an intricate capsule, as an elixir which seeks to protect itself against the light and against frivolous hands by the hardness and strangeness of its casing."[83] Our suspicion will only be confirmed if we now move on to paragraph 132 of the same work, that carries the significant title: *The Echo of Christianity in Morality*. Here, indeed, Nietzsche considers such ideas as the common good, philanthropy, unselfishness, and love of one's neighbor as substitutes, avatars, and residues of the Christian mentality in French free thought.

> The more one liberated oneself from the dogmas, the more one sought as it were a *justification* of this liberation in a cult of philanthropy: not to fall short of the Christian ideal in this, but where possible to *outdo* it, was a secret spur with all French freethinkers from Voltaire up to Auguste Comte: and the latter did in fact, with his formula *vivre pour autrui*, outchristian Christianity.[84]

If we look once more at paragraph 192, we will see that Nietzsche raises Pascal to the head of the rank, in the sense that he distinguishes him through originality, creativity, and a spirit of unity: "There stands Pascal, in unity of fervor, spirit and honesty the first of all Christians—and consider what had to be united here!"[85]

Now, remember that entirely different terms and tones were used to chartacterize Pascal in paragraph 68 of the very same work: "Christianity would long since have ceased to exist: for these pages of the Jewish Pascal (Saint Paul) expose the origin of Christianity as thoroughly as the pages of the French Pascal expose the destiny and that by which it will perish."[86]

The idea of a Pascal representing the instinct of decadence also appears in fragments written during the period in which Nietzsche drafted *Daybreak* (end of 1880), as well as in a text of 1884, where one will find: "Christianity has on its conscience having *spoiled* so many free spirits, for example, Pascal and before him Meister Eckhart."[87]

But it is in *The Antichrist*, when Nietzsche has already unmasked and diagnosed the nihilist forces as forces acting as the will to nothingness and as the will to an end with life, that Pascal will appear as the decadent type, that is, as the product of asceticism and Christian morality:

> Christianity has sided with all that is weak and base, with all failures; it has made an ideal of whatever *contradicts* the instinct of the strong life to preserve itself; it has corrupted the reason of even those strongest in spirit by teaching men to consider the supreme values of the spirit as something sinful, as something that leads into error—as *temptations*.

The most pitiful example: the corruption of Pascal, who believed in the corruption of his reason through original sin when it had in fact been corrupted only by his Christianity.[88]

These considerations and analyses that he develops around Pascal and French free thought allow us to situate Nietzsche himself in the same movement and universe of forces that he tries, continually and paradoxically, to capture, connect and reevaluate. In other words, it is only in and from this very movement, in and from those forces and relations, that Nietzsche's work and thought unfold and break free. In this sense, we can affirm that his enterprise also remains nihilist, nihilist insofar as it is a *destroyer* and at the same time a *creator* of new values. The new values that Nietzsche sets up are no less values. But they are values posed, according to him, from forces that affirm life and acquiesce to its richness, its overflowings, to its excesses and overcomings. In a text of fall 1887, we find this admission:

> It is only late that one musters the courage for what one really *knows*. That I have hitherto been a thorough-going nihilist, I have admitted to myself only recently: the energy and radicalism with which I advanced as a nihilist deceived me about this basic fact. When one moves toward a goal it seems impossible that "goallessness as such" is the principle of our faith.[89]

Nietzsche is and remains paradoxical. And this is accomplished through his thought and expressions, through the movement in which he shifts around and ceaselessly interprets values, inverts them, re-creates them, and turns them to his own use, through art. His "*Gottlosigkeit*" is thus understandable only if one considers nihilism from his own perspective, namely, as a multiform and ambiguous movement which traverses all western history and in which the forces are characterized, precisely, by the capacity to deny, to transform themselves, to disguise or adapt themselves. Thus, the supreme values that Nietzsche sees collapsing: God, Being, the Absolute, the Good, the True, and Perfection, are destroyed by the same forces that produced them. God chokes on theology, morals are gagged by morality—morality that destroys itself, conquers itself, is exceeded by itself.

5

Morality Exceeded by Morality

We wish to be the inheritors of all preceding morality: and *not* begin from zero. Everything we fashion is only the morality that returns against the form that it has taken hold of so far.

—Fragment of 1884

Although Nietzsche has devoted a specific work to the problem of morality (*On the Genealogy of Morals*, published in 1887), one of the most significant questions that appears and reappears throughout his work is that of morality, or that of the forces and relations of forces, in which and from which the different values are constantly created, instituted, transformed, and exceeded.

Nonetheless, it is in this writing, and in other texts of the same period, that he clarifies and specifies in greater detail the insights, analyses, and discoveries already found in his earlier texts. Nietzsche himself claims in paragraph 8 of the Preface: "If this book is incomprehensible to anyone and jars on his ears, the fault, it seems to me, is not necessarily mine. It is clear enough, assuming, as I do assume, that one has first read my earlier writings and has not spared some trouble in doing so."[1] Nietzsche refers then, in this same paragraph, to *Thus Spoke Zarathustra* and to the aphoristic form of his writings. One will also find, in paragraphs 2 and 4, explicit references to *Human, All Too Human, The Wanderer and His Shadow*, and *Daybreak*. Other references to *Daybreak* and also to *The*

Gay Science, to *Human, All Too Human,* and, particularly, to *Beyond Good and Evil* appear in the body of the text itself.[2] On the title page Nietzsche had originally written: "*To Complete and Clarify Beyond Good and Evil, Recently Published.*" And in letters to his editor, Constantin G. Naumann, of Leipzig, he insists that it is imperative to see how *On the Genealogy of Morals* turned out, even in the galley proofs of this work published in 1886.[3]

On the Genealogy of Morals no doubt completes *Beyond Good and Evil,* but it is not for all that a closed work. It is like any other Nietzschean text—a text intended to stand on its own, one that resists and escapes all constraint, all mastery and interpretation. This is why the themes developed in *The Genealogy* are repeated, extended or condensed in the writings that will follow it. This is the case, for example, in *The Twilight of the Idols, The Antichrist,* and *The Case of Wagner,* where one finds, toward the end of the Epilogue, the following note:

> The opposition between "*noble* morality" and Christian morality was first explained in my *Genealogy of Morals:* perhaps there is no more decisive turning point in the history of our understanding of religion and morality. This book, my touchstone for what belongs to me, has the good fortune of being accessible only to the most high-minded and severe of spirits: the *rest* lack ears for it. One must have one's passion in things where nobody else today has it.[4]

In this perspective, we can maintain that *The Genealogy* represents for Nietzsche's later period what *Human, All Too Human* represented for his entire corpus, namely, an *interval,* a passage, a transition. But while *Human, All Too Human* still appears as a kind of chiaroscuro of the history of the moral *affects* that Nietzsche proposes to examine and unmask, *The Genealogy* dissects, analyses, and sets in play the very *forces* that are at work in the history of morality. In other words, the changes of perspective operating in this later period lead Nietzsche to shift the accent away from the symptoms of an *affect of power* toward the symptoms of a *will to power,* that is, toward the forces and relations of forces that express this *Will.* Thus, while *The Genealogy* explores and reevaluates the discoveries and insights that Nietzsche had made up to that point, it will open and prepare other questions that can be newly developed and reinterpreted. This is why it would be a mistake to want to discover through the genealogy, as Nietzsche conceives it, a primal origin or pure genesis in which value, or values would be given once and for all. He even mistrusts the search for origins, as significant and promising as that search might appear, for: "*The more insight we possess into an origin the less significant does the origin appear:* while *what is nearest to us,* what is around and in us, gradually begins to display colors and beauties and enigmas and riches of such significance of which earlier mankind had not an inkling."[5] In the *Wanderer and His Shadow,* Nietzsche shows in a more explicit and distrustful way the unwarranted importance attributed the origin: "To glorify the origin—that is the metaphysical aftershoot that breaks out when we meditate on history and makes us believe that what stands at the beginning of all things is also what is most valuable and essential."[6]

Both in *Human, All Too Human* and *On the Genealogy of Morals* Nietzsche acts as an ausculator, and as someone who dissects, analyzes, and interprets. But in both cases the process can never stop, since a symptom always hides another, an interpretation always calls for another. In this sense the genealogy is a text that must be continually deciphered, reread, rewritten. The color employed by Nietzsche is *gray,* and not *blue,* to where migrate the hypotheses woven by the English genealogists of morals up until that point: "For it must be obvious which color is a hundred times more vital for a genealogist of morals than blue: namely *gray,* that is, what is documented, what can actually be confirmed and has actually existed, in short the entire long hieroglyphic record, so hard to decipher, of the moral past of mankind!"[7]

What is at play, then, is not to merely question values, for there is no definitive value nor is there a value that is self-imposed. What is important, though, is to pose the question regarding the "value" of values, namely, of the forces and the relations of forces that are at work in the creation and institution of values. In this perspective, whenever an evaluation is produced or a meaning is given, the question inevitably arises: What forces have seized them? What forces are seized by them? What morality existed before? What *will* has overcome or exceeded that morality? For all interpretation presupposes the force of interpretation: "In truth, *interpretation is itself a means of becoming master of something.*"[8]

Consequently, all moral judgment, all evaluation and truth have a moving, changing, and fluent character, for they are susceptible to being appropriated, assimilated, or exceeded by the very forces that have produced them. That is to say, no interpretation is self-evident and that meaning has no value in itself. "Is meaning not necessarily relative meaning and perspective? All meaning is will to power (all relative meaning resolves itself into it)."[9]

Thus in *On the Genealogy of Morals,* Nietzsche tries anew to decipher the long-standing hieroglyphic text charged with meaning, questions, and evaluations, a text consisting of the past of human morality. Here he will penetrate anew, bring to light and unmask the different forces and relations of forces that are at work in the tables of values. *The Genealogy,* consisting of a preface, three essays, and which appears to be, from the formal point of view, a systematic treatise, is not for all that easily accessible. Nietzsche sums it up, a year later, in these terms:

> The truth of the *first* inquiry is the psychology of Christianity: the birth of Christianity out of the spirit of *ressentiment, not* as people may believe, out of the "spirit"—countermovement by its very nature, the great rebellion against the dominion of *noble* values.
> The *second* inquiry offers the psychology of the *conscience*—which is not, as people may believe, "the voice of God in man": it is the instinct of cruelty that turns back after it can no longer discharge itself externally. Cruelty is here exposed for the first time as one of the most ancient and basic substrata of culture that simply cannot be imagined away,
> The *third* inquiry offers the answer to the question whence the ascetic ideal, the priest's ideal, derives its tremendous *power* although it is the *harmful* ideal *par excellence*, a will to the end (*ein Wille zum Ende*), an ideal of decadence.[10]

We will try, in this chapter, to avoid a simple *exposition* of the three essays, which would be absurd, in view of the richness of implications and ambiguities that they contain and the innumerable possible readings and interpretations they sustain. Rather, we propose to point out the *paradoxes* where Nietzsche's thought always leads each time it tries—and it never stops trying—to get hold of and to *read* the universe in which these forces move.

"WE THE GOOD"

By attacking the English psychologists and utilitarians, Nietzsche is able to present his own conception and points of view on the developments and metamorphoses that traverse morality up to that point in time. For him these *philosophers* are subject to a certain clumsiness, to a set of platitudes and a total lack of *historical spirit* on the subject of the genealogy of morals.

In what concerns precisely the origin of the judgment "good," their principal weakness consists in always reducing and explaining everything from
the point of view of *utility*. Thus, at the origin, the so-called disinterested
actions would be lauded and considered as good by those in favor of whom
they were accomplished. Later on, however, due to habit and forgetfulness,
they will acquire an independent status appearing then as something good
in-itself. Regarding this theory and the explanations given by Paul Reé in
The Origin of Moral Sensations, Nietzsche saves neither criticism nor irony.
For as far as he is concerned the judgment "good" does not result
absolutely from those to whom one has shown "goodness." "Rather it was
'the good' themselves, that is to say, the noble, powerful, high-stationed
and high-minded, who felt and established themselves and their actions as
good, that is, of the first rank, in contradistinction to all the low, low-
minded, common and plebeian. It was out of this *pathos of distance* that
they first seized the right to create values and to coin names for values:
what does this have to do with utility!"[11] It is thus in the relations between
a superior and dominant group, namely, nobles, lords, and the powerful,
and an inferior group: the herd and everything that is "bad" ("*schlecht*"),
base and petty, that the origin of the word "good" must be sought. "The
lordly right of giving names extends so far that one should allow oneself to
conceive the origin of language itself as an expression of the power on the
part of the rulers: they say "this *is* this and this," they seal everything and
event with a sound and, as it were, take possession of it."[12]

One can quickly grasp the inversion undergone by the judgment
"good and bad" when it is transposed in the perspective of slave morality.
In the aristocratic man the term "good" comes about immediately and
spontaneously from himself, and it only comes afterward that he conceives of the idea of "bad," or "*schlecht.*" In the man given to *ressentiment*,
on the contrary, the word "evil" ("*böse*"), by which he condemns and
judges the powerful and nobles, is uttered first. That is to say, from the
point of view of the failures, the aristocratic man is "dyed in another color,
interpreted in another fashion, seen in another way by the venomous eye
of *ressentiment.*"[13] For the lamb cannot stand seeing the bird of prey; it
must necessarily be evil. But the birds of prey have quite a different view
regarding the lambs. They might even say: "*we* don't dislike them at all.
these good little lambs; we even love them: nothing is more tasty than a
tender lamb."[14] Undoubtedly the weak, the powerless and the wilted
speak from their hearts: "those, those powerful, they are the *wretched*, we
are, as opposed to them, the *good*."

In the First Essay Nietzsche reiterates an idea that was present in one of his earliest writings, *The Greek State*, according to which the beginnings of all civilizations are marked by cruelty, violence and the iron fist of the State. In fact, *On the Genealogy of Morals* associates all conquering and superior civilizations with "barbarians" and beasts of prey:

> One cannot fail to see at the bottom of all these noble races the beast of prey, the splendid *blond beast* prowling about avidly in search of spoil and victory; this hidden core needs to erupt from time to time, the animal has to get out again and go back to the wilderness: the Roman, Arabian, Germanic, Japanese nobility, the Homeric heroes, the Scandinavian Vikings—they all shared this need. . . . It is the noble races that have left behind them the concept "barbarian" wherever they have gone: even the highest culture betrays a consciousness of it and even a pride in it . . .[15]

Thus, it will come as no surprise to see Nietzsche delineate what separates and distinguishes the aristocratic warrior and the priestly caste. In the former, it is an overabundance of force, life, vigor, and good health that governs his creations and judgments. In the priest, it is, inversely, the voice of ressentiment, rancorous rumination, the subterranean hatred and evil eye of impotence that condemns everything that is flowering, overflowing, and affirmative.

> As is well known, the priests are the *most evil enemies*—but why? Because they are the most impotent. It is because of their impotence that in them hatred grows to monstrous and uncanny proportions, to the most spiritual and poisonous kind of hatred. The truly great haters in world history have always been priests; likewise the most ingenious haters . . .[16]

Consequently, the priest appears more intelligent, perspicuous, and masterful in the art of interpretation, refinement, transformation, and "spiritualization" of values. One can recognize the priestly caste by the fact that concepts of political preeminence change into concepts of spiritual preeminence. When the priestly caste is dominant, the oppositions of evaluation tend to be more and more interiorized and accentuated: "It is then, for example, that 'pure' and 'impure' confront one another for the first time as designations of station; and here too there evolves a 'good' and a 'bad' in a sense no longer referring to station."[17]

But the concepts and judgments change only because the nihilist forces of ressentiment are themselves endowed with a malleable power to adapt, to metamorphosize, transform, and to constantly disguise themselves. This is why, out of revenge, the Jewish priest had to necessarily reverse the values that had been set in place, thus lending them new masks and new disguises.

> For this alone was appropriate to a priestly people, the people embodying the most deeply repressed priestly vengefulness. It was the Jews who, with awe-inspiring consistency dared to invert the aristocratic value equation (good = noble = powerful = beautiful = happy = beloved of God) and to hang on to this inversion with their teeth, the teeth of the most abysmal hatred (the hatred of impotence), saying "the wretched alone are the good; the poor, impotent, lowly alone are the good; the suffering, deprived, sick, ugly alone are pious, alone are the blessed of God, blessedness is for them alone—and you, the powerful and noble, are on the contrary the evil, the cruel, lustful, the insatiable, the godless to all eternity; and you shall be in all eternity the unblessed, accursed and damned!' . . .[18]

We can thus understand why, according to Nietzsche, only from the Jewish people, from Jewish soil and a Jewish priest could there arise the message of a *new love* and the anticipation of a Judge, a Savior and a Messiah.[19] This is *not* therefore an *opposition*, but a consequence and an inevitable result of nihilist forces, which, reaching the outer limits of their own course, return again and disguise themselves in new attire, new cloaks, and new forms. Once again the forces of ressentiment triumph and the vengeful instinct of the priest is reproduced.

> Was it not part of the secret black art of truly *grand* politics of revenge, of a farseeing, subterranean, slowly advancing, and premeditated revenge, that Israel must itself deny the real instrument of its revenge before all the world as a mortal enemy and nail it to the cross, so that "all the world," namely all the opponents of Israel, could unhesitatingly swallow just this bait?[20]

Nietzsche presents this vengeance and victory of the forces of nihilist decadence, personified in the Jewish priest and Israel's conquests, in the form of a series of metamorphoses and avatars that have marked Western history up until the present. Thus, from the outset, Rome is defeated by Judea. Later, however, the classical ideal and the noble evaluations will witness a "superb and uncanny" awakening in the Renaissance. But this awakening will be quickly stifled: "thanks to that thoroughly plebeian (German and English) *ressentiment* movement called the Reformation."[21] Finally, with the French Revolution, Judea carried off the most decisive and radical of victories over the classical ideal of antiquity: "the last political noblesse in Europe, that of the *French* seventeenth and eighteenth century, collapsed beneath the popular instincts of *ressentiment—*greater rejoicing, more uproarious enthusiasm had never been heard on earth!"[22]

These successive victories of nihilist forces of ressentiment are understandable only to the extent to which one admits the malleable, mobile, and Protean character with which they are endowed. In order to survive and conserve themselves these forces must constantly borrow, fashion, remodel, and adapt different masks and new disguises. This is why the Greek philosopher already appears as a kind of vestige or as a novel form embodying fatigue, exhaustion, and the will to nothingness typical of the priest. In this sense Nietzsche will argue that the priestly type traverses all of Western thought and that German philosophy is, fundamentally, a concealed theology. This idea, that is summarized and explicitly specified in *The Antichrist*,[23] can be found in some of the earliest works, particularly those that refer to the stink of the seminary and convent emitted by the German philosophers. In a fragment of 1884, one reads in fact: "Fichte, Schelling, Hegel, Feuerbach, Strauss, all of them stink from the odor of theologians and the Church Fathers."[24] Kant also represents the end, fatigue and the extenuation of the old disguised dogmatist. He reflects and prolongs the last rays of the sun, of the Idea of the true world, that is, stable, sublime, eternal, displaced. "The true world—unattainable, indemonstrable, unpromisable; but the very thought of it—a consolation, an obligation, an imperative. (At bottom, the old sun, but seen through mist and skepticism. The idea has become elusive, pale, Nordic, Königsbergian.)"[25]

These considerations lead us to stress that the forces of ressentiment, denier of life, are not a prerogative of the Jewish priest, as great and as extensive as his influence had been in the history of Western nihilism. What Nietzsche emphasizes, and what is central in the analyses of this movement of negation, is the *priestly type* insofar as he represents the forces of decadence, vengeance, hatred, and the *No* to everything that is blooming, overflowing, sensual, and affirmative. One cannot insist enough on the capacity of the forces of ressentiment to change, transform, disguise themselves, so as to better dominate.

But if this is the case, what is the difference between a Jew and an anti-Semite, for example? How can we distinguish the one from the other? Indeed, in one of his later texts (Fall 1888), Nietzsche gives an interesting description of the antisemite:

> *Definition of the antisemite:* envy, *ressentiment*, rage, impotence, as the *Leitmotif* of the instinct, the pretension of the "elect": the perfectly moralistic self-deception—spouting only virtue and big words. And this *typical* trait: they don't even notice that they resemble who they are mistaken about? An antisemite is an envious Jew, that is, the most stupid of all—[26]

In other words, both the Jew and the anti-Semite can embody the forces of ressentiment, express the will to nothingness, the will to an end with life and to everything open, overabundant, in surplus, and powerful. However, even while admitting this malleable power that the forces of ressentiment have to disguise themselves and adopt new masks, this question still haunts Nietzsche: Why, in the final analysis, is it the failures and the decadents who always climb the ladder of life? There is a difficulty here that Nietzsche cannot hide; on the contrary, he admits, stresses, and warns of it: "Strange as it sounds: one has always to arm the strong against the weak; the fortunate against the failures; the healthy against those with a hereditary taint."[27]

This is where one of the principal weaknesses of Darwin's theory lies. For Nietzsche, this theory fails to see or does not want to recognize that natural selection does not work in favor of the exceptions and the lucky strokes; it overlooks the fact that the strong become weak when they have to struggle against the sheer weight of numbers and the cowardice of the weak united by the herd instinct. "My overall view of the world of values shows that in the highest values hanging above mankind today, it is *not* the strokes of luck, the selection types who have the upper hand, but rather the types of decadence—perhaps there's nothing more interesting in the world than this *unwelcome* spectacle . . ."[28]

This spectacle, both the most interesting and the least exultant or the least desirable, reveals itself as an ambiguous and *paradoxical* one. It is paradoxical in the sense that there is no culture or civilization that does not bear the marks of ressentiment and the spirit of vengeance. In fact, the earlier question that we posed regarding the death of tragedy was the following: Can one conceive of both a purely "theoretical" and "artistic" being?[29] This question can also apply in another form to the nihilist forces of ressentiment: Can there be a culture, a people, or an individual totally bereft of ressentiment? Or, as Deleuze puts it: "And we do not really know what a man denuded of ressentiment would be like. A man who would not accuse or depreciate existence—would he still be a man, would he think like a man?"[30]

Aware of the paradox of the forces of decadence that have the upper hand, and at the same time are an indispensable ingredient in the development of cultures and life in general, Nietzsche introduces yet another text in the series of reflections and attacks directed against Darwinism:

> The *instincts of decadence* have mastered the instincts of the *ascendant life* . . .
> The *will to nothingness* has mastered the *will to life* . . .
> —Is it *true*? Has there not been an enormous protection for life, for the species, in this victory of the weak and mediocrities?
> Would this be perhaps the only means in the general movement that both brings to life. and slows down the tempo, a last resource preventing something even worse?
> —even supposing that the strong were masters over everything, and even over value judgments: de we draw the consequences of how they would think of sickness, suffering, sacrifice? This would result in a *contempt of the weak for themselves*. they would seek to disappear and extinguish themselves. . . . And would this be *desirable*?
> —and would we want a world in which the influence of the weak, their finesse, their scruples, their intellectuality, their *flexibility* were totally lacking? . . .[31]

One would thus search in vain in Nietzsche's texts for a pure and simple condemnation of the sick, the weak, the failures, as well as an unconditional rehabilitation of the healthy, strong, superior, and powerful. In *On the Genealogy of Morals*, Nietzsche insists, to be sure, on the loathsome spectacle created by the impotent, the dropouts, the wilted, and sickly poisoned, but he also recalls the fundamental role played by the forces of decadence in the formation and evolution of all civilization (*Cultur*).

> Supposing that what is at any rate believed to be the "truth" really is true, and the *meaning of all culture* is the reduction of the beast of prey "man" to a tame and civilized animal, a *domestic animal*, then one would undoubtedly have to regard all those instincts of reaction and *ressentiment* through whose aid the noble races and their ideals were finally confounded and overthrown as the actual *instruments of culture*, which is not to say that the *bearers* of these instincts themselves represent culture.[32]

In other words, these very forces, as undesirable as they may appear, are nevertheless, and paradoxically, *creators and formers of values.* In the same way we cannot conceive of a man totally "denuded" of *ressentiment,* one cannot conceive of nor find a culture, a civilization, or a people in which the nihilist forces of decadence are not established as indispensable and necessary insofar as they are negators, destroyers, and *creators* of new values, valuations and ideals.

> The slave revolt in morality begins when *ressentiment* itself becomes *creative and gives birth to values:* the ressentiment of natures that are denied the true reaction, that of deeds, and compensate themselves with an imaginary revenge. While every noble morality develops from a triumphant affirmation of itself, slave morality from the outset says No to what is "outside," what is "different," what is "not itself"; and *this No* is its *creative* deed.[33]

These analyses lead us then to consider another form under which the instincts of reaction express themselves, and which is that of "bad conscience." This form is itself also paradoxical to the extent that it both reveals and hides the forces and relations of forces that negate, condemn, contrive, invent and *create.*

GUILT AND BAD CONSCIENCE

Nietzsche, who at several points attacks the lack of historical spirit in the genealogists of morality, such as the English psychologists and the utilitarian philosophers, indulges in an extreme simplification regarding the origins of the feeling of guilt and bad conscience. For him, in fact, the concept of guilt (*Schuld*) derives from an exceedingly material concept of debts (*Schulden*), and punishment, insofar as retaliation is developed entirely aside from the context of hypotheses about the freedom or nonfreedom of the will. Thus, the idea of an equivalence between damage and pain would have drawn its force from the contractual relation between creditor (*Gläubiger*) and debtor (*Schuldner*)—a relation that would have as its basis the fundamental forms of buying, selling, exchange, and trading: "It was here that one person first encountered another person, that one person first *measured himself* against another. No grade of civilization, however low, has yet been discovered in which something of this relationship has not been noticeable."[34]

One knows, however, that all societies, no matter how tribal and elementary, admit already of an aggregate of principles, notions, norms, and ideological ties. Nietzsche no doubt perceives this difficulty. He no doubt reduces the origin (*Ursprung*) of the feeling of guilt to the relation between buyer and seller, creditor and debtor, but he seems reluctant at the same time to introduce in that origin any degree of cause and exclusive priority. This is why he stresses: "Here it was that the oldest kind of astuteness developed; here likewise, *we may suppose*, did human pride, the feeling of superiority in relation to other animals have its first beginnings."[35] He even resorts to a hypothesis when he tries to understand, for example, the link existing between guilt (*Schuld*) and suffering (*Lied*). How, then, would suffering be able to repay or compensate for debts (*Schulden*)? He will say: "This is offered only a conjecture; for the depths of such subterranean things are difficult to fathom, besides being painful; and whoever clumsily interposes the concept of 'revenge' does not enhance his insight into the matter but further veils and darkens it (for revenge merely leads us back to the same problem: 'how can making suffer constitute a compensation?')."[36] And one can add: How can making suffer be a counterpleasure? For, as Nietzsche maintains, seeing others suffer gives us pleasure, and to make others suffer, even more pleasure. We have here a hard, old, powerful, and crucial truth, a *human, all too human* truth. As a result, Nietzsche recalls at what point cruelty was ancient humanity's source of great rejoicing and at what point it was the very ingredient of nearly all joy. But if this is the case, how would one explain that the gnawing worm of bad conscience has bored into man?

Nietzsche proceeds on this difficult and uncertain terrain by way of suppositions and hypotheses. He begins by acknowledging that this change was produced when man, until then adapted to war, to the nomadic and adventurous life, is suddenly held totally within the constraints of society and peace. Unable to flow out to the exterior, man's instincts *turn backward*, that is, *against man himself.*

> The man who, from lack of external enemies and resistances and forcibly confined to the oppressive narrowness and punctiliousness of custom, impatiently lacerated, persecuted, gnawed at, assaulted, and maltreated himself; this animal that rubbed itself raw against the bars of its cage as one tried to "tame" it; this deprived creature, racked with homesickness for the wild, who had to turn himself into an adventure, a torture chamber, an uncertain and dangerous wilderness—this fool, this yearning and desperate prisoner became the inventor of the "bad conscience."[37]

Nietzsche evokes here anew the role of the State and underscores the way in which it took hold of a populace lacking restraint and form to mold it, to tame and render it malleable, in short, to *form* it. Evidently this conquest can only be accomplished by acts of violence and oppression, by tyranny and the dreadful machinery of domination. Nietzsche, as we have seen, is far from conceiving of the birth of the State as issuing from a mutual act of agreement consigned by a "contract." It is just the opposite that occurs:

> . . . some pack of blond beasts of prey, a conqueror and master race which, organized for war and with the ability to organize, unhesitatingly lays its terrible claws upon a populace perhaps tremendously superior in numbers but still formless and nomad. That is after all how the "state" began on earth: I think that sentimentalism which would have it begin with a "contract" has been disposed of.[38]

One can only be shocked at the extreme simplicity with which Nietzsche describes the passage from a savage, free, nomadic life to an institution as complex as the State, even if it is a question of the early formation of the State. In assuming that bad conscience was born from the constraints imposed on life in society, this horde of warriors must nonetheless have a minimum of rules, norms, and precepts, since it was already organized and hierarchical. Nietzsche, however, stresses that bad conscience was not developed following a slow and progressive process, but that it emerged in one leap or abrupt and violent rupture. ". . . this hypothesis concerning the origin of the bad conscience is, first, that the change referred to was not a gradual or voluntary one and did not represent an organic adaptation to new conditions but a break, a leap, a compulsion, an ineluctable disaster."[39]

Perhaps he wants to expressly set himself apart from the other genealogists of morality by making *his* hypotheses, conjectures and insights valuable *to him* vis-à-vis history, or the absence of history. Regarding punishment, he observes in fact: "Today it is impossible to say for certain *why* people are really punished: all concepts in which an entire process is semiotically concentrated elude definition; *only that which has no history is definable.*"[40] It is, however, no less the case that the links that exist between guilt, punishment, bad conscience and ressentiment remain in shadow; they continue to be difficult to grasp. But can they ever be fully understood, if one admits, as we do, that Nietzsche's thought itself moves in a universe of forces, in the interval and the paradox, in a continual play of success and failure? This is why bad conscience and the so-called moral conscience are analyzed in the perspective of one of the most ingenious, subtle, and problematic of Nietzsche's discoveries: the *Will to Power*.

To be sure, he considers bad conscience a serious illness: "bad conscience is an illness, there is no doubt about that, but an illness as pregnancy is an illness."[41] In other words, bad conscience has engendered, developed, and placed in the world an alarming abundance of arts, inventions, machinations, ruses, spirit, and meaning. We already find the questions posed in *Human, All Too Human* that will be eventually reprised and reworked in *On the Genealogy of Morals*. These are questions of the fictions and lies that have enriched humanity, and that have allowed man to lift himself above the animals.

> *The over-animal.*—The beast in us wants to be lied to; morality is an official lie told so that it shall not tear us to pieces. Without the errors that repose in the assumptions of morality man would have remained an animal. As it is, he has taken himself for something higher and imposed sterner laws upon himself. That is why he feels hatred for the grades that have remained closer to animality: which is the explanation of the contempt formerly felt for the slave as a non-man, as a thing.[42]

We can thus see questions arise here that go right to the heart of Nietzsche's concerns: the will to power and the nihilistic forces of *ressentiment* and bad conscience which, as negators of life, create new values and render man and the world at the same time richer, more terrifying, and charged with meanings. In fact, after having described bad conscience, in *The Genealogy*, as an *internalization* of man, that is, as the tearing away of the animal soul that is turned against itself and takes sides against itself, he continues: "was something so new, profound, unheard of, enigmatic, contradictory, and *pregnant with the future* that the aspect of the earth was essentially altered. Indeed, divine spectators were needed to do justice to the spectacle that thus began and the end of which is not yet in sight—a spectacle too subtle, too marvelous, too paradoxical (*zu paradox*) to be played senselessly unobserved on some ludicrous planet!"[43] Nietzsche thus sees man among the lucky throws of Heraclitus's dice game, for whom the world is the kingdom of a child who amuses himself by placing little stones here and there, or building sand piles just to knock them down. Sometimes called Zeus, sometimes chance, this "great child," this *artist* "gives rise to an interest, a tension, a hope, almost a certainty, as if with him something were announcing and preparing itself, as if man were not a goal but only a way, an episode, a bridge, a great promise—"[44]

Now this distention of creations, inventiveness, discoveries, and beauties is only possible because man transforms, fashions, and works the *cruelty* that turns against him. But this is difficult material to work with, recalcitrant and suffering, material branded by critique, discord, self-violation, and a contradiction—in short, by the will to suffer out of the joy of making suffer. From this, one will come to understand the degree of refinement attained by the moral concepts of disinterestedness, self-forgetting, sacrifice, and abnegation that Nietzsche treats as concepts resulting from *cruelty* and from the delight that it arouses.[45] This delight, found in contradiction, self-violation, and in the will to impart a meaning, ends up by placing in the world an incalculable number of evaluations, judgments, arts, and, perhaps, beauty itself. "After all, what would be 'beautiful' if the contradiction had not first become conscious of itself, if the ugly had not first said: 'I am ugly'?"[46] Socrates, that monster of ugliness, no doubt kills tragedy but he creates at the same time science, logic, dialectic and, he allows the plebeian to conquer noble values. He thus erects new ideals, constructs new tables of values and creates, as a result, new meanings. But to do so, the force of interpretation is necessary; for life itself proceeds by infraction, violation, destruction, in short, by the *will to power*.

If the form is fluid—Nietzsche maintains—the "meaning" is even more so. For all evaluation assumes the victory of one will over another, a force or a relation of forces over other forces. This is why he insists:

> The "evolution" of a thing, a custom, an organ is thus by no means its *progressus* toward a goal, even less a logical *progressus* by the shortest route and with the smallest expenditure of force—but a succession of more or less profound, more or less mutually independent processes of subduing, plus the resistances they encounter, the attempts at transformation for the purpose of defense and reaction, and the result of successful counteractions.[47]

In *The Genealogy*, Nietzsche attacks once again the theories supposing such notions as finality, "progress," utility, "adaptation," and self-preservation. For him "adaptation" is only a secondary activity, or a mere reaction whose defenders place it at a first rank, as if life itself could be defined in terms of internal adaptation, an adaptation that would be more and more adequate to external conditions.

Thus the essence of life, its *will to power*, is ignored; one overlooks the essential priority of the spontaneous, aggressive, expansive, form-giving forces that give new interpretations and directions, although "adaptation" follows only after this; the dominant role of the highest functionaries within the organism itself in which the will to life appears active and form-giving is denied.[48]

This vision is notably reinforced if one considers the attacks launched by Nietzsche against the theory of self-preservation in *The Gay Science*, paragraph 349. Here, he stresses equally the springs of life insofar as it aims at *the expansion of power*, while at the same time recalling that the very wish to preserve oneself is an expression of a distressed situation, that is, a symptom of decadence, fatigue, exhaustion, and the will to nothingness. "It should be considered symptomatic when some philosophers— for example, Spinoza who was consumptive—considered the instinct of self-preservation decisive and *had* to see it that way: for they were individuals in conditions of distress." This is why the "Spinozistic dogma" has found in modern Darwinism its most vulgar and unilateral expression in the modern natural sciences. "The whole of English Darwinism breathes something like the musty air of English overpopulation, like the smell of the distress and overcrowding of small people. But the natural scientist should come out of his human nook; and in nature it is not conditions of distress that are *dominant* but overflow and squandering, even to the point of absurdity. The struggle for existence is only an *exception*. a temporary restriction of the will to life. The great and small struggle always resolves itself around superiority, around growth and expansion, around power—in accordance with the will to power which is the will to life."[49]

But if this is the case, if the will to power is will to life, and if what predominates is neither self-preservation nor "adaptation," but a will-to-become-more, a will-to-become-master, a will-to-become-greater, how can one thus explain why the nihilist forces of decadence will precisely the inverse, that is, destroy themselves to the extent that they condemn and deny life? Why create new ideals and new values to the detriment of fundamental life instincts, in the name of negation and depreciation of existence itself? These are the questions we will now consider.

ASCETIC IDEALS

Nietzsche begins the Third Essay of *The Genealogy* by enumerating the various kind of people in whom the ascetic ideal is embodied: artists, philosophers, women, dead-wrongs in general, priests, and saints. He follows by invoking the importance of these ideals for human development—important because they express the fundamental trait of the human will, namely, its *horror vacui, its need for an objective.* This is why he repeats in conclusion what he had affirmed in the beginning: "man would rather will *nothingness* than *not* will."[50] In other words, the ascetic ideal insofar as it is a negation of life and of everything essential to it, like fertility, effusion, joy, overflowing, and excess is, paradoxically, inseparable from that very life it denies, from the earth and nature where it is itself embodied and through which its will to power is deployed, which is also the will to nothingness and the will to ill-fortune.

In his analyses of the ascetic ideal, Nietzsche attacks principally the philosophers and priests. True types, they reveal the mastery and art of nihilistic forces of disguise, of metamophosizing and inventing new tricks that help them to attain the maximum affect of power. He will say of philosophers: "As long as there are philosophers on earth, and wherever there have been philosophers (from India to England, to take the antithetical poles of philosophical endowment), there unquestionably exists a peculiar philosopher's irritation at and rancor against sensuality. . . . There also exists a peculiar philosopher's prejudice and affection in favor of the whole ascetic ideal; one should not overlook that."[51] For Nietzsche the "philosopher beast," like all beasts, aspires instinctively to optimum favorable conditions by which to extend its force and at the same time hinder others from disturbing its march toward the maximal affect of power. "(I am *not* speaking of its path to happiness, but its path to power, to action, to the most powerful activity, and in most cases actually its path to unhappiness.)"[52]

The claim, according to which all philosophers hold a grudge toward anything sensual and have a predilection for the ascetic ideal, is even more surprising when Nietzsche supports it with examples that can, in turn, be opposed and contested by other examples. "Thus the philosopher abhors *marriage,* together with that which might persuade to it—marriage becomes a hindrance and calamity on his path to the optimum. What great philosophers have hitherto been married? Heraclitus, Plato, Descartes, Spinoza, Leibniz, Kant, Schopenhauer—they were not; more, one cannot even *imagine* them married. A married philosopher belongs *in comedy:* that is my proposition."[53] Against this list, however, one can evoke Aristotle, Hegel, Marx, and in our time, Heidegger. It happens, however, that the reader who is unfamiliar with Nietzsche's masks and strategies can easily lose track of what is finally targeted. Nietzsche's texts often involve a deliberately provocative claim, categorical and of a general nature to the sole end of attaining and developing what he wishes to transmit. Here, for example, what is at stake in the interpretation of the ascetic ideal in the philosopher, is *his own will to power in him*, the field of forces and relations of forces in which and by which the "philosopher beast" opens up the road toward the optimum, toward the maximum affect of power. The ascetic ideal thus presents itself in the philosopher not as much as a means of denying "existence," but as that by which he affirms *his* existence, and *only* affirms his existence.

In the texts of 1887–1888, Nietzsche underscores several times the following: the strong man frees himself by the margin of liberty he entrust to his passions, as well as the power with which he knows how to press these "magnificent monsters" into his service.[54] By the sovereignty of willing, he uses and dominates these passions, without for all that weakening or extirpating them. Nietzsche will rework and make known these ideas in *Twilight of the Idols*, where he raises, among other questions, that of the "blond beast":

> In the early Middle Ages, when the church was indeed, above all, a menagerie, the most beautiful specimens of the "blond beast" were hunted down everywhere; and the noble Teutons, for example, were "improved." But how did such an "improved" Teuton who had been seduced into a monastery look afterward? Like a caricature of man, like a miscarriage: he had become a "sinner," he was stuck in a cage, imprisoned among all sorts of terrible concepts. And there he lay, sick, miserable, malevolent against himself: full of hatred against the springs of life, full of suspicion against all that was still strong and happy. In short, a "Christian."[55]

We see in these texts ressentiment and bad conscience at work, as well as the role played by the priest insofar as he is a representative of the ascetic ideal and the forces of decadence that express it. Nietzsche develops this idea in the Third Essay of *The Genealogy*, where he again takes up and analyzes the transformations that ressentiment and bad conscience have undergone in the hands of the priest. The man of ressentiment needs to find those guilty for his sorrows; someone must be evil and wrong so that his suffering can be explained. It is necessary then to vent his passions, seek a narcotic so as to numb his torments. One thus seeks to deaden the pain by another pain, the suffering by a passion more violent and savage that has the effect of anesthetizing it—not only a momentary pain, but a tormenting, secret, unbearable pain. The individual who suffers develops these secret refinements: he enjoys his suspicions, scours his entrails, contriving stories and inventing torturers.

It is at this point that Nietzsche sees the priest enter the scene, deploying all his ability and his art of medication and salvation: "Quite so, my sheep! someone must be to blame for it: but you yourself are this someone, you alone are to blame for it—*you alone are to blame for yourself*!" The direction of ressentiment is thus changed, and suffering is refracted, returned, interiorized. One is henceforth guilty, a sinner, and one must pay for his transgressions. The sick must continue to be sick in order for the priest to survive, he needs it. This is why he must first wound in order to play physician: "when he then stills the pain of the wound *he at the same time infects the wound*—for that is what he knows to do best of all, this sorcerer and animal-tamer, in whose presence everything healthy necessarily grows sick, and everything sick tame."[56]

But the priest himself must be sick and have a deep-seated affinity with the sick if he wishes to understand them, and understand along with them. However, it is necessary for him at the same time to be strong, cunning, powerful, more in control of himself than others, and expert in the art of inspiring fear and instilling confidence. He will thus be for the sick "their support, resistance, prop, compulsion, taskmaster, tyrant, and god."[57] He will defend them, keep them sick so as to affirm his will to power, and to attain the maximum affect of power. He must defend his herd against the healthy and the strong. Consequently, "he must be the natural opponent *and despiser* of all rude, stormy, unbridled, hard, violent beast-of-prey health and might."[58] The ascetic priest reveals himself as the primary form of the animal become *delicate*. He despises more easily than he hates, his war is more a war of trickery than violence. Consequently, he is an expert master of the art of disguise and metamorphosis.

Nietzsche detects everywhere and in all periods the work of undermining and negation to which the ascetic priest dedicated himself: from India to the West, from the most ancient philosophies to the most modern sciences, the ascetic priest is there inflicting pain, fiercely producing suffering to himself and to the other for the pure pleasure of making suffer. In this sense, the philosopher is only another form of the ascetic priest, the relay or the substitute who allows him to survive, to expand, and to manifest his will to power.

To begin with, the philosophic spirit always had to use as a mask and cocoon the *previously established* types of the contemplative man—

priest, soothsayer, and in any case a religious type—in order to be able to *exist at all* . . . for the longest time philosophy would not be *possible* at all on earth without ascetic wraps and cloak, without an ascetic misunderstanding, To put it vividly: the *ascetic priest* provided until the most modern times the repulsive and gloomy caterpillar form in which alone the philosopher could live and creep about.[59]

This is why Kant's success, "this nihilist with his Christian dogmatic entrails," is, for Nietzsche, only the success of a theologian.[60]

But not only Kant; Schopenhauer, Hegel, Schelling, Fichte, and Feuerbach also appear to him as philosophic laborers, or as artful theologians in the service of the nihilist forces of morality. In them morality dresses itself in glittering clothing, flashy, "divine," and "noble." In them we can see a moral transposition of evaluations and herd judgments, of the forces of decadence, of negation and ressentiment in the metaphysical realm. In this perspective, one will read in a text of spring 1888: "I rebel against the translation of reality into a morality: therefore I abhor Christianity with a deadly hatred, because it created sublime words and gestures to throw over a horrible reality the cloak of justice, virtue and divinity—"[61] But in a text written prior to this one (1885–1886), we already see a similar idea: "Fundamental insight: Kant as well as Hegel and Schopenhauer—the skeptical-epochistic attitude as well as the historicizing, as well as the pessimistic—have a *moral* origin. . . . How can Spinoza's position, his denial and rejection of moral value judgments, be explained? (It was *one* consequence of his theodicy!)"[62]

Nietzsche is relentless in his enterprise of dissecting, analyzing, and unmasking the nihilistic forces of decadence. Even the Pre-Socratics, for whom he does not hide his admiration, are included in the long process of degeneration that has marked the history of Western thought. Thus: "Since Plato, philosophy has been dominated by morality. Even in his predecessors, moral interpretations play a decisive role (with Anaximander, the perishing of all things as punishment for their emancipation from pure being; with Heraclitus, the regularity of phenomena as witness to the moral-legal character of the whole world of becoming)."[63]

One will not be surprised, then, to see Nietzsche consider Schopenhauer's atheism also from the standpoint of morality. In paragraph 357 of *The Gay Science*, he presents Schopenhauer as the *first* admitted and inflexible atheist produced by Germany. He is an atheist because he has stripped existence of its divine character and showed it as it is, namely, as something immediate, tangible, and unquestionable. This fact in particular prompts Nietzsche to praise the integrity of Schopenhauer, who will have won a hard-fought victory rich in consequences for the European conscience. With him the spirit of truth is finally set free by forbidding itself the *lie* in faith in God. However, immediately after having recognized these merits, Nietzsche follows: "You see *what it* was that really triumphed over the Christian god: Christian morality itself, the concept of truthfulness that was understood ever more rigorously, the father confessor's refinement of the Christian conscience, translated and sublimated into scientific conscience, into intellectual cleanliness at any price."[64]

This text comes very close to the analyses that Nietzsche develops around modern science and the relations it maintains with the ascetic ideal. In fact, he stresses, it would be a mistake to assume that modern science believes in itself alone, that it has both the will and courage to be only itself, and that it has up till now survived well enough without God, without the afterlife and the values expressed by the ascetic priest. It is precisely the opposite that is true: "science has absolutely *no* belief in itself, let alone an ideal above it—and where it still inspires passion, love, ardor, and *suffering* at all, it is not the opposite of the ascetic ideal but rather *the latest and noblest form of it.*"[65] In other words, the antagonisms that exist between modern science and the ascetic ideal are, all things considered, only a form of reciprocal cooperation: science acts as a force to advance the inner development of the ascetic ideal, while the ascetic ideal, in turn, nurtures science's belief in the inscrutable nature of truth.

Consequently, what science contests is not the ascetic ideal, but only its facades, disguises, its game of masks, its hardness, and its sclerotic character. Science only contributes to what increases the ascetic ideal's capacity to disguise and transform itself.

> This pair, science and the ascetic ideal, both rest on the same foundation—I have already indicated it: on the same overestimation of truth (more exactly: on the same belief that truth is inestimable and cannot be criticized). Therefore they are *necessarily* allies, so that if they are to be fought they can be fought and called in question together. A depreciation of the ascetic ideal unavoidably involves a depreciation of science.[66]

Art, on the other hand, "in which precisely the *lie* is sanctified and the *will to deception* has a good conscience, is much more fundamentally opposed to the ascetic ideal than is science."[67] To be sure, the ascetic ideal and science both share a common "faith" in truth, but this *unconditional will to truth*, this constraint to believe in it, this "*faith in the ascetic ideal itself,* even if it is an unconscious imperative—don't be deceived about that—it is the faith in a *metaphysical* value, the *absolute* value of *truth,* sanctioned and guaranteed by this ideal alone (it stands or falls with this ideal)."[68]

Nietzsche reiterates here what he had already developed in *The Gay Science,* paragraph 344, to which he makes two explicit references. In the text of this book one finds, in effect, the idea according to which the unconditional will to truth—truth at all costs—the fact of sacrificing everything on the altar of truth, of consecrateing and dedicating everything to it, in the end, would end up in a question whose solution may prove more difficult, more problematic and, perhaps, more disturbing: "but it might be something more serious, namely, a principle that is hostile to life and destructive,—'Will to truth'—that might be a concealed *will to death.*"[69]

So if our three exemplars—the priest, the philosopher and the scientist—are presented as types that express the nihilistic forces of the ascetic ideal, if they embody the negative forces of life and of its basic instincts, and if the ascetic ideals are what is most widespread and inherent in human life, can morality still exist? Is good morality still possible? Is all morality evil? It is true that one finds this definition in *Ecce Homo*: "Morality—the idiosyncrasy of decadents, with the ulterior motive of revenging *oneself against life*—successfully. I attach value to this definition."[70] But how does one recognize morality? By the moral phenomena? No! In a fragment of fall 1885 through fall 1886, one will read already: "*My chief proposition: there are no moral phenomena, there is only a moral interpretation of these phenomena. This interpretation itself is of extra-moral origin.*"[71] In this perspective, it would be absurd to ask if such a morality or such values are good or bad, since there is no value in itself. There are only evaluations that proceed from a will, a force or a relation of forces that create, institute, name, affirm, or deny. A meaning is given, an evaluation is instituted, and inevitably, the question returns: What forces have imposed them? What forces have been overcome and which of them have taken over? What will and what relations are at work? All interpretation is thus an interpretation of either an ascendant life or a life in decline, of a will to nothingness that judges life, denies and condemns it, or of a will that elevates life, affirms it, rejoicing in everything strong, powerful, productive, fertile, savage, problematic, and fearful. This is why Nietzsche repeats continuously, in his later phase, that there is only a perspective seeing and a perspective knowing:

> Henceforth, my dear philosophers, let us be on guard against the dangerous old conceptual fiction that posited "a pure, will-less, painless, timeless knowing subject"; let us guard against its snares of such contradictory concepts as "pure reason," "absolute spirituality," "knowledge in itself": these always demand that we should think of an eye that is completely unthinkable, an eye turned in no particular direction, in which the active and interpreting forces, through which alone seeing becomes seeing something, are supposed to be lacking . . .[72]

Seeing something supposes a will that commands and a will that obeys. Similarly, transmitting a meaning, giving a direction and a new evaluation already supposes the force of interpretation and the will that something is otherwise. Thus, in a text written at the end of 1886 through spring 1887, Nietzsche reflects on ethics in these terms:

> Ethics: or "philosophy of desirability."—"Things *ought* to be different," "things *shall* be different": dissatisfaction would thus be the germ of ethics. . . . It [i.e., ethics] expresses a need that desires that the structure of the world correspond to our human well-being; also the will to bring this about as far as possible.
>
> On the other hand, it is only this desire "thus it ought to be" that has called forth that other desire to know what *is*. For the knowledge of what is, is a consequence of that question: "How? is it possible? why precisely so?" Wonder at disagreement between our desires and the course of the world has led to our learning to know the course of the world. But perhaps the case is different: perhaps that "thus it ought to be" is our desire to overcome the world—[73]

We might ask then: Can one have a desire for knowledge entirely without the limits imposed by all knowledge? Can one have the will to dominate and master the world without there being somewhere a resistance to conquering, overcoming, and enjoying it? These questions lead us nearer to considering the eminently paradoxical character manifested by the ascetic priest insofar as he is representative of the highest degree of negation and dissatisfaction regarding the world.

For Nietzsche, there is no doubt: "The ascetic priest is the incarnate desire to be different, to be in a different place, and indeed this desire at its greatest extreme, its distinctive fervor and passion."[74] But only a first-order necessity could explain why this *life-inimical* species continues to increase and prosper; it must be *in the interest of life itself* that such a self-contradictory type does not die out.

For an ascetic life is a self-contradiction: here rules a ressentiment without equal, that of an insatiable instinct and power-will that wants to become master not over something in life but over life itself, over the most profound, powerful and basic conditions; here an attempt is made to employ force to block up the wells of force . . . while pleasure is *sought* in ill-constitutedness, decay, pain, mischance, ugliness, voluntary deprivation, self-mortification, self-flagellation, self-sacrifice. All this is in the highest degree *paradoxical*: we stand before a discord that *wants* to be discordant, that *enjoys* itself in this suffering and even grows more self-confident and triumphant the more its own presupposition, its physiological capacity for life, *decreases*.[75]

If the ascetic ideal is in this sense the struggle of life *for* and *against* death, it becomes clear that this ideal is in the end only a ruse for the *preservation* of life itself. The ascetic priest insofar as he is a type that reproduces the negation of life and its fundamental instincts is basically, and paradoxically, inherent in that very life in which he is incarnate, on which and by which he exercises his will to power. The desire of the ascetic priest for a life outside of life, and a life elsewhere, reveals the *power* that connects him to the world and enables him to persuade to existence the whole herd of the "ill-constituted" and all those who suffer of themselves. With such a guide and shepherd they can struggle against death, or, more precisely, against the disgust of life, against exhaustion, and the desire for the "end." Thus, "this ascetic priest, this apparent enemy of life, this *denier*—precisely he is among the greatest *conserving* and *yes-creating* forces of life."[76]

But what is the source of this sickness? For, for Nietzsche, man is a sick animal; he is the most sick, uncertain, changeable and indeterminate of all animals. And why thus?

Certainly he has also dared more, done more new things, braved more and challenged fate more than all other animals put together: he, the great experimenter with himself, disconnected and insatiable, wrestling with animals, nature, and the gods for ultimate dominion—he, still unvanquished, eternally directed toward the future, whose restless energies never leave him in peace, so that his future digs like a spur into the flesh of every present—how should such a courageous and richly endowed animal not also be imperiled, the most chronically and profoundly sick of all sick animals?[77]

And nonetheless, it is through his very dissatisfaction, his discord, inner pain, and his will to dominate and master that man, that sick animal par excellence, has, from the earliest known times, been able to create, transform and transfigure the world and his existence. "The No he says to life brings to light, as if by magic, an abundance of tender Yeses; even when he *wounds* himself, this master of destruction, of self-destruction—the very wound itself afterward compels him *to live.*—"[78] For the forces of decadence and morality that manifest ascetic ideals deny precisely, and paradoxically, what they preserve and the source of their expression of power. Following their course toward nothingness, they collide against their own limits and contrive new transformations, metamorphoses, and unforeseen creations: this is morality turning against itself, denying itself, overcoming itself, by morality . . .

ZARATHUSTRA, MORALIST

We understand then why Nietzsche had chosen Zarathustra to destroy what had been up until that point venerated under the name of *morality*. Zarathustra was the first to see in the struggle between good and evil "the very wheel in the machinery of things: the transposition of morality into the metaphysical realm, as force, cause and end in itself. . . ."[79] Thus only Zarathustra is capable of bringing forth the truth, since he is well aware of the lie. Only Zarathustra can be a destroyer, for he is a creator. Zarathustra the destroyer, the breaker of tables of values, in whom pleasure and the power of annihilation, to "render" negative, and to "speak" in the affirmative is intermingled. But, we ask again, why Zarathustra, if the splintering of morality runs quite counter to what constitutes the unique personality of this Persian moralist? The answer lies in what the very name Zarathustra means for Nietzsche:

> Zarathustra *created* the most calamitous error, morality; consequently, he must also be the first to *recognize* it. Not only has he more experience in this matter, for a longer time, than any other thinker—after all, the whole of history is the refutation by experiment of the principle of the so-called "moral world order"—what is more important is that Zarathustra is more truthful than any other thinker. . . . To speak the truth and to *shoot well with arrows*, that is a Persian virtue.—Am I understood?—The self-overcoming of morality, out of truthfulness; the self-overcoming of the moralist, into his opposite—*into me*—that is what the name of Zarathustra means in my mouth.[80]

The self-overcoming of morality is clearly found in every one of Nietzsche's works, but it is especially in his later period, beginning with *Daybreak*, that this movement is employed with greater insistence and clarity.
Thus, in the *Preface* written in 1886 for the second edition of this text,
one will read:

> And if *this* book is pessimistic even into the realm of morality, even to
> the point of going beyond faith in morality—should it not for this very
> reason be a German book? For it does in fact exhibit a contradiction
> and is not afraid of it: in this book faith in morality is withdrawn—but
> why? *Out of morality!* Or what else should we call it that informs it—
> and *us?* . . . we still feel ourselves related to the German integrity and
> piety of millennia, even if as its most questionable and final descen-
> dants, we immoralists, we godless men of today, indeed in a certain
> sense as its heirs, as the executors of its innermost will—a pessimistic
> will, as aforesaid, which does not draw back from denying itself because
> it denies with *joy!* In us there is accomplished—supposing you want a
> formula—the *self-overcoming of morality*—[81]

In *Ecce Homo*, one of Nietzsche's very last writings, he will no longer
be a simple descendant of German morality, even if it involves one of the
latest and most problematic descendants of a millennial tradition. From
this point on, he sees himself vested with a cosmic mission: he is the dyna-
mite that will cleave human history in two, his name will be linked with
the most profound collision of conscience and an inexorable decision
against everything that had been believed, demanded, and hallowed so far.

> I contradict as has never been contradicted before and am nevertheless
> the opposite of a No-saying spirit. *I am a bringer of glad tidings* like no
> one before me; I know tasks of such elevation that any notion of them
> has been lacking so far; only beginning with me are there hopes again.
> For all that, I am necessarily also a man of calamity. For when truth
> enters into a fight with the lies of millennia, we shall have upheavals, a
> convulsion of earthquakes, a moving of mountains and valleys, the like
> of which have never been dreamed of.[82]

Even though in less grandiose dimensions, he also ends the penulti-
mate paragraph of *The Genealogy* with an apocalyptic scenario. Here, in
fact, he asserts that Christianity insofar *as it is a dogma* has been ruined by
its own morality, and it is also *as a morality* marching today toward its
own destruction. For Nietzsche we stand at the threshold of this event. It

will occur "after Christian truthfulness (*Wahrhaftigkeit*) has drawn one inference after another, it must end by drawing its most *striking inference*, the inference *against* itself. . . . As the will to truth thus gains self-consciousness—there can be no doubt of that—morality will gradually *perish* now: this is the great spectacle of a hundred acts reserved for the next two centuries in Europe—the most terrible, most questionable, and perhaps the most hopeful of all spectacles—"[83]

We notice here a striking reversal of direction: in the ascetic ideal the pure will to truth is revealed in the end as faith in a metaphysical value, in a value *in itself of truth*; besides, the constraint acting on all sacrifice on the altar of truth would be secretly a *will to death*. Now, the will to truth turns against itself, becomes conscious of itself and problematic. This happens to the extent that it allows the enjoyment beforehand—and to a greater degree—of an act rich in consequences and formidable transformations: the collapse of morality, the reversal of the highest values, and the exploding of an ancient lie that has supported a multimillennial tradition.

One should be wary, however, of too quickly depending on Nietzsche's anticipation of an event, a situation or a change caused by a particular era. To be sure, it is not rare for him to resort to history to shore up his analyses, Nonetheless, it is contrary to Nietzsche's philosophy to conceive of events as unfolding according to some plan, finality or internal logic. In what concerns history precisely, his vision is as uncertain, changeable, and variable, as is his thought in general. And, as regards his idea of morality in particular, the will to nothingness, expressed by the ascetic ideal and the *Yes*-creator who affirms life on earth are presented as two impulses deployed in a play of forces that are continually—and paradoxically—rearranged, in difference, plurality, multiplicity, overcoming, and change.

What stands out in Nietzsche's texts, and above all those of his later period, is a continual construction-destruction, and eternal creation that ceaselessly recommences, since it ceaselessly overcomes, goes beyond and conquers itself. Destruction supposes creation, the will to construct supposes the delight of becoming and the delight of annihilation. Zarathustra builds morality through the metaphysical struggle of good and evil. Moreover, Zarathustra shatters morality and everything that has been venerated until then under the name of "truth," by truthfulness. Can one understand this? "Am I understood?—The self-overcoming of morality, out of truthfulness; the self-overcoming of the moralist, into his opposite—into me—that is what the name of Zarathustra means in my mouth."[84]

6

Beyond Good and Evil

A philosopher—alas, a being that often runs away from itself, often is afraid
of itself—but too inquisitive not to "come to" again—always back to himself.
—*BGE* (292)

Beyond Good and Evil was published in 1886. This work, that immediately follows *Thus Spoke Zarathustra* and is thus situated in the later
period of Nietzsche's productive life, includes themes that have already
been touched on previously and which will be, in turn, reviewed, reread,
rewritten, and reevaluated in the texts that mark the period of intense
activity in the years 1887–1888. If one Nietzschean text always calls forth
another, without for all that confirming that there is some logical and
necessary thread guiding and uniting them in their intelligibility and
inner development, it is precisely because they imply a multiplicity of perspectives, ruptures, rereadings, and new interpretations. In a letter written
September 22, 1886, to Jakob Burckhardt, Nietzsche refers to *Beyond
Good and Evil* in the following terms: "Please read this book (even though
it says the same things as my *Zarathustra*—only in a way that is different—very different)."[1] And, as we have mentioned above, on the title
page of *On the Genealogy of Morals*, he had written originally: "*To Complete and Clarify Beyond Good and Evil, Recently Published.*"

If we consider *Human, All Too Human* as a chiaroscuro or interval in
the development of Nietzsche's thought, and if *On the Genealogy of Morals*
constitutes, in certain respects, a transitional work of the third period, the

task of situating *Beyond Good and Evil* is rendered even more difficult in view of the colossal mass of fragments connected with it and which have been reassembled from as far back as summer–fall 1881. In *Ecce Homo*, Nietzsche will say of this writing: "This book (1886) is in all essentials a *critique of modernity*, not excluding the modern sciences, modern arts, and even modern politics. . . ."² But more than a critique of modernity, of modern science, art and politics, this work recaptures and reevaluates the themes that Nietzsche had already developed in his earliest writings, as well as in *Human, All Too Human*. The aesthetic conception presented in the writings on tragedy will be here reevaluated and shored up in its essential points, and the philosopher will henceforth be someone who knows how to experiment, command, and legislate.

But what is really at stake in *Beyond Good and Evil*? Schutte observes that if metaphysics troubles Nietzsche in such an intense way, it is because he, too, seeks a beyond as the ground of values: "But his ground of values differed significantly from that of the traditional metaphysician. The metaphysical beyond to which Nietzsche objected rested on dualism, whereas he claimed a reality beyond good and evil, that is, beyond the human being's alienation from the flow of life."³ And not beyond *the* good and *the* evil, since seeking a transcendent ground for two opposing values would still be a symptom of decadence, of ressentiment, exhaustion and the will to nothingness. It is precisely this opposition or this antithesis that sets up the spirit of decadence between *the* good and *the* evil that Nietzsche contests. What he craves in return is a "beyond good and evil" (*Jenseits von Gut und Böse*). This is why he insistently emphasizes:

> Whoever has endeavored with some enigmatic longing, as I have, to think pessimism through to its depths and to liberate it from the half-Christian, half-German narrowness and simplicity in which it has finally presented itself to our century, namely, in the form of Schopenhauer's philosophy; whoever has really, with an Asiatic and supra-Asiatic eye, looked into, down into the most world-denying of all possible ways of thinking—beyond good and evil and no longer, like Buddha and Schopenhauer, under the spell and delusion of morality—may just thereby, without really meaning to do so, have opened his eyes to the opposite ideal: the ideal of the most high-spirited, alive, and world-affirming human being . . .⁴

Beyond Good and Evil thus remains an open book—open to the extent that it is a rereading of previous themes and a route, a possibility and a preparation for new interpretations. If Nietzsche's writings are already a succession of ruptures, rewritings, and reevaluations, this work holds a particular interest in that it recaptures, in its reinterpreting, the insights and discoveries that are already found in the early writings, those of the period of *The Birth of Tragedy*. This is why, taking into account the multitude of perspectives and readings manifest in this text, we will limit ourselves to emphasize some reevaluations that reflect this earlier period, and which are related to the meaning and diversity of meanings that issue from the interpretational forces and relations of forces.

OF READING AND REWRITING

In *The Birth of Tragedy*, we can clearly see the influence of Schopenhauer and that of Kant through him. Tragic wisdom, through Apollonian illusion and Dionysian music, reproduces the most intimate ground of things, nature, of the will, in short, of the originary One. Dionysiac music is the very mirror in which the universal will is reflected; which comes to us as eternal truth, as the truth gushing from the wellspring of the One. But already in *The Birth of Tragedy*, and even in writings that precede and prepare for this work, there begins a declension of their respective positions that, later on, will mark a clean break between Nietzsche and Schopenhauer. Thus, the metaphysical consolation embodied in tragedy and which is incarnated in the satyric chorus is, for the Nietzschean vision, pure pleasure—pleasure in its indestructible, affirmative, and transformative power of life, despite the changing character of phenomena. In other words, tragic art admits of the universal suffering, but transfigures it in the affirmation, in the *Yes* to life, to the eternal life, to the surplus and overabundance of life. The *pessimistic* look to which Nietzsche refers in *Beyond Good and Evil* is thus already evoked in *The Birth of Tragedy*, precisely where it is a question, for either art or life, of transforming that suffering in affirmation: "With this chorus the profound Hellene, uniquely susceptible to the tenderest and deepest suffering, comforts himself, having looked boldly right into the terrible destructive forces of so-called world history, as well as the cruelty of nature, and being in danger of longing for a *Buddhistic negation* of the will. Art saves him, and through art—life."[5] This idea will be taken up again and developed in a text dated fall 1885–fall 1886: "Tragic art, rich in these two experiences, is defined as the reconciliation of Apollo and Dionysus. Dionysus imparts the most profound meaning to appearance, and that appearance can nevertheless be denied with *sensual pleasure*. This is directed, like the tragic vision of the world, against the Schopenhauerean doctrine of *resignation*."[6]

And yet, in paragraph 16 of *The Birth of Tragedy*, Nietzsche refers to Schopenhauer as the only thinker "among the great thinkers" to whom the formidable opposition between plastic art (Apollonian art) and music (Dionysian art) has been revealed. To him alone goes the merit of having recognized that music has "a character and origin different from all the other arts, because, unlike them, it is not a copy of the phenomenon, but an immediate copy of the will itself, and therefore complements *everything physical in the world* and every phenomenon by representing *what is metaphysical*, the thing itself."[7] Later on, in paragraph 18, Nietzsche already envisions the looming horizon of a new era, a "tragic" culture, whose appearance is due to the most difficult and prodigious victories by Kant and Schopenhauer. They have prosecuted, by prodigious courage and sagacity, a war at the very heart of science and its pretensions to a universal validity, they have achieved "the victory over the optimism concealed in the essence of logic—an optimism that is at the basis of our culture."[8]

Now already in *Schopenhauer as Educator*, which appeared two years after *The Birth of Tragedy*, Nietzsche considers the differences that separate the scholar (*der Gelhehrte*) from the philosopher, and he ranks Plato and Schopenhauer on the philosopher's side, while Kant is cast as a docile servant of the State: "Kant clung to the university, submitted to authority, sustained the pretense of religious faith, put up with colleagues and students; so it is only natural that his example has begotten university professors and professorial philosophy."[9] In this sense, a scholar will never become a philosopher, since a philosopher is not only a great thinker, but also a real human: "And when has a scholar ever turned into a genuine human being?"[10]

Human, All Too Human appeared four years after *Schopenhauer as Educator*. In this work, Nietzsche not only pursues his critiques of Kant, but he attacks directly Schopenhauer's metaphysics and presents the thing in itself, the essence of things, and the phenomenal world as a sum total of errors, illusions and passions that man has created to deceive himself and, in so doing, achieve a stable, durable and profound existence and good fortune.[11]

> It is true, there could be a metaphysical world; the absolute possibility
> of it is hardly disputed. We behold things through the human head and

cannot cut off this head; while the question nonetheless remains what of the world would still be there if one had cut it off. This is a purely scientific problem and one not very well calculated to bother people overmuch; but that has hitherto made metaphysical assumptions *valuable, terrible, delightful* to them, all that has begotten these assumptions, is passion, error, self-deception.[12]

Thus the *thing in itself* that reproduces Dionysian music in the writings on tragedy, appears henceforth as "worthy of Homeric laughter: that it *appeared* to be so much, indeed everything, and is actually empty, that is to say empty of significance."[13]

These ideas will be newly developed, reworked and deepened in *Beyond Good and Evil*. In fact, one will find here a new version in paragraph 2 of what Nietzsche had already written in the first paragraph of *Human, All Too Human*. In this paragraph he begins by attacking the age-old vice of metaphysics, that consists in establishing oppositions between values and in seeking, for things assessed superior, an origin flowing immediately from the *thing in itself*. "Almost all the problems of philosophy once again pose the same form of the question as they did two thousand years ago: how can something originate in its opposite: for example rationality in irrationality, the sentient in the dead, logic in unlogic, disinterested contemplation in covetous desire, living for others in egoism, truth in error?"[14] In *Beyond Good and Evil*, this very same question posed by prejudice of the metaphysicians appears at the beginning of paragraph 2: "How *could* anything originate out of its opposite? for example, truth out of error? or the will to the truth out of the will to deception? or selfless deeds out of selfishness? or the pure and sunlike gaze of the sage out of lust?"[15] Some lines further down, he observes: "The fundamental faith of the metaphysicians is the *faith in opposite values*. . . . It might even be possible that *what* constitutes the value of these good and revered things is precisely that they are insidiously related, tied to, and involved with these wicked, seemingly opposite things—maybe even one with them in essence."[16]

One quickly grasps what is at blame here, namely, the antithesis between good and evil, the oppositions between good and bad, as well as the religious-moral background that animates them. What is in play is a translation, into metaphysics, of values and moral judgments. The question, however, is not one of actually knowing those values and what judgments one finds in place, but rather what will, what forces, and what relations of forces judge and evaluate. The will to nothingness establishes judgments concerning *the* good and *the* evil; therefore, it establishes a domain going beyond *the* good and *the* evil. That is to say, it both denies earthly values and seeks to erect a principle that will transcend them. This is why, though denying God and the world, Schopenhauer remains nonetheless the handmaiden and faithful adorer of morality. His philosophy exudes the noxious odor of morality and religion: "Even in the background of the most recent philosophy, that of Schopenhauer, we find, almost as the problem-in-itself, this gruesome question mark of the religious crisis and awakening. How is the denial of the will *possible?* how is the saint possible? This really seems to have been the question over which Schopenhauer became a philosopher and began."[17]

In *Beyond Good and Evil* one can nearly everywhere sense the presence of Schopenhauer: he sometimes appears indirectly, sometimes all alone, or side-by-side with other representatives of metaphysics (Kant, Spinoza, Descartes, Berkeley, etc.), who Nietzsche unmasks as dogmatists embodying the nihilistic forces of morality. Yet, in the Preface to *On the Genealogy of Morals*, published a year later, he will refer to *Human, All Too Human* and to Schopenhauer in these terms: "What was at stake was the *value* of morality—and over this I had come to terms almost exclusively with *my great teacher* Schopenhauer, to whom that book of mine, the passion and the concealed contradiction of that book, addressed itself as if to a contemporary."[18]

If Nietzsche's position toward Schopenhauer and Kant is paradoxical and ambiguous, it will be different regarding Socrates, with nonetheless this important detail: unlike Schopenhauer and Kant, Socrates is presented, already in *The Birth of Tragedy*, as the killer of tragic wisdom through Euripides; he introduces dialectic, which in turn establishes science and engenders the theoretical man and his optimism about logic. Still, in the intermediate phase of *Human, All Too Human*, and contrary to Schopenhauer and Kant, he will attribute to Socrates the role of sage and mediator "this simplest and most imperishable of intercessors."[19] In Nietzsche's later period, however, Socrates will reappear as someone who embodies the forces of corruption. Only, Nietzsche's intuitions of the *The Birth of Tragedy* era are now enriched by his discoveries and analyses centered around the will to power and nihilism. Henceforth, Socrates is presented, most often, as a buffoon, decadent type or evil-minded plebeian corrupter of the noble Plato.

It is no less surprising to see *Philosophy in the Tragic Age of the Greeks*, a posthumous writing composed a year after the publication of *The Birth of Tragedy,*[20] position Socrates in the line of "pre-Platonic" philosophers and assert in paragraph 2: "With Plato, something entirely new has its beginning. Or it might be said with equal justice, from Plato on there is something essentially amiss with philosophy when one compares them to that 'republic of creative minds' from Thales to Socrates."[21] Even in *Human, All Too Human* (1878–1880) one will find two references to Socrates, one in volume I and the other in volume II, that show how Nietzsche can be paradoxical in one and the same work. Thus, "With the Greeks everything goes quickly forwards, but it likewise goes quickly downwards; the movement of the whole machine is so accelerated that a single stone thrown into its wheels makes it fly to pieces. Socrates, for example, was such a stone; in a single night the evolution of philosophical science, hitherto so wonderfully regular if all too rapid, was destroyed."[22] In volume II of the same work, one will nonetheless read: "If all goes well, the time will come when one will take up the memorabilia of Socrates rather than the Bible as guide to morals and reason . . . Socrates excels the founder of Christianity in being able to be serious cheerfully and possessing the *wisdom full of roguishness* that constitutes the finest state of the human soul. And he also possessed the finer intellect."[23]

Socrates will reappear in *Beyond Good and Evil,* but this time as an expression of the forces hostile to life, to a plurality of interpretations and to the meaning it contains. In the *Preface* of this work, Nietzsche in fact presents the tasks and aspirations of free spirits: they are both physicians and creators, they dissect and combat the great error of dogmatic philosophy, they have the "magnificent tension of the spirit," the force and energy of those who affirm life and everything multiple, abundant, changeable, and plural. Their "truth" is perspective, for to deny Perspectivism is to deny life.

> To be sure, it meant standing truth on her head and denying perspective, the basic condition of all life, when one spoke of spirit and the good as Plato did. Indeed, as a physician one might ask: "How could the most beautiful growth of antiquity, Plato, contract such a disease? Did the wicked Socrates corrupt him after all? Could Socrates have been the corrupter of youth after all? And did he deserve his hemlock?"
>
> But the fight against Plato or, to speak more clearly and for "the people," the fight against the Christian-ecclesiastical pressure of millennia— for Christianity is Platonism for "the people"— has created in Europe a magnificent tension of the spirit the like of which had never yet existed on earth: with so tense a bow we can now shoot for the most distant goals.[24]

The considerations we have developed regarding Schopenhauer, Kant, Socrates, as well as Plato, reveal how Nietzsche's thought is changeable and "contradictory." These different viewpoints bid us likewise to compare three lists of names in which Nietzsche recognizes his predecessors and teachers. Thus, in paragraph 408 of *Assorted Opinions and Maxims* (1879):

> There have been four pairs who did not refuse themselves to me, the sacrifer: Epicurus and Montaigne, Goethe and Spinoza, Plato and Rousseau, Pascal and Schopenhauer. With these I have had to come to terms when I have wandered long alone, from them will I accept judgment, to them will I listen when in doing so they judge one another.[25]

In a fragment of spring 1884:

> Man is something that must be overcome—it is a question of knowing to what tempo: the Greeks deserve our admiration: without haste,—my predecessors *Heraclitus, Empedocles, Spinoza, Goethe.*[26]

In another fragment of the same year (summer–fall):

> The great philosophers are rarely successful. This is why Kant, Hegel, Schopenhauer, Spinoza! are so impoverished, so narrow! One understands why an artist can image that he is more important than they are. The knowledge imparted by the great Greeks has educated me: there is in Heraclitus, Empedocles, Parmenides, Anaxagoras, Democritus more to admire, they are *more complete.*[27]

One will not be less surprised to read in another fragment dated also from summer–fall 1884: "Fichte, Schelling, Hegel, Feuerbach, Strauss— all of them stink from the odor of theologians and the Church Fathers. Schopenhauer is *free* enough from this, one breathes a fresher air, one smells Plato even. Kant, over-elaborate and loutish: one sees that the Greeks have not yet been discovered. Homer and Plato do not ring in those ears."[28]

As one can note, the first three texts listing the names of thinkers to whom Nietzsche lays claim is a clear indication as to how difficult it will be to discover a definitive evaluation concerning Socrates, Schopenhauer, Kant, and Plato. The name of Socrates is, moreover, completely absent from these three lists, Schopenhauer appears twice but in totally different perspectives, and the one allusion to Kant reveals the increase in the gap separating Nietzsche's present vision and that of the earlier writings, that is, those of *The Birth of Tragedy* period. Although Nietzsche is sometimes ambiguous, hostile, and hesitant regarding the Pre-Socratics, it is ultimately to these philosophers, the Dionysian poets and the Homeric Greeks that he attributes a primary role: "The real *philosophers of Greece* are those before Socrates (—with Socrates something changes)."[29] And yet, in *Beyond Good and Evil* one sees the name of Plato ranked with that of Heraclitus and Empedocles: "Let us confess how utterly our modern world lacks the whole type of a Heraclitus, Plato, Empedocles, and whatever other names these royal and magnificent hermits of the spirit had. . . ."[30] Plato's evaluation just two years later will be totally different: "[Let us take] the philosophers of Greece, e.g., Plato. He severed the instincts from the *polis*, from contest, from military efficiency, from art and beauty, from the mysteries, from belief in tradition and ancestors— He was the seducer of nobility: he himself was seduced by the *roturier* [commoner] Socrates . . ."[31]

These texts lead us to confirm once again the ambiguous and paradoxical quality of Nietzsche's attitude toward Schopenhauer, Kant, Socrates, and Plato. It will be in fact misleading to try to find a final word, a definitive evaluation or a text tying together a thought marked by a continual movement of success and failure. That is to say, Nietzsche's writing moves and deploys itself in and from a universe of forces that are continuously overcome, read and reread, stated and *retracted*, for they always include the one in the other. The characteristic principles of the forces expressed in Nietzsche's texts and thought are their constant mobility and their variable malleability. What is affirmed at one point about a subject reappears later in another perspective, in another interpretation and under another relation. There are several meanings because there are several forces and several relations of forces that take hold of them.

In *Nietzsche and Metaphysics*, Michel Haar makes this remark regarding the split between Schopenhauer and Nietzsche:

> Also it could very well be that a *very different* thought was making its way through a Schopenhauerian terminology and was being shaped. And, conversely, in spite of the rupture, we may witness a sort of faithfulness, on another plane than the ideas, to the one he called to the end "my great master," in spite of the vehemence with which he condemns him.[32]

The author further pursues this line of reasoning by stating:

> Two formulas whose blatant contradiction, however, is *merely apparent*, summarize this double, *but unambiguous* position:
> 1. "My confidence in him was immediate, it is now still the same as nine years ago" (*Schopenhauer as Educator*, 1874).
> 2. My distrust with respect to his system was there *from the very beginning*" (*Posthumous Fragments*, 1878).[33]

Now, to speak of a "mere contradiction" and of a "double, but unambiguous position" in the work of Nietzsche tends to neglect, ignore or fail to admit this vital question: the writing that Nietzsche deploys in his texts is not a writing of reconciliation, but a *writing of paradox*. Nietzsche is and remains *ambiguous* throughout his work. He makes absolutely no effort to cancel or synthesize the "contradictions" produced by the different perspectives and interpretations. Moreover, a mere contradiction is no longer a contradiction. Why continue to talk about it? In doing so, Haar mimics the discourse so dear to traditional Nietzsche commentators like Kaufmann, Jaspers, and Wahl. These authors, apart from their different points of view, all seek a unity, a principle or a synthesis that will reconcile, explain or at least diminish the "contradictions" in Nietzsche's work. He, however, never stops stating and "retracting," evaluating and reevaluating. His writing advances by continual ruptures, attempts, experimentations, and reprises. If Schopenhauer, Kant, Socrates, and Plato haunt him until the end, if Spinoza, Rousseau, Goethe, Christ, and Wagner are mentioned in almost every text, it is because they all lay claim to new reevaluations, to new reinterpretations, and new overcomings.

Multiplicity of meanings and perspectives is a leitmotif that traverses and animates all of Nietzsche's writings. "Interpretation, *not* exposition. There is no state of fact, everything is fluctuating, ungraspable, evanescent; what are still durable are our opinions. Project-a-meaning—in most cases, a new interpretation superimposed over an old interpretation that became incomprehensible, and which is now only itself a sign."[34] In other words, there is no value in itself, that the value of the world resides in the capacity to interpret and organize for oneself a piece of that world. All interpretation then supposes the force that interprets, surpasses itself, re-creates itself. All extension of power opens new perspectives and new horizons, since the world is not a state of fact, but poetic invention, fiction, and continuous creation, the will to take in and be taken in. This is why Nietzsche objects vehemently to the positivism that states "there are only facts":

I would say: No, facts is precisely what there is not, only interpretations. We cannot establish any fact "in itself": perhaps it is folly to want to do such a thing.

"Everything is subjective," you say; but even this is *interpretation.* The "subject" is not something given, it is something added and invented and projected behind what there is.—Finally, is it necessary to posit an interpreter behind the interpretation? Even this is invention, hypothesis.

In so far as the word "knowledge" has any meaning, the world is knowable, but it is *interpretable* otherwise, it has no meaning behind it, but countless meanings.—

"Perspectivism."[35]

In other words, the subject is itself also a poetic invention, the sheer creation of the force that evaluates and imposes a meaning: "'The subject': interpreted from within ourselves, so that the ego counts as a subject, as the cause of all deeds, as a doer."[36] Consequently, there is no subject: "The 'subject' is only a fiction: the ego of which one speaks when one censures egoism does not exist at all."[37]

The notions of interpretation, perspective, fiction, and creation are increasingly present in Nietzsche's work, starting from the texts immediately preceding *Beyond Good and Evil* up to the last writings of his productive life. In fact, the insights and discoveries found as early as the first writings are illuminated and sharpened as Nietzsche analyzes and develops them from the will to power and the relation of forces. *Beyond Good and Evil,* and the texts connected with it, raises to the highest level the notions of appearance, illusion, fiction, and falsity, whereas the antitheses of good/evil, true/false, essence/appearance are considered, dissected, and unmasked as expressions of a will to deny and to condemn life. Thus, Nietzsche reverses these oppositions or, more precisely, he *inverts* these values by erecting another table of values, one that gives future priority to the false, the uncertain, the apparent, and the untrue.

THE TRUE, THE FALSE, APPEARANCES

Already in a fragment written prior to *The Birth of Tragedy*, one finds this confusing statement: "My philosophy is *inverted Platonism* (*umgedrehter Platonismus*): the further one is from the true being, from the purest, from the most beautiful, the better it is. Life in appearance as an end."[38]

The primacy of appearance has influenced more than one commentator to underscore the risk to which Nietzsche exposes himself: precisely that of "ontologizing" appearance and of re-establishing the very opposition that he wishes to avoid, namely, the Platonic opposition between truth and illusion, between the Same and the Other, as well as the Kantian and Schopenhauerian opposition of the thing in itself and the phenomenon. Nevertheless, Nietzsche's stubbornness is all the more surprising as he affirms and reaffirms appearance to the point of, paradoxically, stripping away and voiding the appearance proper: "The true world—we have abolished. What world has remained? The apparent one perhaps? But no! *With the true world we have also abolished the apparent one.*"[39]

Notice that it is not the world, but the *true* world and the *apparent* world that have been abolished. But what remains then? Has Nietzsche abolished all opposition and antinomy, or has he been caught in the trap of the language and metaphysical structures that he contests? This question remains open and susceptible to different interpretations. We will return to it.

In the abovementioned text, which dates from his last productive year, Nietzsche employs the expression "*apparent world*" (*scheinbare Welt*). In the fragment cited above, that was part of his very earliest production, he uses the concept of appearance (*Schein*). The expression "Life in appearance" (*Das Leben im Schein*) invites us then to consider the word *Schein*, which can mean resemblance, deceptive appearance, pretense or sham, illusion, and also, in relation with the verb *scheinen* (shine, give light, seem, appear), what appears by and emits light, by rays, by gleaming. In *The Birth of Tragedy*, in fact, Apollo is evoked as *der "Scheinende,"* as the "shining one," the sculptor god of the solar gaze, who exercises measured restraint; he is "the glorious divine image of the *principium individuationis.*"[40] Dionysus is the god of intoxication and ecstasy, who breaks the chains of the *principium individuationis* and makes the most intimate ground of things, of nature, of the will, in short, of the originary One, express itself.[41]

Although these two forces are presented sometimes separated, sometimes together, here in struggle, there reconciled, Nietzsche does not for all that conceive of them as two drives independent from one another; on the contrary, Apollonian appearance is the very manifestation of the Dionysian. These two deities belong mutually and fundamentally to each other. In musical tragedy, however, a paradoxical phenomenon occurs: the spectator "sees the tragic hero before him in epic clearness and beauty, and nevertheless rejoices in his annihilation. . . . He sees more extensively and profoundly than ever, and yet wishes he were blind."[42] In other words, the spectator and the tragic artist themselves create the figures that their Dionysian impulse destroys, in order to let themselves sense, behind the destruction of the phenomenal world, a higher and more primordial aesthetic joy. All this happens as if the destruction of the visible was the very condition of access to the heart of the One and primordial joy, *Ur-freude*. But music also produces a similar phenomenon: as one desires in tragedy to both see and go beyond seeing, in the musical usage of dissonance one experiences the same will to simultaneously hear and to go beyond the audible. In both cases, it is as if the destruction of visibility and audibility was the condition and passageway to a delight, to an originary pleasure, to an *Ur-lust*. "That striving for the infinite, the wing-beat of longing that accompanies the highest delight in clearly perceived reality, reminds us that in both states we must recognize a Dionysian phenomenon: again and again it reveals to us the playful construction and destruction of the individual world as the overflow of primordial delight (*einer Urlust*)."[43]

If there is one question that truly obsesses Nietzsche, it is the question of the relations of forces and that other that issues from it: the problem of creation and destruction, with that of interpretation. It is in fact in the universe of forces and in the movement of destruction-construction that the problematic of perspective, of interpretation, and evaluation are situated and developed. These readings never cease to change, since they themselves are constantly exceeded, overcome, and recommenced. Already in the very earliest writings, and thus before the development of the major lines and multiple implications of the earth-shaking discovery of the *will to power*, one finds the question of Perspectivism as vision resulting from the force that interprets and evaluates. Thus, in a fragment of summer 1872 through the end of 1873:

> There is no *form* in nature, for there is neither an inside nor an outside there.
> All art reposes in the mirror of the eye.[44]

But the artist is not content to merely contemplate the world, he also wants to transform it: "It is undoubtedly *beauty* that man's sensorial consciousness seeks, it transfigures the world. Why don't we pursue something else? What is it we seek beyond our senses?"[45]

These two texts resonate in yet another text of fall 1880:

> There is no world when there is no mirror" is an absurdity. But all our relations, as exact as they may be, are of descriptions of man, *not of the world*: these are the laws of that supreme optics beyond which we cannot possibly go. It is neither appearance nor illusion, but a cipher in which something unknown is written—quite readable to us, made, in fact, for us: our human position toward things. This is how things are hidden from us."[46]

In other words, to know things, is to organize, create and construct them from the continual activity of the eye thrown on the world. This is why Nietzsche insists: "The point of departure is the illusion in the mirror, we are *living images in a mirror*."[47] But the mirror in itself does not exist: "When we try to examine the mirror in itself we discover in the end nothing but things upon it. If we want to grasp the things we finally get hold of nothing but the mirror.—This, in the most general terms, is the history of knowledge."[48] This is human optical knowledge, visual acuity, a movement of things that are enlarged or diminished by the incessant activity of the eye trained on the world.

In this sense, the basis of knowledge is error, appearance; for there is no single unit of measure for sensation: "Everywhere that the mirror and the organs of touch are encountered, a sphere is born. . . . The limitation of force and constant that sets that force in relation to others thus constitutes 'knowledge.' *Not* the relation of a subject to an object; but something else. It presupposes an optical illusion of rings that surround us *but which in fact do not exist*. Knowledge is essentially *appearance (Schein)*."[49] Appearance that is created from a relation, a limitation and a game that our senses make use of. "Our *thought* is in fact nothing more than a web very subtly woven from *seeing, hearing*, and *touch*, the logical forms are the physiological laws of sensory perceptions. Our senses are centers of highly developed sensations, with resonances and powerful mirrors."[50] That is to say, knowledge evolves not only from the eye, but from the eye, hearing, touch and the entire body. The body is great reason, assures Zarathustra, and what is called "mind" is only small reason, the instrument and the little toy of great reason. This is why Nietzsche writes in a fragment of summer 1886 through fall 1887:

> Everything that arrives in consciousness as a "unity" is already monstrously complicated: we have only an *appearance (Anschein) of unity*.

The phenomenon of the body is a phenomenon more rich, more clear and more seizable: it needs to be placed ahead of method, without concern for its ultimate meaning.[51]

These texts lead us to affirm that the world is nothing other than an extension of our body: we embellish, transform, transfigure, and create from a constraint, a resistance, and a desire to expand and increase our power. It is only to this extent that we render things beautiful, attractive, alluring, and desirable, for they are not that way themselves. This is why Nietzsche sees artists as models worthy of imitation: they know how to falsify, lie, dissimulate, and give things a surface, a skin, and a veil of colors, of nuances, gradations, shadow, and light.

The question of meaning and multiple interpretations occupies an increasingly larger place in the Nietzschean text. During the third period, when he elaborated on and enriched the analyses around the will to power, the problem of art as fiction, as illusion and the will to deceive took on a perspective that enlarged, prolonged, and clarified what had already begun in the two preceding periods. The role played by the genius in the tragic writings would be increasingly assumed, and transformed, by the individual, the researcher, the experimenter, and the artist. In *Beyond Good and Evil*, Nietzsche will present a new type of philosopher, who is at the same time philosopher, legislator, *dissector* and artist. Philosophers of the future are artists inasmuch as they are the *creators of values*: "With a creative hand they reach for the future, and all that is and has been becomes a means for them, an instrument, a hammer. Their "knowing" is *creating*, their creating is legislation, their will to truth is—*will to power*."[52]

We can see that these philosophers of the future are sculptors. They carry a hammer, smash the old table of values, write on stone, cut and refashion material, and thus the resistance, the limit. Besides, they examine and sound the idols, they reveal the cracks in them.[53] Their paradox resides in the fact that they create in destroying and destroy as creators. This is why it would be more accurate to speak of a construction-destruction, which is delight of creating and will to becoming, forging, purifying, transfiguring. The philosophers of the future create their own truth and their tables of values. What does their truth of the others, the truth of the masses, the truth of the herd matter to them! "It must offend their pride, also their taste, if their truth is supposed to be truth for everyman—which has so far been the secret wish and hidden meaning of all dogmatic aspirations. "My judgment is *my* judgment":

no one else is easily entitled to it—that is what the philosopher of the future perhaps says to himself."[54]

The question of the truth and the untruth of a judgment, that Nietzsche had already taken up in *Human, All Too Human*, will be newly resumed, deepened, and enriched as a result of the analyses in *Beyond Good and Evil* centered on the will to power, the relation of forces and perspective. In *Human, All Too Human I*, a work that witnesses a considerable distancing from Kant and Schopenhauer, one reads in paragraph 19:

> The invention of the laws of numbers was made on the basis of the error, dominant even from the earliest times, that there are identical things (but in fact nothing as identical with anything else); at least that there are things (but there is no "thing"). The assumption of plurality always presupposes the existence of *something* that occurs more than once; but precisely here error holds sway, here already we are fabricating beings, unities that do not exist. . . . To a world which is *not* our idea the laws of numbers are wholly inapplicable: these are valid only in the human world.[55]

Further on, in the aphorism entitled *The Illogic Necessary*, Nietzsche will state:

> Among the things that can reduce a thinker to despair is the knowledge that the illogical is a necessity for mankind, and that much good proceeds from the illogical. It is implanted so firmly in the passions, in language, in art, in religion, and in general in everything that lends value to life, that one cannot pull it out of these fair things without mortally injuring them. . . . Even the most rational man from time to time needs to recover nature, that is to say his *illogical original relationship with all things*.[56]

These questions will reappear already at the beginning of *Beyond Good and Evil*, paragraph 4, for example, not only recognize the fictions that have been woven into logic and the representation of number, but it insists again on the necessary and indispensable role these same fictions have played in the preservation and augmentation of life:

> And we are fundamentally inclined to claim that the falsest judgments (which include the synthetic judgments *a priori*) are the most indispensable for us; that without accepting the fictions of logic, without

measuring reality against the purely invented world of the unconditional and self-identical, without a constant falsification of the world by
means of numbers, man could not live—that renouncing false judgments would mean renouncing life and a denial of life. To recognize
untruth as a condition of life—that certainly means resisting accustomed value feelings in a dangerous way; and a philosophy that risks
this would by that token alone place itself beyond good and evil.[57]

As one can note, Nietzsche not only admits the necessity of the false
and the untrue for the preservation and promotion of life, but he sees in
untruth the very condition of that life. Not the true and false linked paradoxically, but the untrue, the false, and fiction presented as indispensable
and in an exclusive way. Nietzsche pushes this necessity to such an
extreme that one can hardly keep from again posing the question: isn't he
once more getting bogged down in the dualism he wants to avoid? This
insistence, however, becomes all the more misleading as in the end he lays
claim to a philosophy beyond good and evil.

In fact, the reader unfamiliar with Nietzsche's strategies and masks,
can easily be led astray by rhetorical effects, inordinate laudatory praise,
hyperboles, absolute statements, the subtle contrasts or gradations that
enliven his texts. He often resorts to a deliberately provocative claim to
the sole end of conveying his vision. In the aforementioned paragraph, for
example, it is not the game of true and false that is stressed, but rather the
necessity of the false and the untrue, of fiction and of the creation of a
purely imaginary, unconditional and self-identical world.

Thus, already in the following paragraph (5), he tilts his weapons at
the tricks of the old dogmatists: he attacks "the hocus pocus of mathe-
matical form," with which Spinoza, "the sick hermit," clad his philosophy. He makes fun of the addresses and secret expedients of the old Kant:

> The equally stiff and decorous Tartuferry of the old Kant as he lures us
> on the dialectical by-paths that lead us to his "categorical imperative"—
> really lead astray and seduce—this spectacle makes us smile, as we are
> fastidious and find it quite amusing to watch closely the subtle tricks of
> old moralists and teachers of morals.[58]

The problematic of truth and untruth shows up again in paragraph
24. This time, however, it is analyzed from the point of view of the inter-
twining of forces which the will to knowing—which is also the will to not
knowing—expresses and develops itself.

And only on this now solid, granite foundation of ignorance could knowledge rise so far—the will to knowledge on the foundation of a far more powerful will: the will to ignorance, to the uncertain, to the untrue! Not as its opposite, but—as its refinement . . . here and there we understand it and laugh at the way in which precisely science at its best seeks most to keep us in this *simplified*, thoroughly artificial, suitably constructed and suitably falsified world—at the way in which, willy-nilly, it loves error, because, being alive, it loves life.[59]

Thus, no longer the exclusivity of truth and untruth, but the will to knowing assumes the will to not knowing. A science that props itself up, edifies, and creates itself on the ground of ignorance. Knowledge and ignorance are here linked paradoxically, imbricated paradoxically insofar as they are a condition, conservation and expansion of life. In fact, this paragraph is a reprise and reelaboration of what Nietzsche had already developed in paragraphs 59 and 107 of *The Gay Science*. In the latter paragraph, art is presented as a necessary fiction by which we maintain ourselves in life and understand the errors and the illusion (*Wahn*) contained in human knowledge:

If we had not welcomed the arts and invented this kind of cult of the untrue, then the realization of general untruth and mendaciousness that now comes to us through science—the realization that delusion and error are conditions of human knowledge—would be utterly unbearable. *Honesty* would lead to nausea and suicide. But now there is a counterforce against our honesty that helps us to avoid such consequences: art as the *good* will to appearance. . . . As an aesthetic phenomenon existence is still *bearable* for us, and art furnishes us with eyes and hands and above all the good conscience to be *able* to turn ourselves into such a phenomenon . . . we need all exuberant, floating, dancing, mocking, childish, and blissful art lest we lose the *freedom above things* that our ideal demands of us. . . . We should be *able* to stand *above* morality—and not only stand with the anxious stiffness of a man who is afraid of slipping and falling any moment, but also to float above it and play.[60]

In paragraph 24 of *Beyond Good and Evil*, it is science itself that becomes the art of taking in, of eluding, of rendering light, airy, floating, dancing, and mocking:

How we have made everything around us clear and free and easy and simple! how we have been able to give our senses a passport to everything superficial, our thoughts a divine desire for wanton leaps and wrong inferences! how from the beginning we have contrived to retain our ignorance in order to enjoy an almost inconceivable freedom, lack of scruple and caution, heartiness and gaiety of life—in order to enjoy life![61]

For knowledge alone pushes us toward despair, annihilation, madness. "Not doubt, *certainty* is what drives one insane."[62] Truth is ugly, but we have art, we have science, we have error so as not to perish. In this sense, religion is also the art of dealing with anguish, the means by which we transmute into surface, harmony, and benefaction an otherwise incurable pessimism. In other words, religious interpretation fosters the instinct that makes man aware of approaching truth *too soon*. Along with piety, religion has, for Nietzsche, the paradoxical characteristic of manifesting fear and at the same time counteracting it and transforming it into a work of art. "Piety, the 'life in God,' seen in this way, would appear as the subtlest and final offspring of the *fear* of truth, as an artist's worship and intoxication before the most consistent of all falsifications, as the will to the inversion of truth, to untruth at any price."[63]

Regarding *Beyond Good and Evil,* Lou Salomé quite correctly observes: "several of its sections could just as well have been titled *Beyond Good and Falsehood.* For it is here that he explicates in great detail the *unjustified opposition* of such values as 'true and untrue,' which in respect to their origin are no less expendable than the contrasting of values of 'good and evil.'"[64] But if one considers certain paragraphs, the work could well be entitled *Beyond True and False.* To be sure, Nietzsche accentuates and reaffirms to the point of exaggeration the importance of the false, of the untrue and of the apparent; he sees in the art of deception, evasion, falsification, and creation the symptoms of an ascendant life; but he does not denounce any less the oppositions between true and false as so many symptoms of a declining life, as the expression of the spirit of decadence, of the will to nothingness, and of the ressentiment of the weak. Thus in paragraph 24, cited above: "the will to ignorance, to the uncertain, to the untrue! Not as its opposite, but—as its refinement. Even if *language,* here as elsewhere, will not get over awkwardness, and will continue to talk in opposites where there are only degrees and many subtleties of gradation."[65] Ten paragraphs later, Nietzsche rails against the nonsense of the bourgeois world, against its claims, its subterfuges and power plays that have produced the philosophies of Descartes, Kant and all *advocatus dei*: "The faith in 'immediate certainties' is a *moral* naïveté that reflects honor on us philosophers; but—

after all we should not be '*merely* moral' men. Apart from morality, this faith is a stupidity that reflects little honor on us."[66]

For Nietzsche, in fact, it is by a strictly moral bias that philosophers up to the present have accorded more value to truth than to appearance. He sees in the prevalence of truth the most ill-founded of hypotheses, since life is only possible on the grounds of estimations and appearances that issue from this very perspective.

> . . . and if, with virtuous enthusiasm and clumsiness of some philoso-
> phers, one wanted to abolish the "apparent world" altogether—well,
> supposing *you* could do that, at least nothing would be left of your
> "truth" either. Indeed, what forces us at all to suppose that there is an
> essential opposition of "true" and "false"? Is it not sufficient to assume
> degrees of apparentness (*Scheinbarkeit*) and, as it were, lighter and
> darker shadows and shades of appearance—different "values," to use the
> language of painters? Why couldn't the world *that concerns us*—be a fic-
> tion? And if somebody asked, "but to a fiction there surely belongs an
> author?"—could one answer simply: *why*? Doesn't this "belongs" per-
> haps belong to the fiction, too? Is it not permitted to be a bit ironical
> about the subject no less than the predicate and object? Shouldn't
> philosophers be permitted to rise above faith in grammar?[67]

Regarding the philosopher of the future, Nietzsche thus arrogates to him the right to abolish all barriers that the spirit of decadence and the forces of ressentiment have erected between true and false, between good and evil. While the limited perspective of the nihilistic forces sees only antinomies and contradiction, the philosopher of the future, as legislator, *dissector*, experimenter, and artist perceives degrees, transitions, nuances, and different values. In a text dating from the period of *Beyond Good and Evil*, Nietzsche discusses his earliest writings in the following terms:

> One can see in my early writings a clear will to open up horizons, a cer-
> tain guileful prudence before convictions, a certain distrust toward the
> traps set by conscience and the magic tricks entailed in all vigorous
> faith . . . that taste which rebels against oppositions that are too exact,
> *desires* in things a good part of uncertainty and the suppression of
> oppositions, as a friend of half-tones, shadows, afternoon light, and
> infinite seas.[68]

These texts, along with the considerations we have developed, allow us to now better understand the problematic formula cited at the beginning of this section, namely, "The true world—we have abolished. What world has remained? The apparent one perhaps? But no! *With the true world we have also abolished the apparent one.*" This assertion, which comes at the end of a text brief in form and dense in content, is in point of fact open to multiple interpretations and opposing points of view. From the title, *How the "True World" Finally Became a Fable*, Nietzsche traces and reviews the different stages that European thought has traversed and that have culminated in the total inversion of all values—that is, in the teaching of Zarathustra. With Zarathustra both the true world and the world of appearance are anihilated, for noon has arrived: "(Noon: moment of the briefest shadow; end of the longest error; high point of humanity; INCIPIT ZARATHUSTRA.)."

These two formulas mark both an end result and a new departure: at the same time that they announce an end they initiate a horizon, an era and a new beginning. They can likewise express the thought of the eternal return as nihilism insofar as it is a movement that exceeds, surmounts, transforms, and shifts into new values. But they can just as well clarify and confirm the discoveries and insights concerning oppositions, or more precisely, the destruction of oppositions which is the method of *Beyond Good and Evil*. Moreover, the suppression of the true world and the apparent world is placed in a new perspective if one considers it from the analyses that have developed, and from *Beyond Good and Evil*, and the texts connected to it.

In the course of the third period, in fact, the elabortions and diagnostics that operate around the will to power and the forces and relation of forces become progressively more clear and precise: the oppositions set up between a true and an apparent world, between good and evil, just and unjust, good and bad are revealed as just so many symptoms of a will to nothingness, as the expression of the ressentiment of the weak and a flight toward the afterlife.

To be sure, the philosopher of the future also seeks a beyond, but the beyond that he lays claim to presents itself as a reality that goes *beyond good and evil, beyond truth and falsity*. To seek a transcendent ground for both opposed values would end in restoring the same values and antinomies that one believed he was contesting in the first place. This is why it would be more accurate to state that the philosopher of the future *creates* reality, a reality that produces, becomes, builds and destroys in a constantly renewed movement. In other words, reality is not something there to be found, but rather something that is to be created and invented: one *names* it, designs it, and imposes a meaning on it. The philosophers of the future and the free spirits are paradoxical to the extent that they are *able* to detect, invent, and create several meanings, several interpretations, and thus, several realities, that incorporate one in the other, that are tied together and incessantly overcome themselves.

But if this is the case; that is, if with the philosophers of the future, and the free spirits who anticipate them the oppositions built up between true and false, good and evil will be and already are abolished, how can one explain that the upper hand belongs precisely to the valuations that establish these oppositions? This question can be clarified if we refer to a text written a year after the publication of *Beyond Good and Evil*:

> *Psychology of Metaphysics,*—The world is apparent: consequently there is a true world;—this world is conditional: *consequently* there is an unconditioned world;—this world is full of contradiction: consequently there is a world free of contradiction;—this world is a world of becoming: consequently there is a world of being:—all false conclusions (blind trust in reason: if *A exists*, then the opposite concept *B* must also exist). It is *suffering* (*Leiden*) that *inspires* these conclusions: fundamentally they are *desires* that such a world should exist; in the same way, to imagine another, more *valuable* (*werthvolle*) world is an expression of hatred for a world that makes one suffer: the *ressentiment* of metaphysics against actuality (*das Wirkliche*) is here creative.[69]

The last paragraph is rich in implications, since the hatred that it presents as the expression of the incapacity to transform suffering is, paradoxically, creator and progenitor of new values: one creates another world because this one makes us suffer. The metaphysicians' ressentiment thus becomes creative and this world becomes a bridge, a means and an occasion to invent a beyond. The suffering is in itself paradoxical to the extent that it is both delight and the means to more joy, to create more and will more. A will to overcoming is displayed here that is neither an end in itself nor a raison d' être. But metaphysicians and religious people overlook the double character of suffering. Instead, they see in it as a lack that must be filled or suppressed at all costs:

> That they see the problem of pleasure and pain in the foreground reveals something weary and sick in metaphysicians and religious people. Even morality is so important to them only because they see in it as an essential condition for the abolition of suffering.

In the same way, their preoccupation with appearance and error: cause of suffering, superstition that happiness attends truth (confusion: happiness is "certainty," in "faith").[70]

Happiness would then be the total absence of doubt and error, the suppression of all *lacunae* and insufficiency, the plenitude of meaning, and the abolition of all "on the side of" and, thus, all "beyond." This would be equivalent to the glacial silence of death, of the absolute void of two mirrors placed face to face, as Roland Sublon has said regarding the suffering in the analytic experience: "The certitude of an eternal life that suppresses all elsewhere and all alterity would render life itself impossible, because it will be frozen by anxiety; and the final word uttered, the belief in which would also die out, for there ould be no object still capable of saying something."[71]

If, on the one hand, the forces of decadence lay claim to a beyond *the* true and *the* false, *the* good and *the* evil, *the* just and *the* unjust, and if, on the other hand, the forces of an ascendant life insist upon a beyond every opposition and antinomy, it remains, nonetheless, the case that all these drives express a will to delight that knows neither repose nor end. It is the pure pleasure of a new beginning at the very moment lack is ready to be filled. Another departure is announced, the bird takes flight, the explorer lifts anchor sailing into the boundless, gaping, open sea, driven on by the joy of unknown places and the uncertainty of ever finding a port.

> It will seem to us as if, as a reward, we now confronted an as yet undiscovered country whose boundaries nobody has surveyed yet, something beyond all the lands and nooks of the ideal so far, a world so overrich in what is beautiful, strange, questionable, terrible and divine that our curiosity as well as our craving to possess it has got beside itself—alas, now nothing will sate us anymore![72]

"IN THE HORIZON OF THE INFINITE"

The metaphor of the sea, and the other figures that it reflects (ships, sails, the sun, breadth, the horizon, land that comes into view or disappears) appear frequently in Nietzsche's work. Thus Zarathustra, who proclaims himself a soothsayer and wanders along on a high ridge between two seas, confesses:

If I am fond of the sea and of all that is of the sea's kind, and fondest when it angrily contradicts me; if that delight in searching which drives the sails toward the undiscovered is in me, if the seafarer's delight is in my delight; if ever my jubilation cried, "The coast has vanished, now the last chain has fallen from me; the boundless roars around me, far out glisten space and time; be of good cheer, old heart!"[73]

Zarathustra wanders on a high ridge between sea and sea, between past and future. Such a heavy cloud, pregnant with lightning flashes, he says yes to all that is creation, dazzling brightness, yet to come. Zarathustra is creator and soothsayer. At noon, under a pure autumn sky, he says to his friends:

And out of such overflow it is beautiful to look out upon distant seas. Once one said God when one looked upon distant seas; but now I have taught you to say: overman.[74]

In a style rich in metaphors, nuances, gradations, and in poetry, this text establishes in its entirety the relations between the affirmation of man, the will to create and the resultant overman. It is extremely important that the first announcement of the overman is made at the *edge* of the forest;[75] now Zarathustra speaks anew of the overman, but at the *edge* of the water, in the heart of overabundance, his gaze turned toward the distant seas. In *The Gay Science*, Nietzsche again employs the metaphor of the sea to recall that "the old god is dead" and to reassure man that the horizon is open anew to daring knowledge:

Indeed, we philosophers and "free spirits" feel, when we hear the news that "the old god is dead," as if a new dawn shone on us; our heart overflows with gratitude, amazement, premonitions, expectation. At long last the horizon appears free to us again, even if it should not be bright; at long last or ships may venture out again, venture out to face any danger; all the daring of the lover of knowledge is permitted again; the sea, *our* sea, lies open again; perhaps there has never been such an "open sea."—[76]

This text contrasts in a striking way with the famous paragraph 125, which is also found in *The Gay Science*, and where the madman, after having announced the death of God, poses some distressing questions to his listeners:

But how did we do this? How could we drink up the sea? Who gave us the sponge to wipe away the entire horizon? What were we doing when we unchained this earth from its sun? Whither is it moving now? Whither are we moving? Away from all suns? Are we not plunging continually? Backward, sideward, forward, in all directions? Is there still any up or down? Are we not straying as through an infinite nothing? Do we not feel the breath of empty space? Has it not become colder? Is not night continually closing in on us? Do we not need to light lanterns in the morning?[77]

It is not a simple coincidence that the text directly preceding the above paragraph refers to the awesome immensity of the Ocean, of the "land" that disappears, as well as the homesickness that affects anyone who ventures toward distant horizons. In paragraph 125, the madman enumerates one after the other the acts that have resulted in the earth now being plunged in the void and the infinite nothingness: the sea has been emptied, the horizon wiped away, and the earth has been unchained from its sun. In paragraph 124, on the other hand, it is man who embarks, who leaves the land and breaks the ties that attach him to it:

In the horizon of the infinite.—We have left the land and have embarked. We have burned our bridges behind us—indeed, we have gone farther and destroyed the land behind us. Now, little ship, look out! Beside you is the ocean: to be sure, it does not always roar, and at time it lies spread out like silk and gold and reveries of graciousness. But hours will come when you will realize that it is infinite and that there is nothing more awesome than infinity. Oh, the poor bird who felt free and now strikes the walls of this cage! Woe, when you feel homesick for the land as if it had offered more *freedom*—and there is no longer any "land."[78]

As one can see, there is a progression animating these two texts: in the paragraph cited above, it is man himself who embarks, who burns his bridges and crosses the awesome immensity of the Ocean. In paragraph 125, there is a step, or there are some steps further toward achieving nihilism: the sea has been drunk up, the horizon wiped up and the earth rolls along dis-oriented in the void and infinite nothingness. Heidegger, who in his study of Nietzsche analyzes these four figures (sun, earth, horizon, and sea) from the point of view of the development and implications of metaphysics in its historical movement, makes this observation:

When Nietzsche names the relationship between the sun and the earth he is not thinking merely of the Copernican revolution in the modern understanding of nature. The word "sun" at once recalls Plato's allegory. According to the latter, the sun and the realm of its light are the sphere in which that which is appears according to its visible aspect, or according to its many countenances (Ideas). The sun forms and circumscribes the field of vision wherein that which is as such shows itself. "Horizon" refers to the suprasensory world as the world that truly is. This is at the same time that whole which envelops all and in itself includes all, as does the sea. The earth, as the abode of man, is unchained from its sun. The realm that constitutes the suprasensory, which as such, *is* in itself no longer stands over man as the authoritative light. The whole field of vision has been wiped away. The whole of that which is as such, the sea, has been drunk up my man. For man has risen up into the I-ness of the *ego cogito*. Through this uprising, all that is, is transformed into object. That which is, as the objective, is swallowed up into the immanence of subjectivity.[79]

The horizon has been wiped up, the sea drunk up, and the earth is rolls along *dis-oriented* in the void and infinite nothingness. Nihilism is thus fully achieved, for all values, the most "noble" and high-placed, have been inverted. The supersensible world and the earthly world are reduced to nothing.

Noon, time of the briefest cast shadow, has arrived. New mutations are developing, new metamorphoses begin, for it is at the very moment of the inversion that new values and new tables occupy their places. In other words, they appear to the extent that old values collapse and old idols fall away. This is why it is better to say, not a construction and destruction, but a construction-destruction, or a creation that presupposes annihilation and voluptuousness in destroying. Nihilism overcomes itself by itself, surmounts itself by itself in an incessant act of creation.

Nietzsche completes paragraph 343, cited above, by recalling that the sea is newly open and that daring knowledge is permitted again. In paragraph 382, also found in *The Gay Science*, an undiscovered country seems to point to the horizon, a beyond "all the lands and nooks" known so far, "a world so overrich in what is beautiful, strange, questionable, terrible, and divine that our curiosity as well as our craving to possess it has got beside itself—alas, now nothing will sate us any more!"[80] That is to say, the will to delight is insatiable, that it has neither an end nor a raison d'être. It passes beyond all limits, all pain and suffering, all pleasure and

unpleasure. Pleasure and unpleasure are only consequences or epiphe-
nomena accompanying an originary pleasure (*Ur-lust*), an original joy
(*Ur-freude*), in short, a will to delight, to become more, to become master, to become greater. Each victory assumes a resistance overcome, each
going beyond a call to another, each overcoming is overcoming a force or
a relation of forces that impart a meaning, impose an interpretation, create a perspective and instate a new value or values. This will to delight that
knows neither limit nor satiation, and which can push on to the point
beyond death, is expressed by Nietzsche in the form of a fable that relates
and depicts in vivid colors the different stages in the seductive travels of
the *Don Juan of knowledge.*

> *A fable.*—The Don Juan of knowledge: no philosopher or poet has yet
> discovered him. He does not love the things he knows, but has spirit
> and appetite for the enjoyment of the chase and intrigues of knowl-
> edge—up to the highest and remotest stars of knowledge!—until at
> last there remains to him nothing of knowledge left to hunt down
> except the absolutely *detrimental*; he is like the drunkard who ends by
> drinking absinthe and *aqua fortis.* Thus in the end he lusts after Hell—
> it is the last knowledge that *seduces* him. Perhaps it too proves a disil-
> lusionment, like all knowledge! And then he would have to stand to all
> eternity transfixed in disillusionment and himself become a stone
> guest, with a longing for a supper of knowledge which he will never
> get—for the whole universe has not a single morsel left to give to this
> hungry man.[81]

It is striking to note that the works of Nietzsche we have examined
more closely are never come to a final conclusion. If the Nietzschean text
as divergence, resistance, and a plurality of perspectives is never a closed
text, a look at the end of the writings with which we ourselves are particularly concerned will show that they all end by forging a new beginning.
Thus, in the last section of *The Birth of Tragedy* Nietzsche asks the reader
to transport himself, if only by dream, into the life of ancient Greece,
where he can walk "under lofty Ionic colonnades" and to hear, in the end,
a call to attend a tragedy and to sacrifice on the altar of Apollo and Dionysus. Regarding *Human, All Too Human I*, his last paragraph introduces
precisely *the Wanderer*, and he presents the free spirits as wanderers and
philosophers who live in mountains, forests, in solitude, and who *seek* the
Philosophy of the Morning.[82] The second part of *Human, All Too Human
II* ends by resuming the dialogue at the beginning of the Second Part

between the Wanderer and his Shadow. The Shadow says to the Wanderer: "Step under these trees and look out at the mountains; the sun is sinking." The Wanderer answers: "Where are you? Where are you?"[83]

Sunset calls for, or recalls another sunrise. Setting and rising are a new end and new beginning. An end and beginning that return and repeat themselves, in difference. Curiously enough, *Thus Spoke Zarathustra* begins and ends with a sunrise, and the poems at the end of *The Gay Science* create a play of colors, tonalities, nuances, shadow, and light. In the next to last poem, *Sils Maria*, one reads:

> Here I sat, waiting—not for anything—
> Beyond Good and Evil, fancying
> Now light, now shadows, all a game,
> All lake, all noon, all time without all aim.[84]

Looking at *The Antichrist*, the last words seal the end of an era and open a pathway to a reevaluation and a total re-creation of history: "And time is reckoned from the *dies nefastus* with which this calamity began—after the *first* day of Christianity! *Why not rather after the last day? After today?* Reevaluation of all values!"[85]

The third and final Essay of *On the Genealogy of Morals* begins and ends with the question of the will to nothingness that characterizes the ascetic ideal, namely, the *horror vacui*, the need for some end, a life that cares more about destroying itself than being paralyzed and frozen by a nothingness of the will: "And, to repeat in conclusion what I said in the beginning: man would rather will *nothingness* than *not* will. . . ."[86] In this sense nihilism remains paradoxically creative, for in *willing* death, the "Sabbath of Sabbaths, the end of ends," it insitutes nonetheless tables of values, which can in turn transform themselves and bring about a multiplicity of creations.

Nietzsche ends *Beyond Good and Evil* by adding an aftersong (*From High Mountains*), in which he hails the arrival of Zarathustra and celebrates the wedding of light and dark.

Seen in its totality, Nietzsche's work is an attempt to link differences through a woven thread of success and failure that is writing. A thought that is developed in and through a universe of forces expresses, by the very movement of creation-destruction that it produces, a diversity of meanings, perspectives, interpretations, and new evaluations. The writing of paradox tries constantly to seize and link the plurality of meanings issuing from force, or from the relation of forces that evaluate, interpret, name, and create. But this writing is itself force, since it manifests the will to inscribe a meaning, to fill a gap, and shore up a difference that always displaces itself and never even approaches "truth," for there is no "truth." There are only differences of perspectives and interpretations. Consequently, the weaker and more weary the will, the more it will want to *find* the basis of all truth and the reason for all opposition produced by its ressentiment toward everything that is strong, powerful, fertile, full, overflowing, and beautiful. Inversely, the will to power that characterizes the ascendant life affirms itself in difference, multiplicity, becoming, change, and everything that escapes constraint and mastery. This will only delights in what resists it and remains to be conquered and possessed. Innumerable lands are yet to be discovered and explored, and infinite suns have yet to rise in the horizon of the unknown. "There are so many days that have not yet broken," are the words taken from the *Rig Veda* and inscribed on the title page of *Daybreak*—a clear, serene work which, according to Nietzsche, "is not inconsiderable when it comes to fixing to some extent things that easily flit by, noiselessly—"[87]

This lucid and serene book is nonetheless rich in ambiguities. The clarity that it projects is full of hope, promise, of the unknown, and things at the same time beautiful, strange, disturbing, serious, and frivolous. According to Nietzsche own words: "almost every sentence of this book was first thought, *caught* among that jumble of rocks near Genoa where I was alone and still had secrets with the sea. Even now, whenever I accidentally touch this book, almost every sentence turns for me into a net that again brings up from the depths something incomparable: its entire skin trembles with tender thrills of memory"[88] Like Nietzsche's other works, *Daybreak* is far from a closed book. Its final paragraph points toward other directions, it leaves the road open or, what is even more, it launches forward, it *wills* moving further onward, more joyously, beyond all Oceans, all horizons, and all infinity.

> *We aeronauts of spirit!*—All those brave birds which fly out into the distance, into the farthest distance—it is certain! somewhere or other they will be unable to go on and will perch on a mast or a bare cliff-face— and they will even be thankful for this miserable accommodation! But who could venture to infer from that, that there was *not* an immense open space before them, that they had flown as far as one *could* fly! . . . *Other birds will fly farther!* This insight and faith of ours vies with them in flying up and away; it rises above our heads and above our impotence

into the heights and from there surveys the distance and sees before it the flocks of birds which, far stronger than we, still strive whither we have striven, and where everything is sea, sea, sea!—And whither then would we go? Would we *cross* the sea? Whither does this mighty longing draw us, this longing that is worth more to us than any pleasure? Why just in this direction, thither where all the suns of humanity have hitherto *gone down*? Will it perhaps be said of us one day that we too, *steering westward, hoped to reach an India*—but that it was our fate to be wrecked against infinity? Or, my brothers. Or?—[89]

Notes

CHAPTER 1

1. *KSA* (*Kritische Studienausgabe*), 13, p. 228. From this point onward, all the italicized words in Nietzsche's quotations are by Nietzsche himself, save when it is a question of words in Latin, or if there is an explicit indication on my part.

2. The term "dialectic" is not intended here in the Hegelian sense, despite the questionable assertions of Gilles Deleuze, leading to his claim that Nietzsche's works are traversed by "anti-Hegelianisms" (See Gilles Deleuze, *Nietzsche and Philosophy* [New York: Columbia University Press, 1983], p. 8).

3. *KSA* 13, p. 228. The *KSA* is the most recent Colli-Montinari edition of Nietzsche's works in the original German (Walter de Gruyter, 1988), and the one most commonly referred to by English-speaking Nietzsche scholars (translator).

4. Friedrich Nietzsche, *The Birth of Tragedy*, translated by Walter Kauffman (New York: Vintage, 1967), (14), p. 93. (Will be noted as *BT* from this point onward.)

5. *BT*, *Attempt at a Self-Criticism* (6), p. 24.

6. Ibid., (19), p. 119.

7. Ibid., (2), p. 19.

8. Ibid., (1), p. 33.

9. Ibid., (1), p. 36.

10. Friedrich Nietzsche, *Ecce Homo*, translated by Walter Kaufmann (New York: Vintage, 1969) (1), p. 270. (Will be indicated *EH* from now onward.)

11. Even Nietzsche's later Dionysus carries ambiguous traits, those of both Apollo and Dionysus. (See *Twilight of the Idols, Skirmishes of an Untimely Man*, in *The Portable Nietzsche*, translated by Walter Kaufmann [New York: Viking, 1967], pp. 519–520. Will henceforth be abreviated as TI.) By a spiritualistic reading of this text, Kaufmann sees in the later Dionysus the "passion controlled" and the "synthesis of the two forces represented by Dionysus and Apollo in *The Birth of Tragedy* . . ." (See Walter Kaufmann, *Nietzsche: Philosopher, Psychologist, Antichrist* [Princeton, N.J.: Princeton University Press, 1974], p. 129.) With regard to the term *Aufhebung*, Sarah Kofman observes: "The Nietzschean *Aufhebung* which implies no work of the negative, has nothing to do with the

Hegelian *Aufhebung*. Nietzsche parodies this metaphysical concept." (Sarah Kofman, *Nietzsche and Metaphor*, translated by D. Lange [Palo Alto: Stanford University Press, 1993], p. 164).

12. *BT* (10), p. 73.

13. See *BT*, 1: "His (Apollo's) eye must be "sunlike," as befits his origin; even when it is *angry* and *distempered* it is still hallowed by beautiful illusion" (*BT* [1], p. 35) (our italics). In a posthumous fragment of 1871, that Nietzsche uses again in *The Greek State* (1872), these aspects are shown more explicitly: "I believe then that one should know that it is to my liking to occasionally sing a paean to *war*. His silvery bow makes its dreadful sound: and suddenly arriving, like the night, is no less than Apollo, the true god who sanctifies and purifies the State. But he begins, like in the opening of the *Iliad*, by shooting his arrows at the mules and dogs. Then he strikes the men themselves, and everywhere flame the pyres covered with corpses" (*KSA* 7, p. 344). One can thus only be shocked to read in Giorgio Colli, one of the organizers of the Critical Edition of the *Complete Works of Nietzsche* in German, the assertion that Nietzsche has failed to consider Apollo's frightful aspects.

14. *BT* (4), p. 46.

15. Ibid. (21), p. 130.

16. Ibid. (7), p. 59.

17. Ibid. (7), p. 59.

18. *KSA* 12, p. 116.

19. *BT* (22), p. 131.

20. Ibid. (22), p. 132.

21. Ibid. (24), p. 141.

22. *KSA* 13, p. 522.

23. In an approximative manner, Nietzsche alludes to the fragments 52, 124, and 70 of Heraclitus (See Richard D. McKirahan, Jr., *Philosophy Before Socrates: An Introduction with Tests and Commentaries* (Indianapolis: Hackett, 1994. Heraclitus's Fragments, pp. 117–128).

24. *KSA* 13, p. 522.

25. *KSA* 13, p. 522.

26. *BT* (9), p. 72.

27. See Gilles Deleuze, op. cit., p. 14.

28. Bernard Pautrat, *Versions du soleil: figures et système de Nietzsche* (Paris: Seuil, 1971), p. 108 (Pautrat's stress).

29. Ibid. We know that Nietzsche devoted very little time to the reading of Hegel. Whatever reading he did, took place during the period of his studies between Bonn and Leipzig (around 1865). There isn't any systematic development or content regarding Hegel's thought in Nietzsche's work. More often he refers to Hegel in a brief and ironic

manner, or in the form of parody, as is the case in *The Birth of Tragedy*. "An 'idea,'—the antithesis of the Dionysian and Apollonian—translated into the realm of metaphysics; history itself as the development of this 'idea'; in tragedy this antithesis is sublimated (*aufgehoben*) into a unity . . ." (*EH* [1], p. 271).

30. *KSA* 13, pp. 224–225.

31. Friedrich Nietzsche, *Twilight of the Idols*, in *The Portable Nietzsche*, translated by Walter Kauffman (New York: Viking, 1967). (Henceforth abbreviated as *TI*); *Skirmishes of an Untimely Man* (49), p. 554.

32. *EH-Z* (6), p. 306.

33. Immanuel Kant, *Idea for a Universal History with a Cosmopolitan Intent, in Perpetual Peace and Other Essays on Politics, History, and Morals*, translated by Ted Humphrey (Indianapolis: Hackett Publishing Co., 1992), p. 32 (Kant's stress).

34. Ibid., p. 39 (Kant's stress).

35. For more details on the philosophy of Shaftsebury, see Ernst Cassirer, *La Philosophie des Lumières* (Paris: Fayard, 1966). Regarding the question of finality in Kant, we have been inspired by Walter Kaufmann's reading, op. cit. Part Two, *Art and History*.

36. See, in particular, *BT*, 3, 5, and 24.

37. Friedrich Nietzsche, *The Will to Power*, translated by Walter Kaufmann and R. J. Hollingdale (New York: Vintage Books, 1968) (853), p. 452. (Henceforth abbreviated as *WP*.)

38. *BT* (3), p. 44. Nietzsche's position regarding the finality of nature remains, even in the early period, ambiguous and hesitant. However, in a fragment of 1881, he directly attacks the concept: "The so-called finalism of nature—in egoism, in the sexual instinct (*Geschlechstrieb*), where, one might say, it makes use of the individual, in the luminescent effusion of the sun, etc.—is nothing but fabrications. It is perhaps the last form of the representation of *God*." (*KSA* 9, p. 447.)

39. Ibid.

40. Friedrich Nietzsche, "The Greek State," in *The Complete Works of Friedrich Nietzsche: Early Greek Philosophy*, vol. 2, edited by Oscar Levy (New York: Russell & Russell, 1964), p. 10. (Henceforth abbreviated as *TGS*.)

41. *UO*, Schopenhauer as Educator, pp. 202–203.

42. Ibid., p. 11.

43. 7 (153), I, 1, p. 308. This definition is found in the fragments between quotation marks, but Nietzsche does not give the reference.

44. Friedrich Nietzsche, *Unmodern Observations*, edited by William Arrowsmith (New Haven: Yale University Press, 1990), p. 195. (Henceforth abbreviated as *UO*.)

45. Ibid., p. 196.

46. Ibid., p. 199.

47. Ibid., p. 194.

48. See Walter Kaufmann, op. cit., pp. 177–178.

49. Friedrich Nietzsche, *Thus Spoke Zarathustra*, translated by Walter Kaufmann, in *The Portable Nietzsche* (New York: Viking, 1967), pp. 126–127. (Henceforth abbreviated as *Z*)

50. Martin Buber, *Werke* (Munich: Kösel-Verlag, 1962), p. 349.

51. *BT* (14), p. 92.

52. *BT, Atttempt at a Self-Criticism*, 1, 2, pp. 18–19.

53. *BT* (12), p. 82.

54. Friedrich Nietzsche, *Philosophy in the Tragic Age of the Greeks*, translated by Marianne Cowan (Chicago: Henry Regney Company, 1971), p. 69. (Henceforth abbreviated as *PTAG*.)

55. Ibid., p. 40.

56. Ibid., p. 52.

57. *BT* (11), p. 76.

58. Ibid. (12), p. 81.

59. *KSA* 1, pp. 544–545.

60. Ibid.

61. *BT* (9), p. 70.

62. Ibid., p. 71.

63. Ibid.

64. Ibid. (9), pp. 71–72.

65. *BT* (13), p. 88.

66. Ibid. (14), p. 89.

67. Ibid. (14), p. 90.

68. Ibid. (14), p. 93.

69. Ibid. (15), p. 93.

70. Ibid. (15), p. 94. The metaphor of a veil is found, among others, in the *Gay Science*, paragraph 339, as well as in paragraph 4 of the Preface, from which the text will be taken up again, in slightly modified form, in *Nietzsche contra Wagner* (epilogue 2), quoted here: "No, this bad taste, this will to truth, to 'truth at any price,' this youthful madness in the love of truth, have lost their charm for us: for that we are too experienced, too serious, too gay, too *deep*. We no longer believe that truth remains truth when the veils are withdrawn—we have lived enough not to believe this. Today we consider it a matter of decency not to wish to see everything naked, or to be present to everything, or to understand and 'know' everything. *Tout comprendre—c'est tout mépriser*. . . . Oh, those Greeks! They knew how to live. What is required for that is to stop courageously at the surface, the fold, the skin, to adore appearance, to believe in forms, tone, words in the whole Olympus of appearance. Those Greeks were superficial—*out of profundity*. And is this not

precisely what we are again coming back to, we daredevils of the spirit who have climbed the highest and most dangerous peak of present thought and looked around from up there—we who have looked *down* from there? Are we not, precisely in this respect, Greeks? Adorers of forms, of tones, of words? And therefore—*artists?*"

71. *BT* (15), pp. 97–98.

72. *The Pathos of Truth*, in *Philosophy and Truth: Selections from Nietzsche's Notebooks of the Early 1870's*, translated by Daniel Breazeale (Atlantic Highlands, N.J.: Humanities Press, 1979), pp. 55–66.

73. *EH: Why I Am So Clever?*, 4

74. *The Pathos of Truth*, op. cit., pp. 65–66

75. *Z*, p. 127.

76. Ibid., p. 129.

77. *UO*, p. 89.

78. It is important to note here that the book appearing presently under the title of *The Will to Power* is in fact only an arbitrary compilation undertaken by Nietzsche's sister and various editors from the philosopher's notes, rough drafts, and unfinished texts. This book, in whatever edition or language it is published, is not in any way at all helpful in understanding Nietzsche's thought and work. This lacunae has, however, been remedied by G. Colli and M. Montnari in the critical edition of the *Complete Works* of Nietzsche. In this new edition, all the posthumous fragments have been arranged in chronological order.

79. Although the term *nihilism* appeared most frequently from 1885, Nietzsche had already employed it as an adjective in a fragment of summer 1880 (See *KSA* 9, p. 126), and also as a noun in a manuscript of 1881 (see *GS*, paragraph no. 21, note 1 in the French Edition, p. 76; *KSA* 9, p. 125).

80. KSA 12, pp. 350–352. Another possible translation is: "*Let the values placed highest be devaluated.*"

81. *WP* (2), p. 9.

82. Martin Heidegger, "The Word of Nietzsche: 'God Is Dead'" in *The Question Concerning Technology and Other Essays*, translated by William Lovitt (New York: Harper Colophon, 1977), p. 62.

83. *WP* (1) pp. 7–8.

84. *BT* (18), p. 113.

85. See KSA, 12, p. 476.

86. *KSA* 12, p. 455.

87. *WP* (27), p. 19.

88. *UO*, p. 136.

89. Ibid., p. 208.

90. *BT* (18), p. 111.

91. Friedrich Nietzsche, *The Gay Science*, translated by Walter Kaufmann (New York: Random House, 1974), p. 167. (Henceforth abbreviated as *GS*.)

92. *KSA* 7, p. 125.

93. *BT* (11), p. 76.

94. Heidegger, op. cit., p. 307.

95. Friedrich Nietzsche, *The Dionysiac World View*, in *The Birth of Tragedy and Other Writings*, translated by Ronald Speirs (Cambridge: Cambridge University Press, 1999), p. 124.

96. *KSA* 7, p. 185.

97. Heidegger, op. cit., p. 105.

98. *KSA* 12, p. 350.

99. Ibid.

100. KSA 12, p. 354.

101. *BT, Attempt at a Self-Criticism* (5), p. 24.

102. Ibid., p. 23.

103. *KSA* 13, p. 225.

104. *BT* (3), p. 41.

105. *KSA* 13, p. 229.

106. *BT, Attempt at a Self-Criticsm* (5), p. 22.

107. Ibid., p. 23.

108. *WP* (822), p. 435.

109. *KSA* 12, p.114.

110. *KSA* 13, p. 500.

111. *EH-BT* (2), p. 272.

Chapter 2

1. Eugen Fink, *La Philosophie de Nietzsche*, translated by H. Hildebrand and A. Lindenberg (Paris: Minuit, 1965), p. 55.

2. 15 (118), XIV, p. 231.

3. Friedrich Nietzsche, *Human, All Too Human: A Book for Free Spirits*, translated by R.J. Hollingdale (Cambridge: Cambridge University Press, 1986) (128), p. 243. (*OS*) (Henceforth abbreviated as *HAH*.)

4. Ibid. *WS* (19), p. 310.

5. *PTAG* (9), p. 69.

6. Lou Salomé, *Nietzsche*, edited and translated by Siegried Mandel (Redding Ridge, CT: Black Swan Books, 1988), pp. 9–10.

7. *EH, HAH* (1), p. 283.

8. *HAH*, II (1), p. 209.

9. "*Rück-und vorsichtig*": Nietzsche plays here with the prefixes *rück*, aft, and *vor*, before, and with the noun *Sicht*, look, aspect, which gives: "looking cautiously before and aft, with reservations . . ."

10. Friedrich Nietzsche, *Daybreak: Thoughts on the Prejudices of Morality*, translated by R. J. Hollingdale (Cambridge: Cambridge University Press, 1982), p. 5 (henceforth abbreviated as *D*.)

11. *HAH* (9), pp. 15–16. Note that when we give as reference the abbreviation *HAH*, we are referring always to the first book. When referring to the second book the reference will be specified in function of the part which composes it: *MOM* for *Mixed Opinions and Maxims; WS* for the *Wanderer and His Shadow*. For the prefaces we use, *HAH* I and *HAH* II.

12. Ibid. (16), p. 20.

13. Friedrich Nietzsche, *On Truth and Lying in a Non-Moral Sense*, in *The Birth of Tragedy and Other Writings*, translated by Ronald Speirs (Cambridge: Cambridge University Press, 1999), p. 148.

14. *HAH* (9), p. 15.

15. Ofelia Schutte, *Beyond Nihilism: Nietzsche Without Masks* (Chicago: University of Chicago Press, 1986), p. 38.

16. *HAH* (1), p. 12.

17. *On Truth and Lying . . .* op. cit., p. 148.

18. Ibid., p. 148.

19. Ibid., p. 148.

20. *HAH*. (2), pp. 12–13.

21. Ibid. (4), p. 14.

22. Ibid. (39), p. 34.

23. Ibid. (92), p. 49.

24. See *HAH, Assorted Opinions and Maxims* (27), pp. 220–221. We will return to this subject later.

25. *HAH* (26), p. 26.

26. Friedrich Nietzsche, *Writings from the Late Notebooks*, translated by Kate Surge (Cambridge: Cambridge University Press, 2003, p. 149. See also *GM*: I, 1, 2; *BGE*: First and ninth parts. See also *supra*, our chapter V, section 1, and chapter VI, section 2.

27. *KSA* 12, p. 378.

28. *WP* (579), p. 311.

29. *GS* (347), p. 288.

30. *WP* (513), p. 277.

31. *HAH, Assorted Opinions and Maxims* (171), pp. 253–254.

32. *HAH* (163), pp. 86–87.

33. Ibid., (164), p. 87.

34. Ibid. (22), p. 23.

35. *KSA* 12, p. 144.

36. *D* (318), p. 158.

37. This tendency found again in the work of Eugen Fink in the late 1950s, goes back to the work of Lou Salomé, published for the first time in 1894.

38. *MOM*, in *HAH* (205), p. 262.

39. *HAH* (6), p. 15 (italics ours).

40. Ibid. (22), p. 24.

41. *D.* (432), p. 185.

42. *HAH* (37), p. 32.

43. Ibid. (16), p. 20.

44. Ibid.

45. Ibid. (222), p. 105.

46. Ibid.

47. Ibid. (19), p. 22.

48. Ibid. (29), p. 27.

49. *GS* (59), p. 122.

50. Ibid. (59), p. 123.

51. *WP* (572), p. 308.

52. See *BT*, 5 and 24.

53. *GS* (107), pp. 163–164.

54. *WP* (617), pp. 330–331.

55. *HAH, AO* (32), p. 222.

56. Ibid.

57. Ibid.

58. Ibid.

59. Ibid. (244), pp. 116–117.

60. Ibid. (154), pp. 82–83.

61. Ibid.

62. Ibid. (31), p. 28.

63. Ibid., Preface (1), p. 5.

64. Ibid.

65. Ibid. (4), p. 8.

66. Ibid. (151), p. 82.

67. Ibid. (40), p. 35.

68. Among the texts where the *will to power* appears, there are some which are earlier than *Zarathustra* and which are present this concept under other names and in different perspectives than those of the later period. In Nietzsche's self-published writings, one will find this expression for the first time in *Zarathustra* (On the Thousand and One Goals, On Self-overcoming, and On Redemption). Other important texts are: *BGE*: paragraphs 9, 13, 19, 22, 36, 257, 259; *GM*: in particular, the second and third essays.

The fragments and notes elaborating the *will to power*, originally planned as a book by Nietzsche and then abandoned, can be found numerically and chronologically arranged in the critical edition of Nietzsche's *Complete Works*, edited by G. Colli and M. Montinari.

69. *WP* (620), p. 333.

70. Ibid. (689), p. 367. The preposition *zur* (toward) in the expression *Wille zur Macht* (will to power) accentuates the mobile and fluid character of the will as becoming. This is what is shown in the above fragment, even if the expression as such does not appear in it.

71. Ibid. (702), p. 373.

72. Ibid. (689), p. 368.

73. *Z*, II: *On Self-Overcoming*, p. 226.

74. *WP* (254), p. 148.

75. Ibid. (602), p. 369.

76. Ibid. (604), p. 327.

77. Ibid. (556), p. 302.

78. *HAH* (99), p. 53.

79. Ibid. (102), p. 55.

80. Nietzsche, *Writings from the Late Notebooks*, op. cit., p. 119.

81. In fact, in paragraph 12 of *The Gay Science*, entitled On the Aim of Science, one will read: "What? The aim of science should be to give men as much pleasure and as little displeasure as possible? But what if pleasure and displeasure were so tied together that whoever *wanted* to have as much as possible of the one *must* also have as much as possible of the other—that whoever wanted to 'jubilate up to the heavens' would also have to be prepared for 'depression unto death'" (*GS* [12], p. 85).

82. *WP* (702), p. 373.

83. Ibid.

84. Ibid. (751), p. 397.

85. One cannot entirely overlook Spinoza's influence on Nietzsche with regard to the discovery and explanation of the will to power. In a letter addressed to Overbeck, dated July 30, 1881, Nietzsche admits with great enthusiasm: "I have a precursor, and *what* a precursor! I hardly knew Spinoza." (*Selected Letters of Friedrich Nietzsche*, Edited and translated by Christopher Middleton (Chicago: University of Chicago Press, 1969), p. 177). But there is an essential difference between Nietzsche's and Spinoza's view of power: Nietzsche refuses to accept the Spinozian idea of conservation. In fact, in the third part of Spinoza's *Ethics*, one reads: "Proposition VI: Each thing, in so far as it is in itself, endeavors to persevere in its being" (English translation of *quantum in se* is "is in itself," rather than in the French translation of the *Ethics*, where the phrase reads, literally, "power of being"—translator) And in Proposition VII of the same part: "The effort (*conatus*) by which each thing endeavors to persevere in its own being is nothing but the actual essence of the thing itself." (Benedict de Spinoza, *Ethics* [New York: Hafner, 1960]). Nietzsche, of course, insists on the mobile, changing and fluent character of force. In the perspective of will to power, everything that exists tends not to preserve itself, but rather, to become more. "Spinoza's law of 'self-preservation' ought really to put a stop to change: but this law is false, the opposite is true. It can be shown most clearly that every living thing does everything it can *not* to preserve itself but become *more*." (*WP* [688], p. 367).

86. *GS* (374), p. 336.

87. Ibid. (371), pp. 331–332.

88. *HAH* (107), p. 58.

89. Ibid. (56), p. 41.

90. Ibid.

91. *WP* (402), p. 218.

92. See in particular *On the Genealogy of Morals*, Third Essay: "What Is the Meaning of Ascetic Ideals?" See also the posthumous fragments of fall 1887 to spring 1888.

93. Ibid. (461), p. 254.

94. It is necessary all the same to recall that Socrates is presented in *The Birth of Tragedy* (1872) and in the texts connected with it as responsible for the death of myth and tragic wisdom. Also, in *Philosophy in the Tragic Age of the Greeks*, it is Heraclitus and not Parmenides who appears as the philosopher whose "regal possession is his extraordinary power to think intuitively" (*PTAG* [5], p. 52). See *supra.*, first chapter, section 3 of our text.

95. *WP* (412), p. 222.

96. Ibid. (435), p. 239. This fragment, that is, in part, laid out in a vertical column, does not provide commas between all the terms. The term "adiaphora" is written in Greek characters and could mean, here: "indifferent things, neutralities."

97. *KSA* 11, pp. 261–262.

98. *AC* (11), p. 578.

99. *WP* (101), p. 64.

100. *HAH, AOM* (27), p. 221.

101. *KSA* 13, p. 504. Already in *The Gay Science*, paragraph 349, of the Fifth Book (written in 1886 and added to *GS* in 1887), Nietzsche affirms a propos Spinoza: "It should be considered symptomatic when some philosophers—for example, Spinoza who was consumptive—considered the instinct of self-preservation decisive and *had* to see it that way; for they were individuals in conditions of distress." See also *BGE*, 5; *AC*, 17.

102. *HAH, AOM* (408), 299.

103. Ibid.

104. *KSA* 8, p. 513.

105. Ibid.

106. *KSA* 8, p. 514.

107. *HAH* (463), p. 169.

108. *KSA* 11, p. 151.

109. *EH, BT* (3), p. 273.

110. *HAH* (408), p. 299.

111. *EH, HAH* (4), pp. 287–288.

112. *WS, Introduction.*

CHAPTER 3

1. Although the concept of *decadence* appears more explicity and frequently in the later period, one finds this term already in French, in text written at the end of 1876 through the summer of 1877, where Nietzsche refers to *Don Quixote*: "It is through this success that he plays a role in the decadence (*la décadence*) of Spanish culture; Cervantes is a national disaster" (*KSA* 8, p. 454).

2. One will remember that Book V, which is also the last book of the work (¶¶ 343–383), had been written in 1886 and added to *GS* the following year, at the time of the second edition. It thus forms part of the later years of Nietzsche's productive life.

The themes we speak of are found, particularly, in the three last books, that are, due to their philosophical content, superior to the preceding two.

3. Friedrich Nietzsche, *Selected Letters*, op. cit., p. 223.

4. *GM*, Preface (3), pp. 15–16.

5. Octavio Paz, *El Mono Gramático* (Barcelona: Editoral Seix Barral, 1988), p. 7.

6. Lou Salomé, op. cit., p. 22.

7. *BGE* (289), p. 229.

8. Karl Jaspers, *Nietzsche: An Introduction to the Understanding of His Philosophical Activity*, translated by C. F. Wallraff and F. J. Schnitz (Chicago: Henry Regney Company, 1969), p. 10.

9. Ibid., p. 11.

10. Ibid., p. 398 (stress is ours).

11. *EH, Why I Write Such Good Books* (4), p. 265.

12. Eric Blondel, *Nietzsche, le corps et la culture* (Paris: Presses Universitaires de France, 1986), pp. 57–58.

13. *Z*, part III, *The Convalescent* (2), p. 329.

14. *WP*, fn., p. 293.

15. Ibid. (616), p. 330.

16. Ibid. (482), p. 267.

17. *BGE* (43), p. 53.

18. Alexander Nehamas, *Nietzsche: Life as Literature.* (Cambridge, MA: Harvard University Press, 1985), p. 241, n. 21.

19. *GS* (261), p. 218.

20. *BGE* (296), pp. 236–237.

21. *D* (530), p. 210.

22. *BGE* (278), p. 224.

23. Ibid. (278), pp. 223–224.

24. Ibid. (289), p. 229.

25. *D*, Preface (1), p. 1.

26. *WP* (432), p. 236.

27. *EH*, Preface (2), p. 217.

28. Ibid., *Why I Write Such Good Books* (1), p. 259.

29. *BGE* (40), p. 50.

30. Ibid.

31. *WP* (806), p. 425.

32. *GS, Preface to the Second Edition* (4), p. 38.

33. Ibid. (339), p. 272

34. Friedrich Nietzsche, *Nietzsche Contra Wagner*, in *The Portable Nietzsche*, translated by Walter Kaufmann (New York: Viking, 1967), p. 682 (*NW*).

35. Ibid. This phrase, which is found in French in the text, is in fact a parody on the formula attributed to Madame de Staël: "Tout comprendre, c'est tout pardonner." See the note accompanying this phrase in, *Oeuvres philosophiques complètes*, Gallimard.

36. *GM*, Preface (6), p. 20.

37. *GS* (352), p. 295.

38. *KSA* 13, pp. 139–140.

39. *WP* (15), p. 14.

40. *A* (507), p. 206.

41. Tracy B. Strong, *Friedrich Nietzsche and the Politics of Transfiguration* (Berkeley: University of California Press, 1988), p. 362, note 29.

42. John Calvin, *Institutes of the Christian Religion*, vol. I, translated by John Allen (Philadelphia: Presbyterian Board of Education, 1936), pp. 47–48.

43. See Strong, op. cit., p. 303, where the author also speaks of neo-Calvinist doctrine.

44. KSA 9, p. 353.

45. KSA (8), p. 571.

46. Ibid., p. 572.

47. Ibid.

48. Ibid., p. 575b.

49. All of the above letters can be found in the French version of the Colli-Montinari edition of Nietzsche's complete works, fully cited above. Obviously, they also appear in the *KSA*. The last letter is from: *Selected Letters of Friedrich Nietzsche*, op. cit., pp. 346–347. KSA, pp. 577–579. (trans.).

50. *Z*, part III, *The Wanderer*, pp. 264–265.

51. *Z*, part II, *The Night Song*, p. 218.

52. *D* (14), p. 16.

53. *BGE* (39), p. 49.

54. *GS* (107), p. 164. In two cases Nietzsche uses the word *Narr*, that can mean: sot, madman, and fool. As it appears in this text, Gallimard has translated the first instance (*den Narren*) as fool, and the second (*des Narren*) as madman.

55. *GS* (59), p. 123.

56. Ibid. (368), p. 325.

57. Ibid. (368), p. 326.

58. Ibid. (367), p. 324.

59. *WP* (1050), p. 539.

60. KSA (8), p. 359.

61. Lou Salomé, op. cit., p. 159.

62. *BGE* (270), p. 221.

63. *EH*, Why I Am So Wise (1), p. 223.

64. Friedrich Nietzsche, *Aurore, Oeuvres philosophiques* (Paris: Gallimard) (Dates et événements). (No English translation available, trans.)

65. *Ibid.*

66. *EH*, Why I Am So Wise (1), PP. 222–223 (modified, trans.).

67. *KSA* 13, p. 356.

68. *KSA* 12, p. 319.

69. *KSA* 12, p. 286.

70. *KSA* 12, pp. 156–157.

71. *GM*, Third Essay (4), p. 101.

72. Ibid., p. 100.

73. *EH*, Why I Am So Clever (4), p. 246.

74. Kaufmann, op. cit., p. 132.

75. *KSA* 11, p. 559.

76. *EH*, Why I Am So Wise (2), p. 224.

77. *GS*, Preface to the Second Edition (2), pp. 34–35.

78. Ibid., p. 35.

79. Ibid. (3), pp. 35–36.

80. Ibid., p. 36.

81. *EH, Why I Am So Wise* (2), p. 224.

82. *KSA* 12, p. 108.

83. *WP* (47), p. 29.

84. *WP* (812), p. 430. The long dashes, as well as the ellipses are Nietzsche's.

85. *BT* (3), p. 43. Strictly speaking, Nietzsche distances himself from Schopenhauer's metaphysics in some of the fragments preceding the publication of *The Birth of Tragedy*. This separation, however, will become more explicit only from *Human, All Too Human* onward.

86. Ibid. (25), p. 144.

87. *KSA* 12, p. 405.

88. *WP* (852), p. 450.

89. *WP* (864), p, 460. (Slightly modified, transl.)

90. Pierre Klossowski, *Nietzsche and the Vicious Circle*, translated by Daniel W. Smith (Chicago: The University of Chicago Press, 1997), p. 203.

91. According to Nietzsche himself, up until February 1887, he had absolutely no knowledge of Dostoevsky. In a letter of February 23, 1887, addressed to Overbeck, he in fact claims: "I also knew nothing about Dostoevski until a few weeks ago—uncultivated person that I am, reading no 'periodicals'! In a bookshop my hand just happened to come to rest on *L'Esprit souterrain* (*Notes from the Underground*), a recent French translation (the same kind of chance made me light on Schopenhauer when I was twenty-one, and on Stendahl when I was thirty-five!). The instinct of affinity (or what should I call it?) spoke to me

instantaneously—my joy was beyond bounds; not since my first encounter with Stendahl's *Rouge et Noir* have I known such joy." (Nietzsche, *Selected Letters*, op. cit., pp. 260–261).

92. *WP* (259), pp. 149–150.

93. *EH, Z* (1), p. 295.

94. *GS* (341), p. 273.

95. *EH, NT* (3), pp. 273–274.

96. Jaspers, op. cit., p. 353.

97. *WP* (1066), p. 549.

98. Ibid. (1062), p. 547.

99. Ibid. (1066), p. 548.

100. Ibid., p. 549.

101. Ibid. (1064), 547.

102. Fink, op. cit., p. 103. The theme of the *overman* is found in the Prologue (3), while the first and second part treat the *death of God* and the *will to power*.

103. *Z*, part III, *On the Vision and the Enigma*, pp. 268–270.

104. Ibid., p. 340.

105. Ibid.

106. Ibid., *Prologue* (4), pp. 126–128.

107. Ibid., *On Redemption*, p. 249.

108. Ibid., p. 251.

109. Ibid.

110. Ibid., p. 253.

111. Ibid.

112. *WP* (1041), pp. 536–537.

113. Ibid., p. 536.

114. *EH, Why I Am So Clever* (10), p. 258. This expression appears again in the chapter *The Case of Wagner*, section 4, of the same book, as well as in *Nietzsche contre Wagner*, Epilogue, 1.

115. *WP* (1067), pp. 549–550.

116. *BGE* (22), p. 30.

117. *WP* (1001), p. 546.

CHAPTER 4

1. *HAH* (475) (235), pp. 175, 112.

2. The principal sources that Nietzsche uses in *The Antichrist* are: Ernest Renan, against whom he is unsparing in his criticism, Julius Wellhausen, Tolstoy, and Dostoevsky.

It is true that Nietzsche had been impressed by reading Tolstoy and Dostoevsky from 1887 (for his discovery of the latter, see, *supra*, our chapter III, section 2, note 87). But it would be a mistake to wish to see a radical change made by these readings in Nietzsche's vision of Christ and Christianity in general. On the contrary, these readings have only reinforced, accentuated or enlarged what Nietzsche had developed already from *Human, All Too Human*, and even before.

3. Friedrich Nietzsche, *The Antichrist*, in *The Portable Nietzsche*, translated by Walter Kaufmann (New York: Viking, 1967) (28), p. 600. (Henceforth abbreviated as *AC*.)

4. *AC* (43), p. 619.

5. Nietzsche, *Selected Letters*, op. cit., pp. 239–241. It is in fact in this paragraph that Nietzsche refers to St. Augustine and to the Church Fathers in general: "One need only read any Christian agitator, St. Augustine, for example, to comprehend the *smell*, what an unclean lot had thus come to top. One would deceive oneself utterly if one presupposed any lack of intelligence among the leaders of the Christian movement: oh, they are clever, clever to the point of holiness, these good church fathers!" (*AC* (59), p. 651).

6. *KSA* 11, p. 243.

7. *D* (68), pp. 39–40.

8. Ibid., p. 40.

9. Ibid.

10. Ibid., p. 41.

11. Ibid., pp. 41–42. It is necessary, however, not to forget that Nietzsche's interpretation of Paul is heavily influenced by his reading of Luther, particularly regarding the doctrine of justification through faith. This is why, before several attacks directed against Paul, one cannot avoid the question: Who is the target, Paul, or really Luther?

12. *AC* (24), p. 593.

13. Ibid. (44), p. 622.

14. Ibid. (10), p. 576.

15. Ibid. (26), p. 596.

16. Ibid. (29), p. 601.

17. Ibid. (33), p. 607.

18. See *AC*, 29 and 31, and also KSA, 13, p. 409.

19. *AC* (35), p. 609. It is convenient to find a connection here between Jesus, insofar as he is the man who perishes, and the tragedy resulting from the death of Socrates, as it is interpreted in *The Birth of Tragedy*, section 13. In fact, after having reiterated the divine calling on which Socrates had insisted, Nietzsche continues: "In view of this indissoluble conflict, when he had at last been brought before the forum of the Greek state, only one kind of punishment was indicated: exile. Being throughly enigmatical, unclassifiable, and inexplicable, he might have been asked to leave the city, and posterity would never have been justified in charging the Athenians with an ignominious deed. But that he was sentenced to death, not exile, Socrates himself seems to have brought about with perfect awareness and without any natural awe of death" (*BT* [13], p. 89).

20. See supra, p. ?? and *AC* (28), pp. 599–600.

21. *AC* (29), p. 600.

22. See supra, the Introduction to chapter 3.

23. *AC* (39), p. 612. In underscoring *practice*, it is evidently the doctrine of justification through faith that Nietzsche aims at. In this same section, there is in fact a passage where the allusion to Luther is quite explicit.

24. Ibid., p. 613.

25. Ibid. (31), p. 603.

26. Ibid. (40), p. 614.

27. Ibid., pp. 615–616.

28. Ibid. (41), p. 616.

29. Ibid.

30. Ibid. (44), p. 620. The text of Paul (*UO*, 15, 14), that gives the *Ecumenical Translation of the Bible* (TOB), is thus: If Christ is not risen, our predication is empty and so is our faith."

31. Ibid. (42), p. 618.

32. Ibid. (44), p. 625.

33. Ibid. (24), pp. 593–594.

34. Ibid. (25), p. 594.

35. Ibid. (26), p. 596.

36. Ibid. (16), p. 583. If one objects that Christianity, insofar as it is a religion of "peace" and "love," has, however, found a certain reception and expansion among barbarians and the strong people of northern Europe, Nietzsche would answer, with irony: "That the strong races of northern Europe did not reject the Christian God certainly does no credit to their religious genius—not to speak of their taste" (*AC*, 19). And further, in paragraph 22: "When Christianity left its native soil, the lowest classes, the *underworld* of the ancient world, when it began to seek power among barbarian peoples, it was no longer confronted with *weary* men but with inwardly brutalized, cruel people—strong but bungled men" (*AC*, 22).

37. *D* (424), p. 182.

38. *HAH* (114), p. 66.

39. *AC* (16), p. 583.

40. Nietzsche, *The Greek State*, op. cit., p. 8.

41. Ludwig Feuerbach, *The Essence of Christianity*, translated by George Eliot (New York: Harper & Row, 1957), pp. 12–13 (Feuerbach's stress).

42. Ibid, p. 14 (Feuerbach's stress).

43. Deleuze, op. cit., p. 158.

44. *AC* (42), p. 617.

45. Ibid. (44), p. 621. And nonetheless, in *The Greek State*, cited above, Nietzsche claims: "In fact here and there sometimes an exuberant degree of compassion has for a short time opened all the floodgates of Culture-life; a rainbow of compassionate love and peace appeared with the first radiant rise of *Christianity's most beautiful fruit, the gospel according to St. John.*" (*The Greek State*, op. cit., pp. 7–8) (stress is ours).

46. *GM*, third essay (22), p. 144. See also *BGE* (52).

47. *AC* (25), p. 595.

48. Ibid. (26), p. 596.

49. *WP* (146). pp. 93–94.

50. Ibid. (243), pp. 139–140.

51. *AC* (26), p. 596.

52. *WS* (9), p. 305. See also paragraphs 10–11.

53. *TI*, The Four Great Errors (7), pp. 499–500.

54. *TI*, Skirmishes of an Untimely Man (38), p. 541.

55. Ibid., pp. 542–543.

56. Ibid., p. 542.

57. On necessity (*Amor fati*), see supra, Chapter 3, section 3.

58. *WP* (259), p. 150. See above, Chapter 3, end of section 2.

59. *GS* (277), p. 223.

60. Ibid., p. 224.

61. *KSA* 11, p. 47.

62. *KSA* 13, p. 191. See also *AC* (3) (4), pp. 570–571.

63. *TI*, "Reason" in Philosophy (4), p. 482. In the original we have: "Gehirnleiden kranker Spinneweber," consisting of play on words that is very difficult to translate, for here Nietzsche uses *Spinne* (spider) and *Weber* (weaver) in order to signify the web of concepts the metaphysicians have woven. A similar play on words, this time carrying an explicit allusion to *Spinoza*, will reappear in *The Antichrist*: "Even the palest of the pale were able to master him (God): our honorable metaphysicians, those concept-albinos. They spun their webs around him until, hypnotized by their motions, he himself became a spider, another metaphysician. Now he, in turn, spun the world out of himself—*sub specie Spinozae*. Now he transfigured himself into something even thinner and paler; he became an "ideal," he became "pure spirit," the "Absolute," the "thing-in-itself." *The deterioration of a god*: God became the "thing-in-itself" (*AC* [17], p. 585). One should recall that in *The Antichrist* (paragraph 11), Nietzsche also refers to Kant as a "catastrophic spider."

64. *AC* (47), p. 627.

65. *BT* (3), p. 41.

66. *KSA* 11, p. 193.

67. Ibid. pp. 193–194.

68. *GS* (109), pp. 168–169. This text immediately follows paragraph 108, which begins the third book of *The Gay Science*, where Nietzsche makes the first explicit mention, in the published works, of the "death of God," and where he speaks of the necessity to "vanquish his shadow."

69. *WP* (462), p. 255.

70. *TI* (48), pp. 552–553. I reproduce the version of this text that appears in *Twilight of the Idols*, simply because it is an English translation of Nietzsche's original German text by a reliable translator, Walter Kaufmann. The fragment that the author refers to is not translated. The *TI* version and the fragment version are virtually the same, with the one exception being that the order of the paragraphs is reversed. The citation for the fragment is: *KSA* 12, pp. 402–403 (translator).

71. *WP* (1052), p. 543.

72. Ibid.

73. Karl Löwith, for example, sees in the eternal return a tragic issue of Nietzsche's "atheism": "How little Nietzsche had outgrown Christianity is shown not only by his Antichrist, but also by its counterpart: *the theory of eternal recurrence*. It is an avowed substitute for religion; no less than Kierkegaard's Christian paradox, it is an escape from despair: an attempt to leave "nothing" and arrive at "something." Karl Löwith, *From Nietzsche to Hegel* (New York: Holt, Rinehart and Winston, 1965), p. 373.

Paradoxically, it is Nietzsche himself who sustains this type of interpretation. In a fragment of 1887, he writes in fact: "In place of "metaphysics" and religion, the theory of eternal recurrence (this as a means of breeding and selection)" (*WP* [462], p. 255). Among the theological studies devoted to Nietzsche, and particularly to his "atheism," the note that predominates, regardless of individual differences of interpretation, is that which sees in Nietzsche's attacks against Christianity the expression of an unavowed religiousity. In this perspective, Nietzsche would be, without knowing it, a good Christian or a good believer. Thus the thought, among others, of W. Nigg, P. Tillich, N. Welte, E. Biser, H. Wein, F. Ulrich, P. Valadier, and Y. Ledure.

74. *KSA* 11, p. 200.

75. *WP* (1038), p. 534.

76. *GS* (343), p. 279. In this paragraph, as in *The Antichrist*, one can only be surprised by the dramatic tone with which Nietzsche announces the end of Christianity. He describes it, as we have noted, in apocalyptic terms; he depicts it as the advent of a cataclysm or a universal catastrophe. One is aware, however, that the kind of Christianity that Nietzsche had known, and to which he refers most often, was only the remainder of a millennial practice, ancient, shopworn, and accommodated to petty bourgeois taste.

The death of God doctrine that is related in the Nietzschean texts is susceptible to several interpretations, and this in virtue of the very different forms in which it is presented. Thus, Heidegger attributes it to devalorization and the end of the suprasensible world (see supra, chapter 1, section 4). But it can also be analyzed from the point of view of the death of the father, the death of the law or morality (see, for example, *WS* [84]; *D* [14]; *GS* [153]). Other important passages that allude specifically to the death of God are: *GS* (108) and (125); *Z*, prologue (2) and (3); I (3); II; III (2); IV (1).

77. *GS* (343), p. 280.

78. Nicolas Berdyaev, *The Destiny of Man*, translated by N. Duddington (New York: Scribner's, 1937), p. 167.

79. *GS* (344), p, 283.

80. Ibid. (346), pp. 285–286.

81. *WLN*, op. cit., p. 98. Nietzsche here plays on words using the verb *wachsen*, which means to sprout, to augment, to rise, to grow. In the first case ("by growing we are leaving Christianity"), he employs the verb _entwachsen_ which means "to sprout" (plant), to push out, but also figuratively, to be emancipated, to pass beyond a stage. In the second case ("we have grown *from* Christian roots"), the verb _auswachsen_ is used, which gives us: to germinate, to push out (seed, semen).

82. *D* (192), pp. 113–114.

83. Ibid., p. 113.

84. Ibid. (132), p. 82.

85. Ibid. (192), p. 113.

86. Ibid. (68), pp. 39–40. See supra, section 1 of this chapter.

87. *KSA* 11, p. 151.

88. *AC* (5), pp. 571–572.

89. *WP* (25), p. 18.

CHAPTER 5

1. *GM* Preface (8), p. 22.

2. See in particular the third essay.

3. See the letters of July 17, 29, 1887.

4. *CW*, Prologue, note, p. 192.

5. *D* (44), p. 31.

6. WS (3). The title of the aphorism is: "*In the beginning.*"

7. *GM*, Preface (7), p. 21.

8. *WP* (643), p. 342.

9. Ibid. (590), p. 323.

10. *EH*, *GM*, p. 312.

11. *GM*, essay I (2), pp. 25–26. One will recall that the first essay is entitled "Gut und Böse," "Gut und Schlecht" ("Good and Evil," "Good and Bad"). It is effectively on

the difference of perspective between "*Gut und Böse* (Good and *Evil*) and "*Gut und Schlecht*" (Good and *Bad*) that Nietzsche insists.

These analyses are to be understood in relation with paragraph 45 of *Human, All Too Human* that we have evoked above. See supra, chapter 2, section 3.

12. Ibid., essay I (2), p. 26.

13. Ibid. (11), p. 40.

14. Ibid. (13), p. 45.

15. Ibid. (11), pp. 40–41. We will return later to the question of the *blond beast* (*blonde Bestie*).

16. Ibid. (7), p. 33.

17. Ibid. (6), p. 31.

18. Ibid. (7), p. 34.

19. Regarding this, and what follows, see what we have developed supra, chapter 4, section 1.

20. *GM*, essay I (8), p. 35.

21. Ibid. (16), p. 54.

22. Ibid.

23. See in particular paragraphs 9 and 10. See also what we have developed supra, chapter 2, section 3.

24. *KSA* 11, p. 262.

25. *TI*, "How the 'True World' Finally Became a Fable," p. 485.

26. *KSA* 13, p. 581. This text is comparable to that other, where Nietzsche alludes to the anti-Semitic writer Theodor Fritsch: "Recently, a certain Theodor Fritsch, of Leipzig, wrote to me. There is truly no German clique more impudent and stupid than that of the antisemites. I have administered to him in thanks a serious epistolary kick in the behind. This scum dares to utter the name of Zarathustra! Disgust! Disgust! Disgust! (*KSA* 12, p. 321).

Theodor Fritsch (1852–1933) was the editor of the *Anti-Semitic Correspondence* and the author of a *Manual of the Jewish Question* (1887), which had, by 1923, reached its twenty-ninth edition.

27. *WLN*, p. 259.

28. Ibid.

29. See supra, chapter 1, section 3.

30. Deleuze, op. cit., p. 35.

31. *KSA* 13, pp. 323–324. In the same sense, see what we have developed supra, chapter 3, end of section 2.

32. *GM*, essay I (11), p. 42.

33. Ibid. (10), p. 36. *Ressentiment* and *this* are stressed in the text. The other words are stressed by us.

34. Ibid., essay II (8), p. 70.

35. Ibid.—the stress is ours.

36. Ibid. (6), pp. 65–66.

37. Ibid. (16), p. 85. In the presentation of the origins of "bad conscience," nothing is more contrary to Nietzsche than to dream of the so-called goodness of the natural man, as well as to weep about the misfortunes befalling man's life in society. In another text he marks with insistance: "We enjoy our wilder, crazier, more disorderly moments; we should be capable of committing a crime just to see what this talk of the pangs of conscience is about. We are inured to the everyday charms of the 'good man,' of social order, of well-behaved erudition. We don't suffer because of 'corruption,' we are very different from Rousseau and have no longing for the 'good natural man.'" (*WLR*, p. 137).

38. Ibid. (17), p. 86. See also: *BGE*, 257.

39. Ibid.

40. Ibid. (13), p. 80. (Stress on the last phrase is mine).

41. Ibid. (19), p. 88.

42. *HAH* (40), p. 35. Regarding this, see what we have developed supra, chapter 2, beginning of section 3.

43. *GM*, essay II (16), p. 85.

44. Ibid.

45. Regarding *cruelty*, Nietzsche writes in *Beyond Good and Evil* (paragraph 229): "Almost everything we call "higher culture" is based on the spiritualization of *cruelty*, on its becoming more profound: this is my proposition. That 'savage animal' has not really been 'mortified'; it lives and flourishes, it has merely become—divine" (*BGE*, p. 158). See also, in the same work, paragraph 230.

46. Ibid., essay II (18), p. 88.

47. Ibid. (12), pp. 77–78.

48. Ibid., p. 79.

49. *GS* (349), p. 292. We should recall that the fifth book, where we find this paragraph, was added to *The Gay Science* in 1887, the same year in which *On the Genealogy of Morals* was published.

50. *GM*, third essay (28), p. 163.

51. Ibid. (7), p. 106.

52. Ibid., p. 107.

53. Ibid.

54. See, in particular: *WP* (933), p. 492; *KSA* 13, p. 484; *KSA* 13, ibid.; *KSA* 13, p. 485.

55. *TI*, The "Improvers" of Mankind (2). p. 502. The term "blond beast" has been diversely interpreted. For the Nazi ideology it is a clear reference to the superiority of the

German people, or the Nordic "race" in general. Others see in this expression what would constitute Nietzsche's fully accomplished man, that is, the wild beast of prey and domination, and in whom all instincts work and move freely. For Walter Kaufmann, there is no doubt: the "blond beast" is not a racial concept, neither does it refer to the Nordic people; blondness in this case would be an allusion to a kind of beast often represented by Nietzsche. This could be a lion, according to Kaufmann's hypothesis.

If the Nazis have found solid arguments in the text that we have cited, the task of establishing it becomes even more difficult when it is a question of interpreting the same expression in *The Genealogy*, first essay, section 11. Here, in fact, after having affirmed that the "blond beast" can express itself in the "Roman, Arabian, Germanic, and Japanese nobility, the Homeric heroes, the Scandanavian Vikings," Nietzsche will indicate more explicitly in some lines down: "The deep and icy mistrust the German still arouses today whenever he gets into a position of power is an echo of that inextinguishable horror with which Europe observed for centuries that raging of the blond Germanic beast (although between the old Germanic tribes and us Germans there exists hardly a conceptual relationship, *let alone one of blood*)." (Stress is ours.)

For our part, we consider that all these readings, as well as other different readings, are possible, for regarding this particular subject, too, one would encounter immense difficulty in finding in Nietzsche's texts a position that is absolutely clear and free of all ambiguity, of all paradox and, particularly, of the most varied and opposed interpretations.

56. *GM*, Essay III (15), p. 126.

57. Ibid.

58. Ibid.

59. Ibid. (10), pp. 115–116. In the *Antichrist* (paragraph 12), Nietzsche will say: "When we consider that among all peoples the philosopher is merely the next development of the priestly type, then this legacy of the priest, this *self-deceiving counterfeit*, ceases to be surprising" (*AC*, p. 579).

60. See *AC*, 10 and 11.

61. *WP* (685), p. 364.

62. Ibid. (410), p. 221.

63. Ibid. (412), p. 222.

64. *GS* (357), p. 307.

65. *GM*, Essay III (23), p. 147.

66. Ibid. (25), p. 153.

67. Ibid. (24), pp. 153–154.

68. Ibid., p. 151.

69. *GS* (344), p. 282 (stress is ours). One is no doubt aware of the importance given in Freud's work, from 1920 onward, to the discovery of the life and death instincts. See Sigmund Freud, *Beyond the Pleasure Principle, Standard Edition*, vol. 18. (*Jenseits des Lustprinzips, G.W.*, vol. 13). On this theme in particular, see our study entitled *L'au-delà du plaisir: Une lecture de Nietzsche and Freud*.

70. *EH*, Why I am a Destiny (7), p. 333.

71. *WP* (258), p. 149. See also: *BGE*, 108.

72. *GM*, Essay III (12), p. 119.

73. *WP* (333), pp. 181–182.

74. *GM*, Essay III (13), p. 120.

75. Ibid.,(11), pp. 117–118. Paradoxical is stressed by us.

76. Ibid. (13), pp. 120–121.

77. Ibid., p. 121.

78. Ibid.

79. *EH*, Why I Am a Destiny (3), pp. 327–328.

80. Ibid., p. 328

81. *D*, Preface (4), pp. 4–5.

82. *EH*, Why I Am a Destiny (1), p. 327.

83. *GM* (27), p. 161.

84. *EC*, Why I Am a Destiny (3), p. 328.

Chapter 6

1. Nietzsche, *Selected Letters*, op. cit., p. 255. (*Sämtliche Briefe Studienausgabe, Band 7.*) (Berlin/New York: Walter de Gruyter, 1986, p. 254.)

2. *EC, BGE* (2), p. 310.

3. Schutte, op. cit., p, 38.

4. *BGE* (56), p. 68.

5. *BT* (7), p. 59 (stress is ours).

6. *KSA* 12, p. 116.

7. *BT* (16), p. 100.

8. Ibid. (18), p. 112.

9. *UO*, Schopenhauer as Educator (3), p. 173.

10. Ibid., p. 214.

11. See supra, chapter 2, section 1, in particular.

12. *HAH* (9), p. 15.

13. Ibid. (16), p. 20.

14. Ibid. (1), p. 12.

15. *BGE* (2), pp. 9–10.

16. Ibid. (2), p. 10. *Human, All Too Human*, paragraph 107, employs the metaphor of the tree to express the same idea: "But all these motives, whatever exhalted names we may give them, have grown up out of the same roots as those we believe evilly poisoned; between good and evil actions there is no difference in kind, but at the most one of degree. Good actions are sublimated evil ones; evil actions are coarsened, brutalized good ones" (*HAH*, p. 58).

17. Ibid. (47), pp. 61–62.

18. *GM*, Preface (5), p. 19. Stress on "my great teacher" by us.

19. *HAH, WS* (86), p. 332.

20. In the first months of 1873, one indeed finds, in Nietzsche's manuscripts, several prepatory revisions of *Philosophy in the Tragic Age of the Greeks*. But traces of these studies can be aleady located in the university course of summer 1872, as well as in the early drafts.

21. *PTAG* (2), p. 34.

22. *HAH* (261), pp. 123–124.

23. Ibid., *WO* (86), p. 332.

24. *BGE*, Preface, p. 2.

25. *HAH, AOM* (408), p. 299.

26. *KSA* 11, p. 134.

27. *KSA* 11, p. 151.

28. *KSA* 11, p. 262.

29. *WP* (437), p. 240.

30. *BGE* (204), p. 123.

31. *WP* (435), p. 239.

32. Michel Haar, *Nietzsche and Metaphysics*, translated and edited by Michael Gendre (Albany: State University of New York Press, 1996), p. 37. (Stress in text.)

33. Ibid., pp. 37–38. (Only "from the beginning" is stressed in the text.) (Translation modifed.)

34. *KSA* 12, p. 100.

35. *WP* (481), p. 267.

36. Ibid. (488), p. 269.

37. Ibid. (370), p. 199.

38. *KSA* 7, p. 199.

39. *TI*, "How the 'True World' Finally Became a Fable," p. 486.

40. *NT* (1), p. 36.

41. In relation with these considerations, see supra, chapter 1, section 1.

42. *NT* (22), p. 131.

43. Ibid. (24), pp. 141–142; "*an der deutlich percepirten Wirklichketit*" as "of reality clearly perceived." Philippe Lacoue-Labarthe has oddly translated it as "a clear and distinct perception of reality." Perhaps he wishes, unintentionally (!), to give it a Cartesian tint.

44. *KSA* 7, p. 465.

45. Ibid.

46. *KSA* 9, p. 308.

47. *KSA* 9, p. 311.

48. *D* (243), p. 141.

49. *KSA* 9, pp. 311–312.

50. *KSA* 9, p. 309.

51. *KSA* 12, pp. 205–206.

52. *BGE* (211), p. 136.

53. In *Beyond Good and Evil*, the hammer metaphor appears again in paragraph 62 and also in paragraph 225, where one reads: "In man *creature* and *creator* are united: in man there is material, fragment, excess, clay, dirt, nonsense, chaos; but in man there is also creator, formgiver, hammer hardness, spectator divinity, and seventh day." To the title of *Twilight of the Idols*, the last book published by Nietzsche, he added the subtitle *How One Philosophizes with a Hammer*.

Eric Blondel draws our attention to the reduction operating in the work of a number of authors regarding the use of the hammer metaphor. These nonspecialists, using the subtitle from *The Twilight of the Idols*, effectively assimilate Nietzsche's thought to what they believe to be "nihilism," namely, the massive and blind destruction of so-called moral, metaphyscial, and religious values. They ignore, Blondel argues, the overdetermination of Nietzsche's texts as well as the diverse applications Nietzsche makes of this metaphor. (See, Blondel, op. cit., pp. 25–26.)

54. *BGE* (43), p. 53.

55. *HAH* (19), p. 22.

56. Ibid. (31), p. 28.

57. *BGE* (4), p. 12.

58. Ibid. (5), p. 13.

59. Ibid. (24), p. 35.

60. *GS* (107), p. 164.

61. *BGE* (24). p. 35.

62. *EH*, Why I Am So Clever (4), p. 246,

63. *BGE* (59), p. 71.

64. Lou Salomé, op. cit., p. 93. Stressed in the text.

65. *BGE* (24), p. 35.

66. Ibid. (34), p. 46.

67. Ibid., pp. 46–47. We have reproduced only a part of the text.

68. *KSA* 12, p. 144.

69. *WP* (579), pp. 310–311.

70. Ibid., p. 311.

71. Roland Sublon, *La Lettre ou l'esprit. Une lecture psychanalytique de la théologie* (Paris: Cerf, 1993), p. 206.

72. *GS* (382), p, 346.

73. *Z III*, The Seven Seals (5), p. 342.

74. *Z II*, Upon the Blessed Isles, p. 199.

75. See supra, chapter 1, end of section 2.

76. *GS* (343), p. 280.

77. Ibid. (125), p. 343.

78. Ibid. (124), pp. 180–181.

79. Heidegger, op. cit., pp. 106–107.

80. *GS* (382), p. 346.

81. *D* (327), p. 161.

82. This last paragraph is followed by an epilogue, which ends in the salutation "au revoir!" (auf *Wieder*sehen!) (Goodbye!).

83. *HAH*, II, p. 395.

84. *GS*, p. 371.

85. AC (62), p. 656. After several polemics regarding the exact place of the *Law Against Christianity*, this text finally figured as the "conclusion" of *The Antichrist* in the edition of *The Complete Works* arranged by Colli and Montinari. The text immediately follows the citation of paragraph 62, that we have given above.

86. *GM* (28), p. 163.

87. *EH-D* (1), p. 290.

88. Ibid.

89. *D*. (575), pp. 228–229.

Index